MAURICE MAETERLINCK

Maeterlinck and his wife (1932)

MAURICE MAETERLINCK

A Study of his Life and Thought

BY

W. D. HALLS

GREENWOOD PRESS, PUBLISHERS
WESTPORT, CONNECTICUT

Library of Congress Cataloging in Publication Data

Halls, W. D.
  Maurice Maeterlinck ; a study of his life and thought.

  Reprint of the ed. published at the Clarendon Press,
Oxford.
  Bibliography: p.
  1. Maeterlinck, Maurice, 1862-1949. 2. Authors, Belgian--20th century--Biography.
[PQ2625.A6H25   1978]   848'.8'09 [B]   78-16379
ISBN 0-313-20574-4

© Oxford University Press 1960

This reprint has been authorized by the Oxford University Press.

Reprinted in 1978 by Greenwood Press, Inc.
51 Riverside Avenue, Westport, CT. 06880

Printed in the United States of America

10 9 8 7 6 5 4 3 2 1

CONTENTS

List of Illustrations	vii
Introduction	ix
1. Before 'La Gloire'	1
2. The Symbolist	24
3. The Thinking Reed	43
4. Meeting with Destiny	47
5. 'Union of the Left Hand'	60
6. The Nobel Prizewinner	89
7. Fame is the Spur	107
8. Sélysette	125
9. The Stranger	151
10. Conclusions	166
Bibliography	173
Index	183

LIST OF ILLUSTRATIONS

	Maeterlinck and his wife (1932)	*Frontispiece*	
1.	Maeterlinck: the schoolboy at the Collège Ste-Barbe	*facing page*	10
2.	*Pelléas et Mélisande*: The death of Pelléas	,,	38
3.	*L'Oiseau bleu*: Act II: In the Fairy Palace	,,	84
4.	The Château de Médan (old print)	,,	126
5.	The Countess Maeterlinck in *La Princesse Isabelle*	,,	142
6.	'Orlamonde': Maeterlinck's study	,,	162

INTRODUCTION

Tel arbre, tel fruit, wrote Sainte-Beuve, and whilst this criterion of literary criticism may lead occasionally to false evaluations, Maurice Maeterlinck (1862–1949) supremely exemplifies its truth. The stages of his life are indissolubly linked to his literary development. Belgium, Symbolism, two world wars, and two women, one his mistress and the other his wife: these are the phenomena that determine the pattern of his biography and his works. To understand his enormous literary output, it is important to study his life and times, for an undoubted parallel exists between them.

In his case, therefore, any division of life from works would be artificial, so that ideally it would be best to consider both as a single entity. Yet when, as with Maeterlinck, the span of life is almost fourscore years and seven and almost sixty major works have to be taken into account, some separation becomes indispensable. Fortunately, convenient landmarks exist where both biographer and critic have reasonable grounds for affirming that one epoch of his long career is closing and a new one beginning. These vantage-points are seven in number. The first occurs in 1890, when Maeterlinck finally abandoned his legal career and achieved his first literary success. The second was in 1895, when he met Georgette Leblanc and felt that the literary vein he had hitherto exploited was all but exhausted. The ensuing period of transition did not endure longer than 1897 when, with Georgette Leblanc, he went into voluntary exile in France and thenceforward trod the path to optimism. By 1906, however, their spiritual and literary partnership was all but dissolved. As early as 1911, moreover, although the award of the Nobel Prize for Literature sealed his literary triumph, he was beginning to revert to an earlier pessimism. This date also marked the beginning of his friendship with Renée Dahon, which finally, after the break with Georgette Leblanc, led to marriage. The new beginning thus made in 1919 had little effect upon his work, for henceforth his physical and literary powers steadily declined. The cataclysm of 1939 and another exile, this time in America, ushered in the last stage of his life. In 1949 the curtain falls, and the 'seven ages' of this man pass into the shadows that had so long obsessed him.

It came almost as a shock to the world to realize, at the time of his death, that this once revered literary figure had lingered on so long. In literature he had been a lonely, neglected figure since the end of the First World War. The spate of laudatory criticism that had flowed at its fullest at the time of the award of the Nobel Prize had by 1949 drained away to a mere trickle. Even hostile critics were few, for Maeterlinck was ignored and almost forgotten. Previously, Maeterlinckian criticism had been violently for, or just as passionately against, his works. In the author's camp may be ranged such critics as Harry and Pasquier in Belgium, Le Sidaner and Bailly in France, Thomas and Taylor in England. Violently opposed to him had been Dumont-Wilden and Lecat in Belgium. Only such writers as Bithell and Gerardino had succeeded in giving a balanced view of Maeterlinck's literary achievements. But Bithell's work dates from 1913, and Gerardino's from 1934. At the time of his death no up-to-date study of his life and works existed.

An indication that his vogue had passed was the lack of notice that the literary critics took of his death, whereas the subsequent deaths of Gide and Claudel, his more famous contemporaries, occasioned a host of new critical studies. In fact, since Maeterlinck's death, only three major works of criticism concerning him have appeared: Robert Beachboard has made a specialist study of Maeterlinck's drama in the United States, Gabriel Compeyre a study of his theatre, and Alex Pasquier a general résumé of his life and works. The present writer hopes that this book, which is presented as a study in the parallel development of his life and thought, will help to fill the many gaps in biographical data and in literary criticism. The hitherto unpublished and unused sources upon which he has been privileged to draw have enabled him to throw light upon the writer's inner conflicts and early literary beginnings, as well as upon some hitherto unknown biographical facts. They have also allowed him to establish for the first time the real chronology of the works, which often differs considerably from the dates of publication. It is hoped thereby that a more complete picture of the man and his writings will have been presented.

It would be impossible to mention all to whom my thanks are due, but my gratitude goes chiefly to Dr. Enid Starkie, who has constantly encouraged and advised me. I wish to express my thanksto Mr. D. M. Sutherland, Librarian of the Taylor Institution, Oxford, and his staff. I am also grateful to the following for permission to copy unpublished documents and correspondence: the Bibliothèque Royale, Brussels; the Bibliothèque Jacques Doucet, Paris; the Bibliothèque de l'Arsenal, Paris; Mr. Sheridan Russell; and Professor Robert Van Nuffel, secretary-general of the Fondation Maeterlinck, in Ghent. I am indebted to Photo Hensler, Oudeghem, Brussels, for permission to reproduce the illustration from a performance of *Pelléas et Mélisande*.

Particular thanks are also due to Countess Renée Maeterlinck, the author's widow, who has kindly allowed me to consult unpublished works and given permission for me to quote from hitherto unpublished correspondence, documents, and plays, as well as helping me by personal interviews.

Financially I have also been helped considerably by the generosity of the Trustees of the Heath Harrison Scholarships Award at Oxford, and by the Centre National de la Recherche Scientifique, Paris.

W. D. H.

Oxford
July 1960

I

BEFORE 'LA GLOIRE'

ABOUT 1850 Ghent, like Bruges, its sister-city, was slowly emerging from the torpor in which it had been sunk since the Middle Ages, when its glory had departed. Its sluggish river, dreaming canals, cloistered convents, and gabled medieval streets were at last reawakened by the strident factory hooter and the clangour of the railway. Thus the later nineteenth century is an age of transition, where for a time the old and new live uneasily together. Poets then young suffered under the impact of modernity, experiencing a new *mal du siècle*, a melancholic, wistful longing for a golden, legendary past.

Ghent, although sometimes called 'la ville française des Flandres', has been, more so than Brussels or Antwerp, the true capital of the Flemish lands. There Flemish nationalism flourished, nurtured by men like Willems and Ledeganck. Although primarily political, this movement, by upholding the dignity of the Flemish tongue, sought to restore the literary heritage of Flanders, whose books had once been publicly burnt by the Duke of Alba, its Spanish governor.

Yet, strangely enough, Ghent was to be a centre of the French literary renaissance in Belgium. In the middle 1880's, linked to similar groups in Brussels, Louvain, and Liège, its writers brought a specifically Belgian contribution to the welter of Symbolist ideas current in far-off Paris. Although the linguistic frontier, the northernmost boundary of the French-speaking domain, runs some thirty miles south of Ghent, French was then, as still today, the language of the upper classes and the well-to-do *bourgeoisie* of the city. In Flanders, not until 1873 was Flemish employed in the administration of justice; in 1883 it was adopted in secondary education; in 1889 the Army recognized it. Today both tongues have equal status. This official reluctance to recognize the language of the people demonstrates conclusively how widespread must have been the use of French. To this anomaly French literature owes not only Rodenbach and Verhaeren, both educated in Ghent, but also Maurice Maeterlinck.

Mauritius Polydorus Maria Bernardus Maeterlinck was born on 29 August 1862 at 6 Peperstraat (rue du Poivre), Ghent. He was the eldest son of Polydore Maeterlinck, a notary who had retired early and lived on his income from investments. Physically a tall man, '... stiff, straight as the letter I', the notary was '... just and good',[1] but somewhat of a tyrant. In matters of religion he was a lukewarm, insincere Catholic; Maeterlinck observes, 'I am indebted to him for having freed me from the torments of Hell and purgatory that might have weighed upon my life.'[2]

Intellectually, moreover, Polydore Maeterlinck was a nonentity. Once his son found he was reading *Sagesse et destinée*. Since he sedulously marked his place, the author discovered that his father never read beyond the first few pages. In fact, Maeterlinck declared that his parents never finished reading any work he wrote.

His father had married Mathilde Colette Françoise Van den Bossche, daughter of a rich but tight-fisted Ghent lawyer. A connoisseur of wine, he thought nothing of consuming a couple of bottles of St-Émilion at one sitting. He died when Maeterlinck was very young, but not before his grandson had also acquired a taste for wine,[3] then a rather unusual one for a Fleming. Mathilde Maeterlinck, although she lavished her love upon her son, never really understood him. In fact, neither parent exercised much influence over him.[4]

Maeterlinck recalls his other relatives with mingled affection and dislike. Ernest, his father's second-born son, followed the family tradition by also becoming a notary. Oscar, his youngest

---

[1] M. Maeterlinck, *Bulles bleues, souvenirs heureux*, pp. 31 and 27. Much of the information in this chapter is taken from this autobiographical work, published in 1948, which deals with the author's childhood and youth. It is not, however, entirely reliable.

[2] *Bulles bleues*, p. 34.

[3] M. Maeterlinck, *La Grande Porte*, p. 136. In later years the author often judged people by the quality of their wine-cellar. Of his publisher, for example, he was wont to say: 'Ah, Fasquelle, he has one of the best cellars in France' (communication from Mr. Sheridan Russell). [4] Georgette Leblanc, *Souvenirs*, p. 16.

brother, died tragically in early manhood. One of his aunts had married a rich Gantois, and Louise, their daughter, was at one time considered a possible match for Maurice. His great-uncle, the Abbé Bernard Maeterlinck, was a priest much respected in the locality. Little is known of Maeterlinck's only sister, Marie, who took to painting, but later contracted an unhappy marriage with a lawyer. Maeterlinck's paternal grandfather was tyrannized over by his wife, a very devoutly religious person, whom the grandson heartily disliked. On his mother's side, his grandmother, widowed from her wine-bibbing husband, owned an estate at Swynaerde, near Ghent, where her grandson stayed frequently. It was possibly to her that Maeterlinck was referring when he wrote to Gérard Harry authorizing an English translation of *La Princesse Maleine*, 'with even more pleasure, because English is almost my mother tongue, for a grandmother with whom I spent almost all my childhood was English'.[1] This categorical statement, which would explain his marked predilection for English literature, is nevertheless untrue. To judge by surnames, as far back as his great-grandparents, Maeterlinck was of purely Flemish stock,[2] having neither French, Walloon, nor English blood in his veins.

The family's early origins are undoubtedly Flemish. The name dates back to the fourteenth century and is mentioned by Froissart. In Ronse (Renaix), on the linguistic frontier, a bailie of the town was created a knight in 1395 for having relieved a famine. To each citizen, at the height of the distress, he had meted out a few ladles of grain and thus earned the appellation of *maeterlinck*, 'the measurer'. When created a count of Belgium in 1932 Maeterlinck assumed his ancestor's coat of arms, 'azur aux trois louchets d'argent', and the singularly appropriate device, 'When God shall wish'. He always preferred the Flemish pronunciation of his name to the rather ugly rhyme to *carlingue* enunciated by the French.

From the beginning, Maeterlinck was bilingual, as are many

[1] '... avec d'autant plus plaisir (*sic*) que l'anglais est un peu ma langue maternelle, car une grand'mère, chez qui j'ai passé presque toute mon enfance, était anglaise.' Unpublished letter dated 27 Sept. 1890, Bibliothèque de l'Arsenal, Paris, MS. 13.066(3).
[2] Information supplied to the present writer by the Archives service of the province of East Flanders, Belgium.

wealthy families in Flanders even today. He probably spoke in Flemish save when addressing relatives and friends. In contrast to Verhaeren, he not only knew but continued to speak the language. His friendship with Cyriel Buysse, the Flemish novelist, for example, lasted many years, but whenever they met they conversed in Flemish.[1]

Maeterlinck's background is thus that of the Catholic-professing, conservative, rich, French-speaking *bourgeoisie* of Flanders.

Little is known of his very early childhood. As a baby he cried so much that he contracted a hernia, which, however, had healed up naturally by the age of six. The Peperstraat, where he then lived, led on to the Grand Béguinage. His mother would take him to visit two aunts and a cousin, who had become *béguines* and who indulged him with sweets.[2] Thus the familiar sight of these religious in their white headdress impressed itself upon his imagination. Even when the family moved to 22 boulevard Frère-Orban, they were still close to the Petit Béguinage, whose entrance was opposite the Rodenbachs' home. His father, with shrewd business acumen, bought up several vacant lots on this new boulevard near the station and on one of them built their new home.

Their town house was, however, used mainly in winter. In May the family would move to their summer residence at Oostacker, a small commune not far from the Dutch frontier and some seven miles along the canal from Ghent to Terneuzen. This house, to which his father added a tower and workshops, was flanked by a large garden running down to the canal. There Polydore Maeterlinck indulged a passion for horticulture—a variety of pear was even named after him—and the future poet of *Serres chaudes* played hide and seek among the hot-houses. Another hobby, bee-keeping, earned Maeterlinck's father a passing mention in *La Vie des abeilles* as 'a kind of wise old man, somewhat resembling the old man in Virgil'.

In old age Maeterlinck's memories of Oostacker were happy

---

[1] Personal communication of Countess Maeterlinck to the writer.
[2] M. Maeterlinck, *L'Autre Monde*, p. 153.

ones. There, for example, he composed and performed his first 'dramatic work'. Browsing over the works of Molière he conceived the idea of mixing up the comic 'business' of *Le Médecin malgré lui*, *Les Fourberies de Scapin*, and *Le Malade imaginaire*. The resulting concoction was acted, with the help of his brother and sister, before a dubious audience of parents, relatives, and servants. Nor were more active pastimes neglected. In one corner of the garden stood gymnastic apparatus, on which Maeterlinck was very proficient. Here already he displays one aspect of his bivalent temperament, in which adeptness in physical exercise contrasts with that other facet of his nature, dreamy, melancholic, and morbid.

The canal loomed large in his childhood play. One July afternoon, when still capable of swimming only a few strokes, he went under and was only fished out of the water with difficulty. On yet another occasion he launched himself on the canal in a washtub. Not far off, but unknown to him, a large cargo-boat was waiting for a bridge to open. Had it not been stopped from passing along the fairway he would most certainly have drowned. On a third occasion his yacht capsized and he again just escaped death.

As a young man, however, his recollections of Oostacker were not entirely happy or even exciting. The country estate, with the broad expanse of water bounding its western limits, became identified in his imagination with the sinister, crumbling manors depicted by Edgar Allan Poe. The flat, monotonous, and marshy countryside created within him a sense of isolation. Yet there was also the longing for remote lands engendered by the not far distant sea and the prospect of great ships moving in stately fashion along the waterway. Such an environment awakened corresponding echoes in his soul and inspired the atmosphere of his early poems and Symbolist drama.

In 1868, when six, Maeterlinck's formal education began. The convent school in Ghent run by the Sisters of the 'Nouveau-Bois' was intended for girls of good family, but also took boys up to the age of seven. Here he learned his prayers, the catechism, and some arithmetic. In *Bulles bleues* he recalls with affection one of his teachers, Sister Julia.[1] His schoolroom was hung with biblical scenes, among them a print of Breughel's *Massacre of the Innocents*, a picture that later formed the basis of his first short story.

In his early childhood the Maeterlincks engaged foreign governesses to teach their children English and German. These came and went in bewildering succession because Polydore Maeterlinck had amorous intentions that were constantly being thwarted by the watchfulness of his wife. Thus Maeterlinck never learned these two languages thoroughly, although in reading them he was tolerably proficient. Not until his old age, after seven years spent in America, did his spoken English become at all fluent.

Maeterlinck stayed only a year at the convent school before leaving to become a pupil at the Institut Central, a private school run by a M. Calamus and situated between the Cathedral of S. Bavon and the Belfry of Ghent. His sole recollection of what he learned there was of a stylistic rule enunciated by a teacher, M. Poma: never repeat the same word on the same page. Four years later, moreover, his father grew dissatisfied with his education: on picking up a French grammar manual used at the school he noticed that the rules concerning the subjunctive and the past participle were inadequate. He himself had attended the Jesuit College of Namur. This induced him to enter his son as a day-boarder at the local Jesuit Collège de Sainte-Barbe, situated in the Savaenstraat not far from the banks of the Lys and the Upper Scheldt.

This school had already educated two other youths destined to achieve literary fame, Georges Rodenbach and Émile Verhaeren. According to Albert Mockel, who was not a pupil of it, the establishment was highly esteemed in Belgium for the sound classical grounding it imparted.[2] Maeterlinck entered it in September 1874, a year after he had made his first communion. To his companion of later years, Georgette Leblanc, he must have painted a sombre picture of life within its walls, for she writes:

> One single bad memory in these years of happy wisdom, a single rancour that darkens the fine hours of youth, Maeterlinck will never

---
[1] *Bulles bleues*, pp. 11-12.
[2] Quoted in C. Hanlet, *Les Écrivains belges contemporains*, vol. i, p. 177.

forgive the Jesuit Fathers of the Collège Ste-Barbe for their narrow-minded tyranny. I have often heard him say that he would not have his life over again because of his seven years at college. For him there is one crime that cannot be forgiven, that which poisons the joys and destroys the smile of a child.[1]

In old age, however, Maeterlinck was to declare that his teachers were patient and devoted,[2] and intellectually very competent, although he disliked the tale-bearing atmosphere that was encouraged.[3] This is fulsome praise from one whose works had by then been proscribed by the Church.

Despite a general lack of cleanliness, the pupils' material welfare was well provided for. The food was coarse, but abundant and wholesome. The beer, supplied by breweries run by different pupils' families, was often undrinkable, so that frequently the sins of the fathers were visited upon the heads of their luckless sons. Physically, the young Maeterlinck was a very active boy. In his later school years he was more likely to be seen during recreation busily playing football than hanging, like others, on the words of Charles Van Lerberghe, the future poet, a year older than Maeterlinck, who, with Grégoire Le Roy, was to become his closest friend. In mishaps at games Maeterlinck acquired a permanent scar that turned red in moments of anger and a little finger that remained crooked for life. He learned to fence and continued to practise the art for many years. He appeared to be a completely extrovert youngster.

Intellectually he was not outstanding, although he always put up a creditable performance.[4] Weak at mathematics, he shone only in French composition. One essay, written in 1876, when he was in 4^e latine, earned him special commendation from his French Jesuit teacher. Entitled merely 'Account of a day in the holidays', it purported to describe a visit to Swynaerde in which the animals on his grandmother's estate were endowed with human, super-

---

[1] Georgette Leblanc, *Morceaux choisis de Maurice Maeterlinck*, Introduction, p. (vii) (unnumbered).
[2] *Bulles bleues*, p. 87.
[3] Quoted in C. Hanlet, op. cit., vol. i, p. 177.
[4] For details of his scholastic career see G. Vanwelkenhuyzen, 'Maurice Maeterlinck au Collège Sainte-Barbe', *Annales de la Fondation Maeterlinck*, vol. iii, 1957.

natural, and even symbolic qualities—perhaps the first expression of an artistry later more fully realized in *L'Oiseau bleu*. However, the Jesuits discouraged undue literary indulgence and, in particular, the works of the Romantics and contemporary French poets merited their special condemnation. Verse-writing was strictly forbidden; exceptionally, Van Lerberghe did not come under this ban, because he had won a competition open to all Belgian Jesuit colleges, by writing a hymn to the Immaculate Conception.[1] Maeterlinck was accorded no such dispensation.

Surprisingly, music was not taught in the school, and, as none was heard at home, Maeterlinck developed neither aptitude nor taste for it, a curious fact in view of the many musical settings later made of his works. On the other hand, drama, particularly religious, was encouraged and Maeterlinck performed in several plays. In 1879 he wrote, in collaboration with a fellow pupil, Herman Baltia, an 'eclogue' performed under the title *Notre Dame d'Oostakker*. Three years earlier he had been enrolled in the Congregation of Our Lady of the Angels, and this, coupled with the fact that at Oostacker there was a statue of the Virgin Mary in a grotto resembling Lourdes, probably motivated the piece.

Nevertheless, if Maeterlinck is to be believed, the spiritual education given revolted him. Frequent and compulsory chapel services were the occasion for homilies on the inevitability of death, the carnal sins, and the fire and brimstone awaiting the transgressor. As a result, he declares that he had never had more than a precarious and provisional faith, 'but I had ended up by believing that one must believe and that I *did* believe'.[2] After leaving school he almost acquired what he describes as the 'prejudice' of faith, but this did not seem intellectually honest. His attitude contrasted notably with that of some of his schoolfellows. In the top form, out of sixteen in the class no less than seven declared a vocation for the priesthood; some of these died nobly as missionaries, others, says Maeterlinck, became merely pious hypocrites. From these and others—the sons of nobles, destined for diplomacy—the three future poets, Maeterlinck,

[1] A. Mockel, 'Le Symbolisme en Belgique', *Visages du monde*, 15 April 1936, p. 88.
[2] M. Maeterlinck, *L'Ombre des ailes*, p. 117.

Van Lerberghe, and Le Roy, stood aloof, following their classes as 'distinguished amateurs'.[1]

An atmosphere of gloom and melancholy was present outside as well as inside school.[2] The grim Château des Comtes des Flandres, the brooding, stagnant canals spanned by innumerable bridges, the gaunt outline of the prison, the forbidding asylums for the deaf and dumb: such were the familiar landmarks of the schoolboy, who later used them as a background to some of his Symbolist plays. Moreover, the frequent evocation of death by the good Jesuits reinforced a pessimistic disposition latent already in Maeterlinck and apparent, save for one brief period, throughout his life. Georges Rodenbach, who had passed through the hands of the same teachers a few years previously, wrote of the atmosphere:

> Death was always present to us in our youth. Oh, those years when we should have been taught to love life and when they busied themselves only with making us familiar with death. . . . It [the Collège Ste-Barbe] was as shut off as a seminary. And all around us the dead town made moan in the tearful harmony of its bells. There was a central courtyard, a playground as bare as a beach on which the retreating tide has left behind its sadness. Not even the enlivening note of a few trees. Alone, on a gable, the implacable face of a big clock whose hands now met, now left each other. The chimes of the hour fell upon us so plaintively that they seemed but shadows! One might have said that they were a rain of iron and ashes. Changeless and bleak existence, beneath the high walls of that courtyard that blotted out the sun! There it was that my young soul took flight from life because it had learnt too much of death.
>
> Death! This it was that the priests who were our teachers enthroned among us as soon as term began.[3]

Rodenbach, no less than Verhaeren and Maeterlinck, had been steeped in this cheerless atmosphere. It was doubtless a prime factor in the depression Maeterlinck suffered from for some years after leaving school, and made of him, although physically robust, a hypochondriac.

---

[1] M. Maeterlinck, *Devant Dieu*, pp. 178–9.
[2] For a description of the atmosphere of Ghent see F. Hellens, *En ville morte*.
[3] G. Rodenbach, *Le Rouet des Brumes*, p. 210.

In their later school years Maeterlinck, Van Lerberghe, and Le Roy gravitated naturally together, linked by a common interest in literature. Maeterlinck soon supplanted Van Lerberghe as the dominant partner in the friendship, although the latter was the eldest of the trio. His parents were dead and his legal guardian was Désiré Van den Hove, an uncle of Maurice, with whom he lived in a house almost opposite the one where Maeterlinck had been born. They sought to outdo each other in French composition and both were piqued when, on rare occasions, the prize was won by Van Melle, whose brother was to be the first publisher of Maeterlinck's works. Grégoire Le Roy, on the other hand, was the most colourful character of the three. His versatility in poetry, sculpture, music, and painting marked him also as the most artistic. On one occasion he fought a pistol duel at Oostacker, with Maeterlinck acting as his second. (Van Lerberghe, for whom the spectacle was too harrowing, retired as the other second in favour of a general's son.) Unknown to both duellists, their respective seconds had agreed not to load the pistols. Thus the powder was fired, a bloodless combat resulted, honour was safe, and the escapade terminated happily in a picnic meal.

It was Grégoire Le Roy who was also the most precocious sexually. A Don Juan, he made the double conquest of two sisters, both school-teachers. In despair at having to share their idol's favours, the pair resolved on suicide: they swallowed a bottle of ink between them, but were only violently sick. Van Lerberghe, by contrast, lived in a perpetual dream fantasy of virgins, princesses, and fairies (the very characters of Maeterlinck's first plays). Thus, without revealing his identity, he would trail after sickly, anaemic, but angelic-looking girls, the incarnation of his ideal. When convinced that he had excited their curiosity, his shadowing would cease and he would congratulate himself that they were pining at the sudden loss of their unknown suitor. On the other hand, Maeterlinck was more mundane: at eighteen he took a milliner's errand-girl for his mistress.[1] She was the first of many.

[1] *Bulles bleues*, p. 127.

1. *Maeterlinck: the schoolboy at the Collège Ste-Barbe*

Writing remained, however, the dominant passion for all three. Occasionally they would agree upon a subject and they would then each write upon it after his own fashion. This method most likely engendered Maeterlinck's play *L'Intruse*, Van Lerberghe's *Les Flaireurs*, and Le Roy's unfinished drama, *L'Annonciatrice*. They would criticize each other's efforts freely. For Maeterlinck it is no exaggeration to say that his schooldays impressed themselves upon his writing in two ways: the one, a haunting preoccupation with death; the other, the no less haunting search for God. With St. Augustine he might say: 'Our hearts are restless till they rest in Thee.'

A literary career for their eldest son was, however, unthinkable to Maeterlinck's parents. Upon leaving school in 1881 he was entered as a student of law at Ghent university. He says that he would have preferred medicine,[1] but was obliged to follow his father's career. Although on occasion he dreamed of becoming a brilliant lawyer, on the whole this early constraint gave him a lifelong abhorrence and contempt for the processes of justice.

Meanwhile he continued ardently to follow his literary bent, interesting himself deeply in the revival of letters then surging up in Belgium. This renaissance, which had received its initial impetus from Charles de Coster, Octave Pirmez, and Camille Lemonnier, had given rise to a number of reviews, which were widely read. *La Jeune Belgique*, Parnassian in tone, edited by Max Waller, around whom were grouped such writers as Albert Giraud, Georges Rodenbach, Verhaeren, and Iwan Gilkin, was launched in December 1881 and Maeterlinck became a subscriber. Its rival, *La Wallonie*, founded by Albert Mockel in Liège in May 1886, became the principal organ of Symbolism in Belgium; its later contributors included not only Verhaeren, Van Lerberghe, and Maeterlinck, but French writers such as Mallarmé, Gide, and Valéry. Another review, *L'Art moderne*, started in 1881 by Edmond Picard and Octave Maus, the lawyer turned art critic, postulated the social mission of art; later it also threw open its columns to the Symbolists. In Brussels literature revolved around the colourful personality of Edmond Picard, the one-time sailor

[1] J. Bithell, *The Life and Writings of Maeterlinck*, p. 5.

who had become barrister, orator, poet, and critic. Both Rodenbach and Verhaeren 'devilled' for him after qualifying as lawyers, and one of his later pupils was Henry Carton de Wiart, another man of letters and also a future Belgian Prime Minister.

The literary revival received its consecration in the 'Banquet Lemonnier', organized by *La Jeune Belgique* in honour of Camille Lemonnier. Held on 27 May 1883, this banquet, which has been termed 'la Pâque des lettres belges', numbered Maeterlinck and his two Ghent friends among its 212 subscribers. The occasion was unique. The government committee appointed to attribute the official Quinquennial Prize for Literature had recently decided that no meritorious works had appeared during the period, thereby rejecting Lemonnier's novels, *Un Mâle* and *Le Mort*. At the dinner Georges Rodenbach paid homage to the slighted novelist, saluting him as 'the Marshal of Belgian letters', and Picard made a vigorous speech attacking officialdom. Thus the 'Jeunes-Belgiques', by honouring Lemonnier, reasserted the rights of literature in Belgium.

This reflowering of literature coincides with Maeterlinck's formative years and runs parallel also with far-reaching political and social changes in Belgium. In 1884 the collapse of the government of Frère-Orban heralded the rout of the liberal *bourgeoisie*. The next decade saw a fierce struggle towards democracy, crystallizing in the fight for universal suffrage. The rapid industrialization of the kingdom, an independent state for only half a century, created social problems and tensions that resulted in miners' riots in Brussels, Liège, and Charleroi in 1886 and 1887. Maeterlinck must have felt acutely the passing of the old order and the birth-pangs of the new. His interest in medievalism and his passion for the English Pre-Raphaelites is symptomatic of his yearning to escape from reality.

His literary ambitions received their first fillip when, in November 1883, *La Jeune Belgique* published 'Les Joncs', his first poem to appear in print. But the verse, written in triolets, appears uninteresting and conventional. Another effort submitted drew a broadside of criticism from Max Waller, published in the correspondents' column of the review in July 1884:

M. Maeter.—bad, your verses to your friend Charles V[an] L[erberghe], supremely bad.

The truth was that his style was too patently imitated from the Parnassians, and indeed remained so until Grégoire Le Roy read him one day a poem by Verlaine whose vaguely mystical images evoked corresponding echoes in his own poetic imagination.[1] But the following months brought none of the three Ghent friends any further literary success. Maeterlinck, preparing for his final examinations, was probably too engrossed in his law studies. However, the death of Victor Hugo in May 1885 gave the trio a pretext to approach Georges Rodenbach, whom they admired for his speech at the Lemonnier banquet. Although he had ceased to live in Ghent since 1883, Van Lerberghe and Le Roy caught sight of him one Sunday on the Place d'Armes and inquired whether *La Jeune Belgique* would be represented at the French poet's funeral. Van Lerberghe also seized the opportunity to say that he wrote poetry and was immediately invited by Rodenbach to submit some verses for criticism.

In June 1885 Maeterlinck graduated as a doctor of law. Sponsored by Maître Auguste Verstraeten, he took the barrister's oath on 21 July and was duly enrolled in the register of lawyers of the Ghent appeal court. His name remained on the roll for many years after he had ceased to practise.[2]

A decisive opportunity then presented itself to him: he persuaded his parents that a stay in Paris would enable him to study at first hand the eloquence and technique of the French Bar. To convince them he no doubt adduced the example of Rodenbach, his recent acquaintance, who had gone to Paris in 1878 with a similar intention. Although he may have vaguely dreamed of forging a reputation as a barrister, he was certainly hankering in secret to plunge, if only for a while, into the literary maelstrom of Paris. Despite the expense, his father surprisingly agreed to the project.

[1] F. Hellens, 'Maurice Maeterlinck', *Annales de la Fondation Maeterlinck*, vol. iii, 1957, p. 12.
[2] Editor's notes, pp. 71–73, to a special number, devoted to Maeterlinck, of *Gand artistique*, 1 Mar. 1923.

Thus, in October 1885, the *annus mirabilis* of Symbolism, Maeterlinck and Le Roy, followed some months later by Charles Van Lerberghe, installed themselves in the Parisian Mecca. They made little attempt to study French juridical oratory. Indeed, Maeterlinck later averred that four or five visits to the Palais de Justice had sufficed to convince him that the eloquence of the Paris Bar, like that of its Brussels counterpart, wallowed in the same kind of iniquitous quibbling.[1] This appraisal doubtless allowed him to concentrate on literature with a clear conscience.

The pair took rooms at 22 rue de Seine, than a quiet backwater near the river, now a busy thoroughfare full of art dealers and sellers of literary autographs. Le Roy, contemplating painting as a career, enrolled as a student at the École St-Luc and the Atelier Gervex & Humbert.[2] Maeterlinck was more anxious to contact the literary lions of the day. The two young Belgians quickly found a favourite haunt in the Brasserie des Culs de Bouteille (later known as the Brasserie Pousset), in the rue Drouot, almost on the corner of the rue Lafayette. There they met a few young writers—Mikhael, Pierre Quillard, Rodolphe Darzens, Jean Ajalbert, and Saint-Pol-Roux (then still known as Paul Roux); they were also occasionally joined by Catulle Mendès. But the literary idol of them all, to whom they listened in respectful admiration, was Villiers de l'Isle Adam. The poet, already in his fifties, treated these young men as his equals, although they were still literary nonentities. At that time, only three years before his death, he was completing the writing of *L'Ève future* in his squalid, cheerless lodgings. His tragedy of *Axël* was then appearing in a monthly review. The great man read aloud to his enraptured audience pages of *Akëdysseril* and recounted some of the *Nouveaux Contes cruels*, which only reached publication in 1889.

Maeterlinck always retained vivid memories of this first personal contact with the Breton writer. Although the young hopefuls were far from rich, Villiers was even poorer than they and they treated him willingly to the 'bocks' he drank far too readily. In the early morning hours they would all accompany the master to his room and then silently disperse, 'some dumbfounded,

---

[1] *Bulles bleues*, pp. 195–6. [2] J. Bithell, op. cit., p. 6.

others, unknown to themselves, mellowed or regenerated at their contact with genius, as if they had consorted with a giant from another world'.[1] Maeterlinck paid unceasing tribute to Villiers: 'All that I have done', he wrote, 'I owe to Villiers, more to his conversations than to his works.'[2]

From this literary coterie sprang, inevitably, a review, *La Pléiade*, an ephemeral periodical not unimportant in the history of Symbolism. Théodore de Banville, the Parnassian poet, was its patron, although, save for a brief introductory note in its first issue, he did not seem to interest himself in its fortunes. The review's title is significant, because it was doubtless intended to signify the band's poetic vocation; it was only settled upon after long discussion and was finally fixed at a meeting between Mikhael, Quillard, and Saint-Pol-Roux at the latter's house, after alternatives such as *Le Symbole* and *L'Arche d'alliance* had been rejected.[3] The last meeting before going to press was held at Quillard's house, but for some reason Maeterlinck did not attend it. On his behalf Le Roy read the short story, *Le Massacre des innocents*, and a few poems of *Serres chaudes* that Maeterlinck had already written: these contributions were accepted for publication in a later number. When Le Roy returned to their lodgings late that night he found Maeterlinck in bed, but awake and burning to know if his work had passed muster.[4]

Thus from 26 rue de Condé, in March 1886, there appeared the first number of *La Pléiade*, 'revue littéraire, artistique, musicale et dramatique'. Maeterlinck's name, with his Christian name, Mooris, spelt in the Flemish fashion, appeared with others on the title-page, including those of Le Roy and Van Lerberghe, who by then had arrived in Paris. Darzens was the general editor. This new constellation of the Symbolist firmament survived six monthly issues and boasted only eighteen subscribers. Its April number announced:

For future publication: Mooris Maeterlinck, *Les Symboliques*, poetry, and *Histoires gothiques*, prose.

---

[1] *Bulles bleues*, p. 199.   [2] J. Huret, *Enquête sur l'évolution littéraire*, p. 128.
[3] Saint-Pol-Roux, 'Souvenirs', *Visages du monde*, 15 Apr. 1936, p. 78.
[4] G. Le Roy, 'A l'aube de sa gloire', *Gand artistique*, 1 Mar. 1923, p. 47.

In May there appeared the first and only *Histoire gothique*, 'Le Massacre des Innocents', followed in June by six of Maeterlinck's poems. These represent his first published work in France.

The short story was a semi-Realist transposition of Breughel's picture. One is inevitably reminded of Flaubert who in 1845, at the same age as Maeterlinck was when he went to Paris, was deeply impressed in Genoa by a reproduction of Breughel's *Temptation of St. Anthony* and in 1849 elaborated the first draft of *La Tentation de Saint Antoine*. Maeterlinck's tale, perhaps written even before he went to Paris, strikes an authentically Flemish note. By a subtle transformation the Holy Land has become Flanders. Pity and impotence before the sudden blow of Destiny would seem to be the message its writer seeks to convey. Villiers, who read this first effort, remarked: 'Very good, your *Massacre des Innocents*. But all this too solid Realism does not suit you. Music before everything! Your path lies elsewhere.'[1] By good fortune Maeterlinck accepted this trenchant advice and was thus at the outset diverted from Realism to Symbolism. Nor was this the sum of his debt to Villiers: the Breton gave to the Fleming the desire to explore the mysterious and the mystic aspects of life. He counselled him to read Ruysbroek the Admirable, the unlettered medieval Flemish monk of Groenendael, whose *Adornment of Spiritual Marriage* Maeterlinck translated in 1889. So was awakened the mystical sense latent in his Flemish nature.

The reverse of the medal, the Flemish capacity for enjoyment, was no doubt also exercised to the full by the three Belgian friends in Paris. French food, however, did not please them. In the guttural Flemish patois of Ghent they would often commiserate with each other in restaurants, 'ten es da goe vloamsch rosbifken niet zulle' (Because there aren't any good Flemish beef-steaks!).

Before returning to Belgium Maeterlinck introduced to Villiers Georges Rodenbach, then on a second visit to Paris.[2] This contact led Rodenbach in 1887 to attempt to arrange a lecture tour

---
[1] Quoted in A. Pasquier, *Maurice Maeterlinck*, p. 29.
[2] F. Ruchon, *L'Amitié de Mallarmé et de Rodenbach: lettres et textes inédits 1887–98*, p. 53 note.

in Belgium for Villiers. The plan fell through, but through the intervention of Huysmans with Jules Destrée it was realized the following year.[1] Thus in March 1888 Villiers came to Ghent to address the Cercle artistique et littéraire, of which Maeterlinck was a member. In the spring of 1886 Maeterlinck also met Verlaine, to whom he was introduced in a café.[2] This first encounter seems to have left no lasting impression on either, although later Verlaine was alleged to refer somewhat cruelly and cynically to the Belgian as 'a bit of a mountebank'.[3] Verlaine could not understand—although who better than he should have done so?—the curious blend of sincerity and insincerity that characterized the early Maeterlinck, both in literature and in life.

In June 1886, however, the three young Belgians packed their bags for home. Their first literary excursion was over, but it had merely excited their longing for more. In particular, it had incited Maeterlinck to despise the legal career upon which he was now to embark.

What impression did this young poetaster make about this time on others? Describing their meeting in Paris, Rodenbach wrote:

Maurice Maeterlinck, a boy of 22 at the most, beardless, with short hair, protruding forehead, clear, distinct eyes, with a straightforward gaze, his face harshly set, the whole denoting will-power, decision, stubbornness, a real Flemish face, with undertones of reverie and colourful sensibility. At heart a taciturn person, who is very reserved, but whose friendship must be reliable.[4]

Save for the slight error in age, and adding a possible *caveat* as to his strength of will and resoluteness, the description is exact. Particularly characteristic and significant is his silent nature, which later earned him the gibe of being *le grand taiseux*. Such hidden depths might conceal abundance or emptiness: time alone would tell.

Meanwhile Maeterlinck settled down again reluctantly in Ghent, from 1886 to 1889, practising somewhat half-heartedly as

[1] R. Baldick, *Life of Huysmans*, p. 115, gives details of Huysmans's arrangements.
[2] G. Rodenbach, *Évocations*, p. 165.   [3] A. Wade (ed.), *Letters of W. B. Yeats*, p. 255.
[4] G. Rodenbach, 'Trois nouveaux poètes', *La Jeune Belgique*, 5 July 1886, p. 318.

a barrister. His father being comparatively well off, he had little incentive to work hard in his profession. Relatives and friends of the family retained him for their affairs, but his father made him an allowance to supplement his income. Indeed, he would have been hard put to it to earn his own living. He had none of the eloquence and facility of the successful lawyer. His voice was reedy and harsh. His experience in the courts was so repugnant to him that in later years it was only with the utmost reluctance that he consented to speak in public, and even when he did so he was conspicuously unsuccessful.

He divided his life between Oostacker and Ghent. Outdoor pastimes, such as bee-keeping and horticulture, occupied him. He maintained his cult of physical fitness by bicycling, boating, and sailing on the canals. In winter he would go out on long skating expeditions along the waterways from Ghent to Terneuzen or from Bruges to Sluis, through the marshy borderlands separating Belgium from Holland. His artist eye was alive to the 'Northern scenery', as Van Lerberghe refers to it in a letter to Mockel dated 2 January 1889: 'Then polar moonrisings, adored by Maurice Maeterlinck. He is interested, too, in leaves beneath the ice, the terror abroad in the sterile countryside, the naked trees, and in a host of strange sensations.'[1] Moonlight, frozen vegetation, a barren and desolate landscape: these are the images employed to such effect in *Serres chaudes*.

A spur had been given to his literary ambitions by the publication in 1887 of twelve of these poems in a Paris anthology entitled *Le Parnasse de la Jeune Belgique*, in which seventeen other Belgian poets were also represented. He scored another minor success when a Brussels review, *La Revue générale*, published his second, and only other, short story, *Onirologie*, a curious study in dream clairvoyance that owes much to Edgar Allan Poe.

Encouraged by Van Lerberghe, always over-eulogistic in regard to his friend's work,[2] Maeterlinck decided to collect those poems already published, together with new ones, in a selection

[1] 'Quelques lettres de Charles Van Lerberghe', *Vers et prose*, Jan.–Mar. 1914.
[2] Cf. the letter from Van Lerberghe to Maeterlinck quoted at the end of M. Hamel's article, 'Deux heures au château de Médan avec Maurice Maeterlinck', *Revue belge*, 15 Aug. 1929, p. 323.

entitled *Serres chaudes*. Its printing was undertaken by Louis Van Melle, a former school friend. A small hand machine with Elzever characters was used, and Grégoire Le Roy and another friend, the budding Ghent sculptor Georges Minne, were pressed into service to help with the printing. As the type was needed for other work during the day the printing took place by night. To finance the book Maeterlinck borrowed money from his family. Eventually 155 copies of *Serres chaudes* were run off and sent to a Brussels bookseller for sale. The poems caused hardly a ripple on the literary pond, very few copies were sold, and in March 1890 Maeterlinck wrote asking for the return of the remainder.[1]

The poems of *Serres chaudes*, however, interest the reader by their very strangeness: an aura of mystery surrounds them. Torpor, ennui, melancholy, languor permeate them—sentiments the poet half felt in sincerity, half wore as a literary pose. In these pieces the values are both genuine and false. The explanation of this is to be sought in the mental and spiritual crisis through which their author was then passing. In Paris Villiers had initiated him into the atmosphere of the occult and he had begun to ponder deeply all the inexplicable phenomena of life. Death fascinated him above all, a mental fixation that was never to leave him until he had drawn his last breath. Materialistic Belgium, to be powerfully depicted later in Verhaeren's *Les Villes tentaculaires*, was anathema, yet circumstances forced him to live in it. The soulless monotony of provincial life gripped him, that life brilliantly described by Rodenbach in his novel *Bruges-la-morte*. His legal career was destined to failure. At twenty-seven he was neither in love nor loved, although he yearned to be:

> Seule la lune éclaire enfin
> De sa tristesse monotone
> Où gèle l'herbe de l'automne,
> Mes désirs malades de faim.
>
> (*Désirs d'hiver*)

Nor had he any faith to cling to. Although the poetry is imbued

---

[1] Unpublished letter of Maeterlinck dated 3 Mar. 1890, Bibliothèque Jacques Doucet, Paris, MS. 7247-16.

with a vague religiosity, he had already discarded religion and religious standards, whilst remaining loath to embrace more worldly ones. Life was running through his fingers like the barren desert sand.

Sincerity and insincerity: Maeterlinck, like all angry young men, was the child of his generation. The literary spirit of the age was the enemy of hope. Symbolism, iconoclastic, had revolted against the vulgarity and materialism of the Naturalists and the scientific dogmatism of the Positivists, but no Chateaubriand had emerged to re-enthrone Christianity on the broken altars. The plight of Verhaeren was typical: he also was in the throes of a spiritual agony of which the poetic trilogy, *Les Soirs, Les Débâcles, Les Flambeaux noirs* (1887-90), is the literary testimony. For him the crisis was resolved in 1891 by a happy marriage. Maeterlinck was to wait until 1895 before, as Lemonnier put it, he met a similar destiny in the person of Georgette Leblanc. An unpublished letter, dated 12 August 1890, which the poet wrote to Verhaeren, betrays his psychological state about this time; he writes: 'I think that illnesses, sleep, and death are feasts of the flesh, profound, mysterious, and not understood; I think there is much to seek and find in this domain that you have been the first to explore, and that the hospital is perhaps the temple of Isis.'[1] The title-poem of *Serres chaudes* reflects this pessimism:

> Mon Dieu! Mon Dieu! quand aurons-nous la pluie
> et la neige et le vent dans la serre!
>
> (*Serre chaude*)

But for the younger man the moment was not yet. The literary god that he besought offered him back nothing but his own despair.

His translation of Ruysbroek's *Adornment of Spiritual Marriage* which appeared in *La Revue générale* in October 1889 is, however, a clearer indication of his philosophical position at the time

---

[1] '...je crois que les maladies, le sommeil et la mort, sont des fêtes profondes, mystérieuses et incomprises de la chair; je crois qu'il y a beaucoup à chercher et à trouver, de ce côté que vous avez exploré le premier, et que l'hôpital est peut-être le temple d'Isis.' Unpublished letter of Maeterlinck to Verhaeren, dated 12 Aug. 1890, from Oostacker. Bibliothèque Royale, Brussels, Fonds Verhaeren.

than his poetry. Although his poems expressed his aspiration towards God and had even moved one of his earliest critics, Gérard Lelong, a Ghent Catholic writer, to speak of the 'Catholic breeze' that blew through them, there is disillusionment in them also. But Ruysbroek had led him on to the study of other mystics. The introductory essay to his translation, probably written about this time, demonstrates a wide reading of other mystical and semi-mystical works: Plato, the pseudo-Dionysius, Plotinus, Jakob Boehme, Novalis, Emerson, Coleridge—all these authors had been studied. Revealed religion had been weighed in the balance and found wanting, but the mystical way of direct communication with God still lay open. He was not alone in this belief: Huysmans's preface to Rémy de Gourmont's *Le Latin mystique* (1890) spoke of a revival of the mystical tradition in literature, but declared it would only be fruitful if identified with a return to faith. Huysmans had already been led to conversion and at one stage Maeterlinck might well have walked the same Damascus road.

Literature now occupied more and more of his leisure. In 1889 his first play, *La Princesse Maleine*, was written and by the end of the year was appearing serially in another Brussels periodical, *La Société nouvelle*. A first limited edition of the play was printed on Van Melle's hand-press in December 1889, after Maeterlinck had borrowed 200 francs from his mother to pay for the printing.

Doubtless this financial dependence upon his parents was irksome. He still lived with them in the house on the boulevard Frère-Orban, whose drawing-room was opened only on high days and holidays. The dining-room was the true focal point of the family, although with his father Maeterlinck now shared only a love of food and a delight in country pursuits. If free to do so he would have liked to live far from the city and devote himself to his writing. In December 1889 Van Lerberghe wrote of him:

... Maeterlinck's ideal is to retire to the country; he is a field rat. He dreams of silence, trees, guiltless animals, the sky and water, one unique, chosen woman, and his work in his retreat. I am only a sham town rat and this lofty ideal appeals to me too. But then this demon of a man is so superior to me, so fine, so indestructible, that I am captivated by the most simple of his ideas....[1]

But this idyll of rural retirement still lay far in the future, a remote dream.

Nevertheless, 1890 was to be a momentous year for the would-be recluse. On 13 February Mallarmé, already the high priest of Symbolism, spoke in Ghent to the Cercle artistique et littéraire on Villiers de l'Isle Adam, who had just died. Maeterlinck was present, and very probably Rodenbach, a frequenter in Paris of Mallarmé's 'Tuesday evenings' in the rue de Rome, introduced him.

In March Maeterlinck was himself the subject of a lecture. Picard, in a room in Brussels where Mallarmé had spoken a week or two before, spoke on Verhaeren, Maeterlinck, and Van Lerberghe. Through over-attention to Verhaeren the critic was, however, only able to give cursory attention to the other two poets. Nevertheless, for the first time Maeterlinck found himself the object of some interest in the Belgian capital.

This fact may have again induced him to reach out to a wider public. In June 1890, on the same press as before, he had printed a fresh edition of 150 copies of *La Princesse Maleine*. Owing to shortage of characters, every few pages the type had to be broken up and reset. The volumes were dispatched to Paul Lacomblez, a Brussels bookseller who was to become a lifelong friend of their author and who had already rendered some service to the Belgian literary movement. Once more, sales were negligible and only some fifteen copies were sold.

Apart from the usual dedicatory copies to friends—among them one to the Belgian Parnassian writer, Iwan Gilkin, with whom he had become friendly in 1887—Maeterlinck also sent a copy to Mallarmé in Paris.[2] This simple action was to save the play from oblivion and at last to launch the name of its Belgian author upon the world in a spectacular fashion. Favourably impressed by it, Mallarmé passed on the copy to his friend Paul Hervieu with the suggestion that Octave Mirbeau should review

---

[1] 'Quelques lettres de Charles Van Lerberghe', *Vers et prose*, Jan.–Mar. 1914. Letter to Mockel headed 'Gand, Déc. 88'.
[2] C. Mauclair, *Mallarmé chez lui*, p. 43.

it in *Le Figaro*. Mirbeau, who was if anything rather anti-Belgian, eventually agreed to read it and some days later Hervieu received a note from the critic bearing the one word 'Thanks'. On 24 August 1890 Mirbeau's article appeared in *Le Figaro*. Lauding the play to the skies, it was wildly exaggerated in tone:

> I know nothing of M. Maurice Maeterlinck. I do not know from where he comes or what he looks like. Whether he is old or young, rich or poor, I know not. I know only that no man is more unknown than he; and I know also that he has written a masterpiece, not a masterpiece labelled as such, a masterpiece beforehand, as are published every day by our young masters, sung on all the notes of the squeaking lyre—or rather the squeaking flute of the present day; but an admirable and pure and eternal masterpiece, a masterpiece that suffices to render a name immortal and to cause that name to be blessed by all those that hunger after the beautiful and the great; a masterpiece such as honourable, tormented artists have sometimes dreamed, in moments of enthusiasm, of writing, and as they have never written hitherto. In short, M. Maurice Maeterlinck has given us the work of this age most full of genius, and the most extraordinary and most simple as well, comparable and—shall I dare say it?—superior in beauty to what is most beautiful in Shakespeare. This work is called *La Princesse Maleine*. Are there a score of people in the world who know of it? I doubt it.

For Maeterlinck, at long last, the day of glory had arrived.

2

THE SYMBOLIST

MIRBEAU'S article caused a furore.[1] Critics who were pillars of orthodoxy, such as Sarcey in Paris and Frédérix in Brussels, esteemed the comparison with Shakespeare far-fetched and even ridiculous. On the other hand, Mallarmé wrote approvingly to Mirbeau about the play;[2] in a second letter he confessed he could not understand the uproar about Maeterlinck, whom he had noticed on his visit to Ghent and found to be 'charming, fervent and handsome, very silent'.

As for the new literary discovery himself, he was thunderstricken:

I unfold the daily paper, it is the *Figaro*, and at the top of the two first columns of the front page, I read my name picked out in large capitals: MAURICE MAETERLINCK. Amazed, expecting nothing from fate, which had never engineered such surprises for me, I rapidly scan the article, fearing the *in cauda venenum* of the French press, generally awkward about foreigners; I grow pale, I blush, the sun dazzles me.[3]

But, despite his stupefaction, he wrote immediately to thank his benefactor. Modestly he expressed astonishment that the play merited such high appreciation.[4] He had resolved, he said, to remain in Ghent and not bask in the idolizing of the Paris literary world, for he felt too timid, too awkward, and too young for such celebrity. This reserve doubtless commended itself to Mirbeau, for he and Maeterlinck remained great friends for many years.

[1] R. H. Sherard, an English journalist, claims to have attempted to 'launch' Maeterlinck before Mirbeau (cf. R. H. Sherard, *Twenty Years in Paris*, p. 323). He was told about Maeterlinck by François Coppée and sent a dispatch to his London newspaper that Paris was about to hail a new literary star. But the item was not published because he was suspected of 'puffing' a friend.
[2] Henri Mondor, *Vie de Mallarmé*, p. 754, note.   [3] *Bulles bleues*, p. 206.
[4] Unpublished letter to Mirbeau, dated 27 Aug. (1890), from Oostacker. Bibliothèque Jacques Doucet, Paris, MS. 7247-12. 'Si vous saviez comme cela m'a surpris! Je ne savais pas qu'il y eût vraiment quelque chose de si bon en cette pauvre *Princesse*.'

The stir in Belgium itself was naturally greater even than in France. Reporters besieged the Maeterlinck home. To escape from the glare of publicity the author slipped off to London for a few days, on what was most probably his first trip across the Channel.[1] On his return he found that a Brussels journalist, Léon Dommartin, had published two panegyrics about him. Astutely he wrote twice commenting sardonically upon them. He pointed out that he was not quite the magnificent physical specimen he had been represented to be, 'but let us allow the ladies to dream on'.[2] He categorically disclaims the appellation 'genius', 'which is a kindly but dangerous truculence ... which makes me smile when I consider the wretched sentences -jobber that I am in reality'.[3] In the previous letter he enthuses over London, the English landscape, the English poets, and mentions especially Walter Crane's Toy Books for children. (He states elsewhere that he admires English literature above all and reads especially Shakespeare, Coleridge, Emerson, Carlyle, and Browning.) In another letter to Mirbeau he contrasts his meteoric rise to fame with the disappointments suffered by such French poets as Villiers de l'Isle Adam and Barbey d'Aurevilly who died neglected and in obscurity.[4] Even the publication by Van Melle in July 1890 of two further plays, *Les Aveugles* and *L'Intruse* (both in one act), fails to shake his essential modesty. He confesses that in literature he is still gropingly feeling his way and in writing he is a mere tiro.

The reaction in Ghent to his new reputation was curious.[5] A few acquaintances cut him dead; others greeted him pityingly as if they had suddenly to humour a mental defective. Even his friends could not realize the magnitude of his sudden success. Some of the townsfolk considered the whole affair a hoax; others,

[1] G. Harry, *Maurice Maeterlinck*, p. 14 (English edition).
[2] Unpublished letter to Léon Dommartin, dated 20 Nov. 1890, Ghent. Bibliothèque Royale, Brussels, MS. 5622–20.
[3] 'Je passe sur *le génie*, qui est une truculence aimable mais dangereuse et qui me fait sourire lorsque je considère le misérable tripoteur de phrases que je suis en réalité.' Unpublished letter to Léon Dommartin, dated 2 Dec. 1890, Ghent. Bibliothèque Royale, Brussels, MS. 5622–21.
[4] Unpublished letter to Mirbeau, no date or place, but probably late 1890. Bibliothèque Jacques Doucet, Paris, MS. 7247–9.
[5] M. Hamel, 'Deux heures au château de Médan avec Maurice Maeterlinck', *La Revue belge*, 15 Aug. 1929, p. 319.

that Maeterlinck had engineered the publicity. In far-off Paris the adverse criticism was even worse: Mirbeau was accused of foisting a fraud upon the public in a plot to share increased royalties.[1]

The hubbub over the play brought Maeterlinck another new friend, Gérard Harry. Born in Paris of English extraction, he had settled in Brussels, where for over thirty years he was to engage in journalism and remain on close and friendly terms with Maeterlinck. In 1890 Harry translated *La Princesse Maleine* into English and submitted it to Heinemann's. The publisher's reader acrimoniously described the play as the most appalling plagiarism of Shakespeare he had ever seen. Nevertheless, the translation appeared.

Maeterlinck himself admitted the charge of plagiarism. To Harry he termed the work 'a mere Shakspiterie'. Although it owes something to *Macbeth*, the plot itself is taken from a Grimm fairy tale; nevertheless, the characters are essentially Shakespearian. The setting, if reminiscent of Flanders, also recalls Edgar Allan Poe, the translations of whose works by Baudelaire and Mallarmé were widely known among the Symbolists. The atmosphere is faintly medieval and Pre-Raphaelite. To this extent the play may be described as merely a pastiche of the dramatist's reading.

What is unusual is the theme: love pursued by sombre, hostile powers, the forces of Destiny, eventually succumbing to them in Death. In his analysis of the female soul Maeterlinck poses its two extremes: the wickedness of Queen Anne set as a foil to the purity and innocence of Maleine. Plot, characters, and treatment are a reaction against the Naturalist tradition and a drama that was content to serve up 'slices of life'. Although by 1890 the triumph of Symbolism in poetry was assured, the movement had as yet produced no drama, for Villiers de l'Isle Adam had died leaving no successor. Thus Iwan Gilkin's judgement upon *La Princesse Maleine*, 'an important work that marks a date in the history of the contemporary theatre',[2] is basically correct. The play, although not entirely Symbolist in character, already contains in embryo the sum of Maeterlinck's dramatic originality: the new twist he gave to the age-old belief that men are puppets of Fate, mani-

[1] Cf. p. 25, n. 4.   [2] I. Gilkin, 'Chronique', *La Jeune Belgique*, 1889, p. 399.

pulated in a context of unfathomable mystery; such an enigma was to be *suggested* rather than stated outright.

Despite the excitement caused by this first play it has never been acted on the stage. Several tentative arrangements were indeed made to produce it, but all fell through. In October 1890 it appears that a person passing himself off as M. Albert Carré, then Director of the Paris Théâtre du Vaudeville, even made the journey to Ghent to seek an option on it.[1] The dramatist was not at home and Carré later denied that he had ever been interested in staging the play. In November Maeterlinck wrote to *La Jeune Belgique* protesting that Paul Fort was going to produce it at the Théâtre Mixte without his consent, for he had already assigned sole rights to Antoine of the Théâtre Libre.[2] But Antoine affirmed that he had never seriously contemplated a production, despite strong pressure brought to bear upon him by Henry Bauer and Mirbeau.[3] Belgian newspapers asserted that Antoine had had to bow the knee before French playwrights, jealous of a foreigner's success.[4] Whatever the truth, it is clear that French theatrical producers considered the play a bad risk. Only rarely can a drama acclaimed as a masterpiece have achieved the doubtful distinction of never having been acted. In retrospect, the whole furore about the play appears unjustified, yet it impressed deeply what might be termed the second generation of Symbolists. Nevertheless the Belgian was to have no easy beginning to his dramatic success.

Meanwhile, his personal life resumed its uneventful tenor. He always loved to manipulate military weapons and thus enrolled in the Ghent Civic Guard, where he took his duties seriously. His mornings were devoted normally to writing. Besides his studios at Ghent and Oostacker, he had rented a small *pied-à-terre* in the rue du Marais at Brussels. Here, in a studio whose walls were hung with prints of pictures by Burne-Jones and other

[1] Unpublished letter to Mirbeau, dated 8 Oct. 1890, Oostacker. Bibliothèque Jacques Doucet, Paris, MS. 7247-10.
[2] Unpublished letter to Mirbeau, no date or place, but probably later 1890. Bibliothèque Jacques Doucet, Paris, MS. 7247-8.
[3] A. Antoine, *Le Théâtre: la Troisième République de 1870 à nos jours*, vol. i, p. 252.
[4] A. Mockel, 'Chronique littéraire', *La Wallonie*, 1891, p. 94.

English Pre-Raphaelites, he would sometimes be visited by his friend Gilkin, lodged in the nearby rue Potagère. At noon he met his friends in a café. The afternoons were occupied with sport or long walks. He read a great deal, but surprisingly few French books; in 1890 he maintained that he had finished only four: Villiers's *Axël*, Mallarmé's lecture on Villiers, Huysmans's *Certains*, and Mirbeau's *Sébastien Roch*.[1] Already he sought the ordered, routine-like existence that he clung to in later years.

He was mentally far from well and was plunged increasingly into fits of melancholia. One pretext that he gave to Mirbeau for not visiting him in Paris immediately was that he was suffering from heart trouble.[2] Only a visit to a Brussels specialist finally persuaded him that his palpitations were caused by over-eating! In May 1891 his youngest brother, Oscar, contracted double pneumonia after a skating accident and died. This tragedy imprinted itself deeply on his mind and was the inspiration of the beautiful essay, *Les Avertis*—those predestined to die young—later published in *Le Trésor des humbles*.

Although his literary prospects were now considerably brighter, Maeterlinck had no desire to become a professional writer; that status, of which for him the hack journalist was the most abject example, was one he wholly despised. He in fact was wont to declare that it was virtually impossible for him to write to order. He therefore cast about for some not too onerous official post giving him enough time to pursue writing as a hobby. Senator Vannerus de Solart was asked to use his influence to obtain his appointment as the local magistrate at Waarschot, near Ghent. Until his literary notoriety the senator had expressed a strong desire to help Maeterlinck, but now, fearing writers were not quite respectable, he declined to do so. In any case, since the Belgian government remained implacably hostile to writers, the senator's representations might well have proved unsuccessful.

In early 1891 Maeterlinck was interviewed by Jules Huret, then conducting his *Enquête sur l'évolution littéraire*, which appeared serially in the *Écho de Paris* between 3 March and 25 July. The

---

[1] Unpublished letter to Mirbeau, no date, from Oostacker. Bibliothèque Jacques Doucet, Paris, MS. 7247–11.   [2] Cf. p. 27, n. 1.

journalist confirms that he is simple in his habits, rather shy and modest, yet sincere. He confessed to a 'ferocious appetite', having already developed a typically Flemish love for the pleasures of the table. He had practically given up advocacy, although, he told Huret, 'from time to time a poor peasant comes and asks me to defend him, and I plead—in Flemish'. In art his admiration went to Puvis de Chavannes, in literature to Laforgue and Baudelaire. He also mentioned approvingly Gide's *Cahiers d'André Walter*. (In July 1891 he met Gide for the first time, when the young French writer was travelling in Belgium with his mother. Gide's entry in the *Journal* further demonstrates his enthusiasm for Maeterlinck at that time.)[1] Another incongruous trait in Maeterlinck's personality emerges when in February 1891 he went off to the Cologne Carnival, possibly on his first visit to Germany.[2] But he was a curious blend of intellectuality and sensuality.

Huret's *Enquête* doubtless served to stimulate interest anew in the Belgian author. Percheron and Retté enlisted the help of the young producer, Lugné-Poë, in persuading Paul Fort to include Maeterlinck's one-act drama *L'Intruse* in a matinée programme given by the Théâtre d'Art as a benefit performance to be shared between Verlaine and Paul Gauguin, the painter. Thus, on 21 May 1891, for the first time one of Maeterlinck's plays was publicly performed. It was placed last on the programme, for if the bill, which also included a one-act drama by Verlaine and the recital of various poems, proved too long, arrangements had been made to omit Maeterlinck's play. In fact, it caused a sensation and Quillard said it was 'the revelation of the day'.[3] The dramatist was not present, most possibly because his brother Oscar died the day before the performance.

Written at the end of 1889, *L'Intruse* is a *drame d'attente*. Death is the grim 'intruder' whose arrival, although merely suggested, is awaited with foreboding and terror. There is little Shakespearian about this play, but much that is Flemish. The scene is laid in an old country house in Flanders; a Flemish clock

[1] A. Gide, *Journal*, vol. i, p. 22 (Rio de Janeiro edition, 1943).
[2] Note 7 to Inventory of unpublished letters of Maeterlinck to Mockel, *Annales de la Fondation Maeterlinck*, Ghent, vol. i, 1955, p. 100.
[3] J. Robichez, *Le Symbolisme au théâtre*, p. 123.

occupies a prominent place in one corner, marking not only the passage of the hours but reminding the reader, in this drama which contains an element of Platonism, that 'time is the moving shadow of eternity'. Maeterlinck's own philosophical position is also clearly set out for the first time; concerning the blind old grandfather the uncle remarks: 'Not to know where one is, not to know whence one comes, not to know whither one is going, no longer to distinguish midday from midnight, nor summer from winter . . . and always these shadows, these shadows. . . . I would prefer to cease to live. . . .'[1] Man is blind and irredeemably lost, with only occasional flashes of faint perception—an intuitive knowledge, usually of evil. Such is the substance of this first, truly Symbolist play.

In 1891 Maeterlinck became the storm-centre in one of the final episodes in the conflict between the new generation of writers and officialdom, a struggle that had been intensified since the rebuff to Lemonnier in 1883. This time the fight concerned the Triennial Prize for Dramatic Literature. The chairman of the official committee appointed to make the award was Gustave Frédérix, whose implacable hostility to his younger contemporaries was notorious. In the period 1889–91 the only new Belgian dramatist of note had been Maeterlinck; grudgingly, and with many strictures that damned the author with faint praise, he was recommended. Maeterlinck, mindful of the Lemonnier episode, acidly refused the honour, writing in *L'Art moderne*: 'I have not yet received official notification of this misfortune, but . . . I refuse this unforeseen academic prize.'[2] Picard, in an editorial entitled 'A Well-deserved Lesson', draws a distinction between numskull officialdom and the people who, despite bad leadership, cherish affection for the true artist. It had been Baudelaire who said: 'In Belgium they only think as a herd. In Belgium the great crime is not to conform.'

The quarrel about the prize broadened out into more general issues. The Brussels newspaper *La Nation* had just begun 'an

[1] *Théâtre*, vol. i, p. 244.
[2] Letter to *L'Art moderne*, dated 15 Sept. 1891, reproduced in the editorial to the number dated 27 Sept. 1891.

inquiry into the state of literature' modelled on Huret's. Georges Eekhoud replied to the inquiry: 'Our principal enemies were and are still the bureaucrats, the professors of literature, mere official spokesmen, the snobs and "old women" of criticism.' In a letter to Huret, reproduced in *L'Art moderne*, Maeterlinck made clear that his personal refusal to accept the prize was due to the treatment meted out to his colleagues in the past; for 500 francs, the usual value of the award, '. . . a country thus gives itself, in a fairly commercial fashion, the puny airs of a Maecenas which it is useful to discourage'.[1] The author's foes accused him again of turning the whole affair into a publicity stunt that would net him far more than the prize. Three years later the storm broke out again when the same official committee declared him ineligible for the award because of his attitude in 1891. Not till after 1897, when Maeterlinck had settled in France for good, did the political authorities begin to regard him more favourably. But the author forgot more slowly and it was only in 1914 that he finally buried the hatchet.

The publication in 1891 of *Les Sept Princesses*, written at the end of 1890, provoked another tempestuous outburst. The orthodox critics attacked the play and taunted him with Mirbeau's unwarranted comparison of its author to Shakespeare. Maeterlinck retorted that they wished to dig his grave with this gibe. As for *Les Sept Princesses*, he said, it was 'a mere visiting-card', the last of his little trilogy of death. He was already meditating other works of a different nature, such as one to be entitled *La Beauté dans la maison* and another called *La Destinée dans la maison*. At that time he was also working on a drama of passion which, he hoped, would rid him of being labelled 'the poet of terror'.[2] Indeed, he declared, in writing *Les Sept Princesses* he had striven to the utmost to suppress all elements of dread.

Yet, one must admit, this play, a tableau recalling the albums of the Pre-Raphaelite Walter Crane rather than a drama proper, evokes above all the sentiment of terror. The princely lover who returns to find his beloved dead is indeed a figure of legend, but

---
[1] E. Picard (?), 'L'Incident Maeterlinck', *L'Art moderne*, 4 Oct. 1891, p. 320.
[2] Letter to *L'Art moderne*, 29 Nov. 1891, p. 380.

this is no fairy tale. Rather is it the allegory of Love seeking after the Ideal. This Ideal may be attained only by penetrating Death itself, and yet, once Man approaches, the Ideal itself dies and the barrier remains between the two. The play may be regarded as a symbolical sequel to 'Et s'il revenait un jour', one of Maeterlinck's *Chansons* which is itself based on a poem by Dante Gabriel Rossetti.[1]

The fresh polemic in Brussels stimulated in Paris yet another upsurge of curiosity regarding Maeterlinck. As a result, Lugné-Poë persuaded Paul Fort to stage *Les Aveugles*. Thus, on 11 December 1891 the troupe of the Théâtre d'Art performed the play at the Théâtre Moderne. The occasion was a notable one, for during one item on the bill, a recital of the *Cantique des Cantiques*, perfumes were sprayed about the auditorium in a somewhat derisory attempt to practise the theory of Baudelaire's *Correspondances*! Lugné-Poë acted the oldest blind man in *Les Aveugles*, and a dummy represented the dead priest. At one point, Lugné-Poë, eyes closed, had to guide the dog to the corpse, gripping its coat tightly. The action of course really demands that the dog should lead the blind man. At the crucial point, the animal's attention was diverted, thus making the ruse obvious. The audience, already in high spirits after having seen the young zealots of Symbolism squirting cheap scent everywhere, rocked with laughter. Angry words were exchanged between the 'converted' and the profane, and blows were even meted out.

In *Les Aveugles*, written probably early in 1890, Death is again the protagonist. Out on a walk, the old priest who is conducting a group of blind people suddenly dies. They are left helpless and abandoned in a spot where they are a prey to many dangers, not the least being the terror in their own minds. When their fear reaches its climax there appears on the scene a mysterious Stranger, none other than Death himself, and with his arrival the weird drama closes. Once again the interpretation must be allegoric: this is the plight of humanity, unguided and forsaken. The dead priest may symbolize the Church, religion, or even God Himself. The blind

---

[1] W. D. Halls, 'Maeterlinck and Anglo-American Literature', *Annales de la Fondation Maeterlinck*, vol. i, 1955, pp. 15–16.

cannot even huddle together for comfort. The oldest blind man can foresee their fate, for he is the *seer*; the one sighted person in the party, a young baby, cries with intuitional knowledge when the dread visitor, the harbinger of evil and death, appears. Thus Maeterlinck conveys that Destiny, a force of wickedness, has in its relentless power God's creature, Man, or, more terrible still, has even vanquished God Himself.

The similarity between *L'Intruse* and *Les Aveugles* is patent, and was moreover remarked upon at the time by the critic Jules Lemaître.[1] These two plays, with *Les Sept Princesses*, constitute a dramatic trilogy of death. If the dominant emotions they evoke are horror and terror, their intellectual content reflects despair. In November 1891 Maeterlinck wrote to Verhaeren, 'I am thirsty, at the moment, for life.'[2] But his black mood, 'the dark night of the soul', was not yet to lift.

At the performance of *Les Aveugles* Maeterlinck had met Lugné-Poë. The author, who by then had practically finished the writing of *Pelléas et Mélisande*, suggested that Lugné-Poë should produce it. Shortly afterwards the company of the Théâtre d'Art came to Brussels and staged *L'Intruse* at the Théâtre du Parc. Lugné-Poë then visited Maeterlinck in Ghent.

This marked the beginning of a business friendship between the two. When in Belgium Lugné-Poë would stay with Maeterlinck in Oostacker or Ghent, and on his visits to Paris Maeterlinck would put up at Lugné's rooms in the rue Turgot. This meant that Lugné and his actress companion Suzanne Déprès, whom he was later to marry in London, slept on a mattress on the floor. One night the couple were awakened by a loud crack; the bed on which the heavy Belgian had been sleeping had given way under his weight![3]

Once again, Maeterlinck had the humiliation of seeing one of his plays turned unwittingly into a farce, when *L'Intruse* was put

---

[1] J. Lemaître, review of *Les Aveugles*, *Journal des Débats*, 14 Dec. 1891.
[2] Unpublished letter to Verhaeren, dated 18 Nov. 1891, no place, Bibliothèque Royale, Brussels, Fonds Verhaeren.
[3] For details of the relationship between Lugné-Poë and Maeterlinck, cf. G. H. Lugné-Poë, 'Mes confidences sur Maeterlinck', *Conferencia*, 15 Sept. 1933, pp. 353–68.

on at Caudheil's theatre in Brussels in March 1892. The play depends upon the discreet use of stage effects, such as a lamp that unaccountably dims and brightens. These tricks were bungled, so that, for example, when the dialogue demanded that the light should dim, it brightened. The audience became hilarious. After the performance Lugné-Poë expostulated to the hapless stage manager. The latter, exasperated equally by the fiasco, lunged out at Lugné-Poë, who neatly dodged, with the result that the blow landed fairly and squarely on Berthe Bady, the leading lady. Such was the inauspicious commencement of Maeterlinck's theatrical progress in his own country.

The spring of 1892 saw the completion of *Pelléas et Mélisande*, a work which for the dramatist was more a penance than a pleasure. In a letter to his publisher, Lacomblez, he wrote: 'I reckon on undertaking a fairly long journey, for I have had more than enough of literature and of this empty blind-horse labour.'[1] The long journey' was, however, not embarked upon.

In April 1892 he developed an interest in telepathy. Van Lerberghe, then studying in Brussels, and Maeterlinck in Ghent engaged without much success in telepathy experiments.[2] The first consisted of Maeterlinck sitting with his Civic Guard rifle in front of him, and for half an hour Van Lerberghe concentrated on divining what the object might be. This trivial incident is significant, for much later Maeterlinck was to write many essays in which extra-sensory phenomena were examined. It reveals a different facet of the man then principally known as the poet of 'terror plays'.

During the summer Maeterlinck was again worried about the state of his health. He feared that he was suffering from a serious throat disease and consulted a Dr. Crocq, a well-known Brussels specialist. Once again the doctor dismissed his symptoms as insignificant: he was merely suffering from hoarseness.[3]

With the passage of time Maeterlinck found new friends, who

[1] Unpublished letter to Paul Lacomblez, dated 13 Feb. 1892, Ghent. Bibliothèque Royale, Brussels, MS. II 6629C–6: '. . . je compte entreprendre un assez long voyage, car j'en ai plein le dos de la littérature et de ce vain travail de cheval aveugle.'
[2] C. Van Lerberghe, *Lettres à Fernand Severin*, p. 14.
[3] Ibid., p. 31, letter marked 'début de 1893?'

gradually supplanted the old. Grégoire Le Roy had been forced through financial necessity to take up uncongenial work that left him no time to share Maeterlinck's leisurely mode of existence. Van Lerberghe had moved to the Brussels suburb of Schaarbeek and visited Ghent only infrequently. Although their old friendship was spasmodically renewed he complained bitterly that their former intimacy had gone; in October 1893 he wrote: '. . . that phlegmatic and icy Maeterlinck, who loves me like a brother and never writes to me, because for him it is childish, girlish, to write to each other.'[1] Maeterlinck's indifference to former associates was to become more and more marked as the years went by.

Nevertheless, his circle of friends and acquaintances widened. In 1892 Maeterlinck had joined the committee of a new literary review, *Le Réveil*, published in Ghent under the auspices of the Cercle artistique et littéraire. Through a young Ghent poet, Lucien de Busscher, Charles Doudelet, destined to become Belgium's foremost designer and engraver at the turn of the century, had also joined the committee. Doudelet and Maeterlinck soon became firm friends. On long walks and excursions that took them as far afield as Furnes or Dixmude they would discuss a diversity of topics, ranging from country pursuits to Flemish art. Doudelet said they became 'spiritual brothers',[2] but their friendship, which endured for twenty years and more, developed also a professional aspect: in 1896 they discussed enthusiastically a project to establish a marionette theatre in Paris, with the backing of Lugné-Poë, and later Doudelet designed the sets for at least two of Maeterlinck's plays, *Joyzelle* and *L'Oiseau bleu*.

Another new-found friend was Cyriel Buysse, one of the most outstanding Flemish novelists that Belgium has produced. They met while skating at Drongen (Tronchiennes), near Ghent, and for a while Buysse mistook him for a certain Van der Mensbrugge. Maeterlinck did not bother to correct the error; when it was discovered and he was taxed with it, he merely remarked: 'What was the use? I didn't know whether we should become friends

[1] Ibid., p. 47.
[2] F. de Smet, 'Maeterlinck et Doudelet', *Gand artistique*, 1 Mar. 1923, pp. 62–63.

and, in that case, the mistake was unimportant. Now it's different!'[1] The friendship thus etablished, they met almost daily in the Café Albion in Ghent. Buysse, Doudelet, with three other leading lights of *Le Réveil*, Albert Guéquier and the brothers De Busscher, would forgather there about eleven o'clock. Towards midday Maeterlinck would arrive, fresh from a morning's writing, pipe in mouth, his pockets bulging with newspapers. Light-hearted conversation would be interlarded with earnest artistic and literary debate. Maeterlinck fought shy of discussing his own works and if the talk touched upon one of them would as often as not refer to it as: 'Ah yes, that old story, that old joke', and modestly change the subject.

In March 1893 a great event in Maeterlinck's somewhat humdrum life was a second meeting with Verlaine, whom he had not seen since his Paris visit. A Belgian lecture tour had been arranged for the French poet by Henry Carton de Wiart, with the help of Maeterlinck.[2] Verlaine spoke first in Brussels, then in Antwerp, Verviers, and Charleroi. Another lecture followed in Brussels, when he addressed the members of the Brussels Bar on the edifying subject, 'Mes Prisons', before he departed for Ghent.

On 7 March 1893 a reception committee headed by Maeterlinck welcomed him at the station. The poet greeted the assembled company by shouting from his carriage window, 'Je la prends au sucre', intending to convey that he took his absinthe with sugar.[3] In Ghent Verlaine put up in a grand manner at the Hôtel de la Poste, where his expenses were paid by Jean Casier, a young Catholic poet. It is alleged that the Casier family carriage, with its armorial bearings, was also put at the disposal of Verlaine, who shocked his devout hosts by leaving it conspicuously for some while outside a local brothel—but the story is probably apocryphal. At his lecture, Maeterlinck, Le Roy, and Georges Minne, all handy with their fists, deemed it necessary to stand by in case of a disturbance, but although the talk was a flop, no untoward incidents occurred.

[1] C. Buysse, 'La Jeunesse de Maeterlinck', *Gand artistique*, 1 Mar. 1923, p. 48.
[2] H. Carton de Wiart, *Souvenirs littéraires*, p. 147.
[3] *Bulles bleues*, p. 189.

THE SYMBOLIST

Preparations had begun in February 1893 to stage *Pelléas et Mélisande* in Paris. The Théâtre d'Art secured the half-promise of the Théâtre du Vaudeville at which to give a matinée performance, but eventually Albert Carré, its director, let them down. Nothing daunted, Lugné-Poë, aided by Camille Mauclair, put the play into rehearsal. The company were heartened by a note from the writer Rachilde, who declared herself to be the playwright's most fervid admirer. Financial support was lacking, but Maeterlinck, upon his arrival in Paris, offered to sign promissory notes, which he said he would redeem when he inherited his family's wealth. Lugné-Poë's father was also induced to part with 200 francs. (Incidentally, Lugné-Poë remarks that he always found Maeterlinck generous: he often returned his royalties to the Théâtre de l'Œuvre, the successor to the Théâtre d'Art when Paul Fort gave up.) Mauclair whipped up enthusiasm in the Press, admirably supported by Mirbeau, who allowed his signature to be appended to a propagandistic article Mauclair wrote and published in the *Écho de Paris*.[1] These efforts resulted in several prominent people, among them Henri de Régnier, Rachilde, Robert de Rothschild, and Tristan Bernard, lending their support to the enterprise.

On 17 May 1893 the single matinée of Maeterlinck's masterpiece finally took place at the Théâtre des Bouffes-Parisiens. As usual, the audience consisted largely of the author's most ardent admirers, among them, on this occasion, being Mallarmé, Whistler, Hervieu, and Paul Adam; but his disparagers likewise turned out in full force.

The story of *Pelléas* is too well known to need recounting, but Sarcey's hostile summary of it is interesting: 'This drama, my goodness! ... It is the incestuous love of a married woman for her brother-in-law; the outraged husband surprises the guilty ones, kills the one and wounds the other, who dies afterwards.'[2] And indeed if there were no more to the play than this, little would need to be said. However, Maeterlinck presents the story on two separate planes. As a true-to-life social problem it might

---

[1] C. Mauclair, *Servitude et grandeur littéraires*, p. 101.
[2] F. Sarcey, review in *Le Temps*, 22 May 1893.

well have been tackled by Ibsen or the Naturalists, for it depicts the irreconcilable cleavage between the natural law and the social law. Must a woman, almost tricked, in her extreme youth and innocence, into marriage with one she does not love, remain faithful to him in all circumstances? Society upholds the inviolability of the marriage vow, but a natural law more powerful than social codes bids her prefer her lover to her husband. But to this social problem Maeterlinck propounds no saving solution: the final catastrophe is ineluctable.

Presented thus, the story of brothers who are enemies because rivals in love is banal. Yet Maeterlinck has invested this *Tristan*-like tale with a fresh, Symbolist meaning, on a different level from the moral and social aspects of the dramatic situation. It is the symbol of love which, personified in Mélisande, comes stealing into a bleak and weary world. For a space it illumines the all-engulfing shadows and then is as suddenly extinguished. For love, even love, brings in its train misery and horror, jealousy, murder, and intolerable suffering. Such is the deeper significance of the theme of *Pelléas*.

In the play, Death is enthroned, as before, but Love has come to challenge its hegemony, another force, asserts Maeterlinck, among those invisible powers that weave the pattern of our lives. Hitherto, passion and tenderness had found no place in his plays. In *Pelléas* there is affection and love, but Love is not to be welcomed, for it can only encompass disaster, leaving Death even more firmly ensconced as the arbiter of Man's destiny.

Biographically, the most interesting facet in the play is Maeterlinck's treatment of love and innocence. Mélisande is the prototype of his early heroines, the 'child-wife'. This child heroine is reminiscent of Poe's Annabel Lee, or of the young and innocent females depicted in Pre-Raphaelite painting. But the ultimate choice of such a model obviously lay within Maeterlinck himself.

Grégoire Le Roy, who was under-sexed, also made children his heroines. There are grounds for believing that Maeterlinck, by contrast, was over-sexed. Both lack and excess of sexuality may well lead to psychological regression, thus providing an explanation of characters such as Mélisande. Mockel, early on,

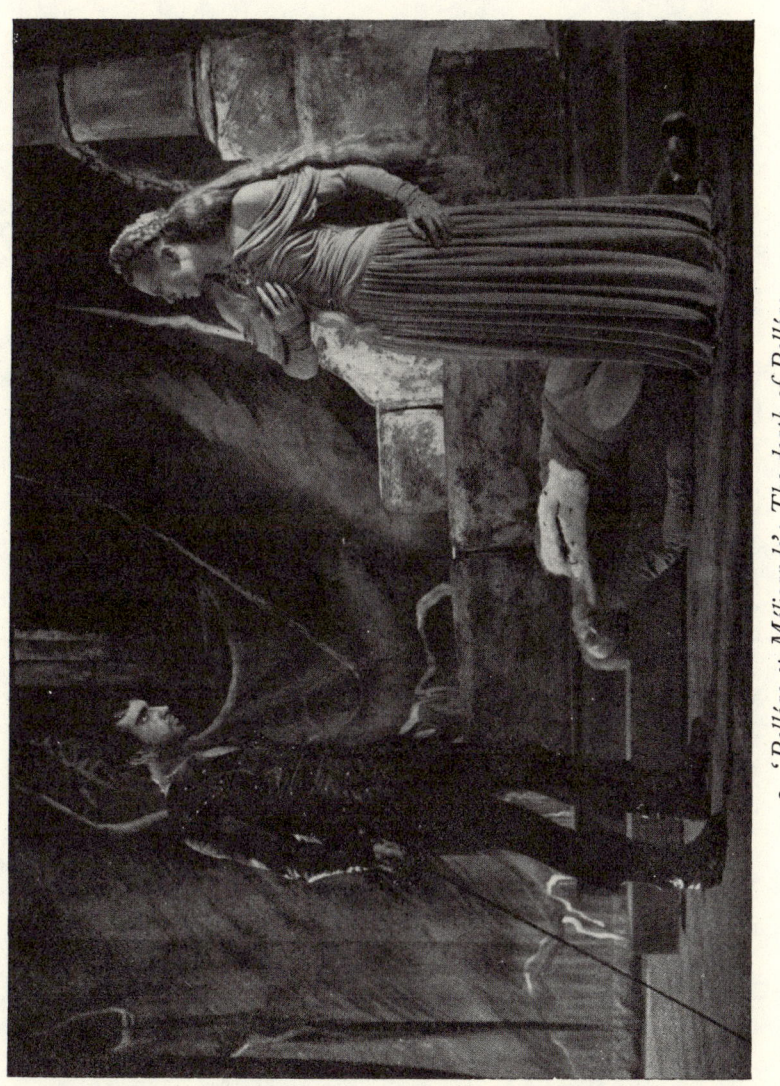

2. *Pelléas et Mélisande*: The death of Pelléas

had attributed the essential form of Maeterlinck's ideas to sadism: in *Pelléas et Mélisande* this expresses itself as a desire to inflict cruelty upon innocence. Maeterlinck himself associates sadism with pity, and certainly the dramatic use of brutality to emphasize the wrong suffered by beauty and virginity heightens the effect of compassion. But this persecution of the innocent may be more than a mere literary device, and represent a state of morbid pathology in the psychology of the poet, whose *Serres chaudes* had betrayed a mind at the end of its tether and, in the wildness of its imaginings, near to dementia.

For the Paris performance of the play the staging was strikingly effective. The set was almost Shakespearian in its bareness. The lighting, shining from overhead, cast grey tones and slight shadows everywhere. The costumes were copied from portraits by Memlinc and from the simple Pre-Raphaelite decorations in the albums of Walter Crane. The stage was separated from the auditorium by a thin gauze curtain. It was hoped thereby to simulate the mysteriousness of the setting, 'out of time and out of place', blurring in shadow the outlines of reality.

During the performance Maeterlinck was so anxious as to the play's reception that he paced the streets round the Palais-Royal and would not observe the spectators. In the main his nervousness was unfounded, for the audience liked the play. The critics, however, gave it a mixed reception: Sarcey, as was to be expected, waxed sarcastic; Rémy de Gourmont commented on the dialogue, which, he claimed, by its provincialisms and general awkwardness proclaimed the dramatist's Belgian origins.[1] On the other hand, Mallarmé registered enthusiastic approval. Financially, the matinée yielded little: a supper for the company ordered in the nearby Gutenberg Café had to be paid for in part by the café-proprietor, a friend of Lugné-Poë.

Nevertheless the performance had been seen by Alhaiza, a director of the Brussels Théâtre du Parc. He arranged for the company to give a performance in the Belgian capital on 5 June 1893, which was followed by another a day or two later. Once again Maeterlinck met with ridicule in his own country.

[1] R. de Gourmont, *Les Jeunes*, p. 239.

Van Lerberghe, who was present at the first performance, described the reaction of the audience:

> The whole legion was there to defend the work of Maeterlinck against the eternal enemy, the *bourgeois*, who also had come in a great procession. . . . The hatred of the *bourgeois* for all that is ideal, great, and beautiful in Maeterlinck is really fierce. Sublime passages were laughed at; a section of the public even went so far as to take advantage of the darkness to imitate the noise of kissing in the great love scene of Act IV. That lovely scene of the sheep told by little Yniold and which is like a sudden pastoral, a distant, melancholic air on a flute between two sombre scenes, was welcomed by gusts of laughter. And it was played by a marvellous young girl.[1]

Sarcey's Belgian counterpart, Gustave Frédérix, writing in *L'Indépendance*, jeered scornfully at the play. The *Patriote* gave it ten lines and dubbed Maeterlinck a *zwanzeur* (leg-puller). For the author it was yet another humiliation, another cause for having no regrets when, like Rodenbach, Verhaeren, and Mockel before him, he went to settle in France.

The Paris performance of *Pelléas et Mélisande* may well have been the first time that he actually met Mirbeau. At any rate, a little while before the performance he wrote thanking his benefactor for what he then believed was Mirbeau's article in the *Écho de Paris* and concluded: 'Thank you again and again and once more, my dear wonderful friend, to whom I owe everything, and forgive me for saying it so badly. Ah, how happy I shall be to see you at last!'[2] Another meeting was with Mallarmé, when, on the eve of the performance, Mauclair took him along to the rue de Rome. Their encounter does not seem to have impressed Maeterlinck, for he does not mention it, although much later he did deplore in a general way the 'affected atmosphere'[3] of the Symbolist leader's 'Tuesday evenings'.

Undaunted by the chilly reception in Belgium of *Pelléas*, in late 1893 Lugné-Poë, accompanied by Maeterlinck, took the

---
[1] C. Van Lerberghe, *Lettres à Fernand Severin*, pp. 38–39.
[2] Unpublished letter to Mirbeau, no date, Paris. Bibliothèque Jacques Doucet, Paris MS. 7247-7.
[3] Phrase in an unpublished letter to Mockel, from Nice, in 1927. Letter No. 49 to Mockel, *Annales de la Fondation Maeterlinck*, vol. i, 1955, p. 105.

play on tour to Holland. It had a successful reception in both Rotterdam and The Hague. Thus, for the first time, the Belgian experienced what was to be his fate: popularity abroad, ridicule or indifference in Belgium or France.

Nevertheless, *Pelléas* was to achieve distinction. Through Henri de Régnier the play came to the notice of Claude Debussy, then a struggling, almost unknown composer. After consulting Mauclair, Maeterlinck gave Debussy permission to compose a score for the work and by August 1893 the composer had embarked on the music that was to ensure for the play a lasting niche in the history of drama.

For over a year Maeterlinck had published nothing save a few of the Rossetti-esque *Chansons* that had been appearing in reviews from 1891 onwards. These were collected later into *Douze chansons*, the original title for which was probably *La Quenouille et la besace*, an obvious borrowing from Rossetti's *The Staff and Scrip*. But 1893 saw another burst of literary activity. The three 'dramas for puppets', *Alladine et Palomides*, *Intérieur*, and *La Mort de Tintagiles*, published in 1894, were probably then in the course of composition. Of *Alladine et Palomides* little need be said save that, on the author's own confession, it is a mere 'decoction of *Pelléas*', but not so skilfully written. The same element of sadism appears, this time in Ablamore, the old king, who takes revenge on Alladine, his young and innocent Greek slave whom he loves. She has given her affections to the knight Palomides, who somewhat resembles the author himself, torn always between his aspirations towards the Ideal and the exigencies of his own sensuality. By contrast, however, just as *Pelléas* is the masterpiece of Maeterlinck's legendary theatre, *L'Intérieur* is the masterpiece of his 'static' theatre, the theatre of everyday life. There is no action in the play, which simply describes the approach of a group of people, bearing the dead body of a girl who has been drowned, to her home, where her family, all unsuspecting as yet, are happily enjoying the evening. Once again the symbolism is apparent: Destiny threatens happiness at every turn. The last of the marionette trilogy, *La Mort de Tintagiles*, closes the first period of the Maeterlinckian drama, and marks the nadir of despair towards which his works had steadily moved in these early stages of his career. The struggle between Love and Death becomes the principal theme in this play, with Death as the inevitable victor. Yet, in one sense, the work foreshadows the dramatist's later development: Ygraine, sister of the doomed little Tintagiles, hurls defiance at Death. The play ends on a note of challenge. For two years Maeterlinck was not to write again for the theatre, and in this period he was to acquire from Emerson, no less than from personal experience, some faith in life and in the possibility—to put it no higher—of some power capable of vanquishing the force of Destiny.

His interest in Emerson had probably been aroused when he had been asked to write a preface to a translation by a Belgian lady, Mlle Mali (who signed herself, perhaps symbolically, I. Will), of seven essays by the American. This work appeared in February 1894, a full year before his meeting with Georgette Leblanc, who is generally alleged to have relieved his pessimism. For him Emerson is a source of consolation and encouragement, 'the good, early-morning shepherd of the pale green fields of a new optimism, natural and plausible'. He makes life appear worth living: 'He came for several at the time when it was necessary to come and at the moment when [men] had mortal need of new explanations.'[1]

But the passage to optimism was not easy. The essay, 'L'Étoile', published in *Le Figaro* on 24 September 1894, marks a relapse into despair before the insoluble problem of Destiny. Maeterlinck's blackest hour had come, but the dawn was now not far off.

---

[1] *Le Trésor des humbles*, p. 132.

3

THE THINKING REED

BETWEEN 1886 and 1894 there germinated in Maeterlinck's mind all the seeds of thought that were to come to full maturity in his later years. Some, indeed, bore early fruits and were already beginning to wither by 1894: of such were his ideas on Symbolism; others had fallen on sterile places and had never grown: such were his religious beliefs. The development of his thought during this first period of his career had followed closely the circumstances of his life and the intellectual contacts he had made. Among these last one personal influence above all must be emphasized, that of Villiers de l'Isle Adam.

The 'Chateaubriand of Symbolism' had stamped with his personality the course of Maeterlinck's thought. Villiers had denounced Positivism and had proclaimed the existence of a universe more real than the visible one—a cosmos of imagination and dream. In the theatre Maeterlinck is the protagonist of the reaction towards Idealism that had begun with Villiers's *Axël*. The Breton had penetrated the mysterious world and discovered with disgust its corruption, even in love. The Fleming had explored behind the façade of materialistic Belgium, and had likewise been revolted. Love, now ugly, now beautiful, exercised no healing or redeeming power. A Catholic, Villiers sought to resolve the mystery of life not through the ways of faith but by a bold probing into the so-called occult sciences of sorcery, spiritualism, and magnetism, and by the study of obscure philosophical concepts. Maeterlinck had studied the works of the mystics, but had turned his back upon his Christian upbringing; instead, he postulated the existence of tremendous occult forces controlling the destinies of men.

To these hidden powers Maeterlinck gave the name of Destiny. They were the arbiter of the soul, whose reality, despite his abandonment of religion, he continued to believe in as the 'essential' part of the self. But Man has no happy Destiny: 'To go in search of destiny, is it not to go in search of human sorrows? There is no destiny of joy; there is no happy star.'[1] Thus in his early plays no exercise of the will or the intelligence can avail against a hostile Fate. Man is helpless, battened upon by misfortune and Death, the helpmeet of Destiny, dreadful because it brings with it the unknown. The soul, hemmed in by disaster, can only stand mute with terror.

This philosophical concept is the basis of his dramatic aesthetic. The typical attitude of his characters is as if benumbed with fear. The family that waits helplessly in *L'Intruse*; the blind that seem petrified into inaction in *Les Aveugles*; the royal couple beating helplessly against the glass partition, not daring to use the subterranean way open to them, in *Les Sept Princesses*—all are imbued with a horror that renders them powerless.

Love is also a weapon of Destiny, whether it be between man and woman or brother and sister, for it likewise encompasses disaster. Maleine and Hjalmar, Pelléas and Mélisande, Alladine and Palomides—these love and are loved, but Death cuts them off irrevocably from each other. Thus also is the child Tintagiles snatched ruthlessly from his sisters. One of the highest sentiments of Man leads him to his doom.

But there are inklings even in these early plays that Love may be bivalent. The instrument of Death may become the key that unlocks the intelligence and the will. Pelléas and Mélisande accept their destruction as inevitable, but Ygraine, the sister of Tintagiles, sets diligently to watch and ward off Death intent upon its victim. With her, reason re-enters the Maeterlinck drama. Though fruitless her striving, the attempt has nevertheless been made. She foreshadows the later Monna Vanna, whose love inspires a will to happiness that finally triumphs over impending catastrophe.

More terrible still, in these early plays, is the fact that Destiny claims its victims singly and solitarily. Maleine is murdered when alone in her bedroom, far from the protecting arm of her lover. As Death approaches, the silent throng around Mélisande withdraw

[1] *Le Trésor des humbles*, p. 184.

to a distance. Alladine and Palomides, feebly calling to each other, meet Death apart. Tintagiles dies alone behind the barrier of a great steel door. The sick mother in *L'Intruse* has no consoling family around her bed. There is an orbit of solitariness about the blind in *Les Aveugles* that arises from the very nature of their affliction. The Ophelia-like character of the dead girl in *Intérieur* plunged unseen to the water's depths. Maeterlinck could not have insisted more passionately upon the essential isolation of the human soul.

Passivity is the keynote of this 'static theatre'. It is the logical upshot of the inertia of will exhibited by the characters. Events, indeed, seem to come to them, rather than they go forth to meet events. Yet often—and in this Maeterlinck demonstrates his belief in intuitional knowledge—they perceive the ill that is to befall them. The character type of the 'seer' or 'sage' seems to possess a kind of elementary wisdom. The baby in *Les Aveugles*, the sightless grandfather in *L'Intruse*, the child Yniold in *Pelléas*, as well as Arkel—these, though powerless to prevent the tragedy, have presentiments of danger. Such characters are significant because, later, through the acquiring of wisdom Maeterlinck saw a way to mitigate the evil effects of Destiny.

It is the females who are shown as the most pitiful toys of Destiny: the most pure, the most innocent, the most weak, are its chosen victims. The evil that falls upon them is all the more pathetic because unmerited. This, though it is feasible to consider it as an exteriorization of the sadism in Maeterlinck's nature, may also be regarded as a manifestation of a great compassion for mankind. In strong contrast to this typical female appear two other types: the ambitious Anne, sensual and disgusting, and Astolaine, the ideal, the personification of physical beauty and spiritual power.

The speech of his characters betrays their consciousness of fear and terror. They indulge in useless repetitions, stammering phrases, and are generally incoherent, lapsing into long and awkward silences—all characteristics of Maeterlinck's own mode of speech. But the silence is active as well as passive. Side by side with the dialogue actually spoken Maeterlinck is concerned to express another dialogue. In *Le Trésor des humbles* he was to affirm: 'There might rather be heard, above the ordinary dialogue of the reason and the sentiments, the more solemn and uninterrupted dialogue of the human being and his destiny.'[1] With Carlyle, from whom he first learnt the virtues of silence, he believed that only thus do souls communicate, and only occasionally do their inmost thoughts rise to consciousness and utterance.

Thus the *frisson nouveau* that Maeterlinck introduced into the drama is one of fear and of the unknown, in which he tried to express his own wonder and bewilderment at the mystery of life. But precisely because, in Symbolist drama, such sentiments can only be suggested, and dialogue, unlike poetry, demands conciseness, this dramatic vein was quickly exhausted. By 1895 the time had come for the Belgian author to *faire du nouveau*.

[1] *Le Trésor des humbles*, p. 162.

4

MEETING WITH DESTINY

The years 1895 to 1897 mark a period of transition in Maeterlinck's career. The public, who had already perceived that he was 'repeating' himself, expected something different from him; if he failed to give it, what reputation he had built up would quickly be forgotten. Hitherto, his pessimism had coloured all his writing. A new inspiration was urgently required to induce him to abandon his fundamental attitude of despair and open up to him fresh creative vistas. Such a renewal of the spirit was brought about by Georgette Leblanc. During this period her paramount influence, combining with other favourable circumstances, was a leaven at work, gradually transforming the author's habits, modes of thought, and environment.

Mme Leblanc, who was to share Maeterlinck's life for a score of years, was born at Rouen in 1869.[1] Her father, Bianconi Leblanc, was of Italian origin; her mother was Norman.[2] Her brother, Maurice Leblanc, achieved fame as the writer of the Arsène Lupin detective stories. Her father, a shipowner, widowed early in life, became a gloomy, melancholic character after his wife's death. Georgette passed her early years in an oppressive atmosphere, often alone with her father, whom she feared.

She took up singing and interested herself in literature, reading intensively Montaigne and Schopenhauer. To escape from her rather unhappy home life she essayed the only remedy open to a young girl of her social circumstances: marriage. At the age of seventeen she eloped with a Spaniard and married him. With this gentleman she declared she had made a pact: 'With my dowry I would buy my liberty.'[3] There is an inconsistency in her story:

---

[1] Much of the information in this chapter is drawn from Georgette Leblanc's autobiography, *Souvenirs*, which, however, is not entirely reliable in facts or dates.
[2] G. F. Sturgis, *The Psychology of Maeterlinck*, p. 20.
[3] Georgette Leblanc, *Souvenirs*, pp. 33–34.

having run away from home, she could hardly expect her father to hand her marriage portion over to the man he would undoubtedly consider as capable of dissipating it as of abducting his daughter. However, there is no doubt that a marriage actually took place and subsisted during all or most of her years with Maeterlinck. Her husband gambled his money away and physically maltreated her. She lived with him for a year and then left him, making a legal complaint about his ill-treatment; afterwards she entered a sanatorium to recover from her experiences. She never lived with him again. She talks of her marriage as one in name only, unconsummated even, and only contracted in order ultimately to be free of all entanglements, both family and matrimonial.

Having recovered from her ordeal, she took up singing lessons again and was then lucky enough to secure a part in Alfred Bruneau's *L'Attaque du moulin*, produced at the Paris Opéra-Comique. She was a success in the role and she seemed to be all set for an operatic career.

In her Paris studio she entertained a very diverse artistic and literary set. 'Sâr' Péladan and the Rosicrucians were regular visitors, as were also writers such as Louis Fabulet (the translator of Kipling and Whitman), the composer Fabre, the artist Le Sidaner, to name only a few who might have influenced Maeterlinck later. Another assiduous caller was Georges Rodenbach, notable, as always, for his pallor and sartorial correctness.

One day, possibly through Rodenbach, there came into Georgette Leblanc's hands the translation by Mlle Mali of Emerson's essays, to which Maeterlinck had written a preface. If the singer is to be believed she stayed up all night reading and re-reading this preface and fell in love immediately with its Belgian author.

Moreover, by a singular coincidence, the opportunity for her to go to Belgium presented itself the very next day. Calabresi, a director of the Théâtre de la Monnaie, offered her 800 francs a month to appear in Brussels. Although a contract held her to Carvalho of the Opéra-Comique and she was being paid more than double this sum, she did not hesitate. Her acceptance would bring her physically closer to Maeterlinck, her new literary idol.

MEETING WITH DESTINY

Thus, in the autumn of 1894, she made her début at the Monnaie in *La Navarraise*.

How far this highly coloured account of her life before she met Maeterlinck corresponds to the truth is difficult to ascertain, since one must needs rely on her own memoirs. Of a sentimental, eccentric disposition, she is likely to have romanticized the circumstances, particularly in regard to Maeterlinck.[1]

The two first met late one evening on 11 January 1895 in Picard's house on the Avenue de la Toison d'Or in Brussels.[2] A party of friends, which included Maeterlinck, had been invited back to supper after having seen a performance of Strindberg's *The Father* at the Théâtre du Parc. At the instigation of Octave Maus, the art critic, Picard had also asked Georgette Leblanc to come along after her performance at the Théâtre de la Monnaie; she was consequently the last to arrive. She had carefully 'engineered' the invitation with the express purpose of being introduced to Maeterlinck.

For this auspicious occasion she had indulged to the full her always extravagant taste in dress. A long black gown of velvet, embroidered with golden flowers that gave it a Pre-Raphaelite air, set off to perfection her Grecian figure. In the middle of her forehead sparkled a massive diamond. As she made her entrance she espied Maeterlinck standing by the mantelpiece. He wore a cape over his evening dress. Tall, with broad shoulders, he had a dark moustache, already turning grey. Below his lower lip he grew a small tuft of hair, a fashionable adornment that rejoiced in the name of an 'imperial'. She was struck by his sensitive face, which bore a troubled, anxious air. His frame was squat and sturdy, like that of a peasant. He was, as usual, a little out of his element: in the countryside, pipe in hand, he felt at home; in the polished atmosphere of the drawing-room he would withdraw into himself. His future lover, who had looked forward with so much ardour to this encounter, could not restrain herself from murmuring delightedly, 'What luck! He's young!'[3]

---

[1] Additional details concerning Georgette Leblanc's early life are given in Jean Cocteau's preface to *La Machine à courage*, a sequel to *Souvenirs*.

[2] C. Lemonnier, *La Vie belge*, p. 173. Lemonnier was present. Cf. also H. Carton de Wiart, *Souvenirs littéraires*, p. 110.   [3] Georgette Leblanc, *Souvenirs*, p. 4.

At supper they sat opposite each other. He appeared awkward to her, particularly in his speech; his gaze often met hers, but he hardly spoke to her. After the meal she was invited to sing, and interpreted in dramatic fashion some of Maeterlinck's *Chansons*, set to music by Fabre. Then, 'I asked the poet if he approved of my interpretations. He showed himself delighted at them, but declared to me that there was nothing beneath all this save a manner of playing with harmonious words.'[1] The evening ended with the pair agreeing to meet again in Ghent, where Maeterlinck would show her round. As she wended her way home, escorted by Octave Maus, she was in ecstasy.

She must also have made an impression on Maeterlinck, for before their second meeting she received from him a book extravagantly inscribed, 'To Georgette Leblanc, the heroine of great dreams.' But the trip to Ghent, made on a rainy day, was a miserable fiasco. After meeting Maeterlinck's parents, they strolled disconsolately through the town, discussing religion and poetry, Maeterlinck admitting that he read above all the English poets.[2] Believing neither in love nor happiness he was accustomed, he frankly told her, to have several mistresses at the same time. What passed for happiness was for him mainly a matter of pleasure and physical well-being.

Maeterlinck returned the visit and was entertained in her Brussels flat. This time his gift was two volumes of Plotinus. She had carefully arranged the *décor* in a manner that she thought would please him: one room had been fitted with black hangings and silver ornaments. He took one glance at it and requested that they stay in the drawing-room, where the furnishings were commonplace and modern. She remarks: 'Thus immediately the statue that his works had caused me to erect in my mind crumbled to give place to an exactly opposing reality.'[3] Nevertheless they kept up their meetings, making trips to Malines and to Dutch Flanders, where they visited Flushing, Veere, and Middelburg. One gathers from her account that on these expeditions he did not exactly impress her by his ardour. But their relationship was maintained.

---

[1] Georgette Leblanc, *Souvenirs*, p. 10.   [2] Ibid., p. 18.   [3] Ibid., p. 23.

Meanwhile, in Paris and elsewhere, Lugné-Poë continued to keep Maeterlinck's name before the public. On 15 March 1895 *Intérieur* was put on in Paris and was well received. The performance was also noteworthy because the bill included Tristan Bernard's *Les Pieds nickelés*, his first dramatic work ever performed. Maeterlinck was present and afterwards, when asked for an interview, modestly replied: 'I don't know what to say to you. ... When a man has given his place and date of birth, he has nothing more of interest to add.'[1]

From Paris the Théâtre de l'Œuvre was again invited to tour with *Pelléas et Mélisande*. Performances were given in Liège and then in Rotterdam and The Hague, where the distinguished Dutch writer, Van Hamel, spoke in honour of Maeterlinck, who had accompanied the troupe on their tour. Arrangements had also been made for it to visit England.

Maeterlinck was already known by repute in England. As early as 1890 an article by Harry had appeared in the *Manchester Guardian*, and the same writer had published English translations of several of the plays. Shaw, Gosse, and Archer favoured Maeterlinck as they favoured Ibsen. The *Yellow Book* had had the same effect upon literary thinking in London as the Théâtre de l'Œuvre had had in Paris. On the other hand, 1895 was not a favourable time to launch the works of Maeterlinck on the English stage. Victorian opinion was in the process of crystallizing against the Symbolists. The translation of Max Nordau's *Dégénérescences* had just appeared, condemning the whole literary movement. Oscar Wilde's trial was about to begin. Thus J. T. Grein had taken a somewhat risky step in inviting L'Œuvre to perform Maeterlinck and Ibsen in London. Grein, a Dutchman, had founded the Independent Theatre, an institution in London similar to the Parisian companies, in that it lacked a permanent home. With the help of Alfred Sutro, later to become Maeterlinck's chief English translator, but then a rising young playwright, he had arranged a week of performances in a theatre in the Strand. Maeterlinck crossed from Flushing with the company. He was welcomed at a banquet given in honour of L'Œuvre

---

[1] G. Leneveu, *Ibsen et Maeterlinck*, p. 140.

by Dorothy Leighton, the co-director of the Independent Theatre.

Disaster threatened the venture from the beginning. When they came to unpack the wardrobe, recounts Lugné-Poë, he found that the costumes for *Pelléas* had been left behind. The situation was desperate as it was Saturday and the shops were shutting. In the street he encountered a Scotch boy clad in kilt, sporran, and glengarry. The boy was allegedly persuaded to lend his attire and it was used as a costume for Pelléas! The repertory week, which opened on 25 March, included Ibsen's *Rosmersholm* and *The Master Builder* as well as *L'Intruse* and *Pelléas*. The *Times* reviewer did not give the company a very enthusiastic write-up, declaring that both *Rosmersholm* and *L'Intruse* had been seen in England before. The English press in general appeared indifferent, and the only notable fact, for example, that the *Daily Mail* printed about the tour was that in an interview Maeterlinck had given as his opinion that Verhaeren was Belgium's greatest non-dramatic poet.[1] Although the performances were not an outstanding success, they afforded Maeterlinck the opportunity of meeting for the first time such writers as Shaw, William Archer, Arthur Symons, W. B. Yeats, and Harley Granville-Barker, to all of whom he was introduced by Sutro.

Maeterlinck's works have often been termed Germanic rather than French in tone. Their Flemishness is undoubtedly manifest, and he certainly owes more to English and American literature than to French or German literatures. His debts to English literature are manifold, ranging from Shakespeare to James Barrie, whereas his debts to French literature, chiefly to Villiers and the Symbolists, are less apparent. It is certain that, between France and Germany, his work is more calculated to appeal to the Teutonic than to the Latin mind. These considerations give his declared attitude to Germany in 1895 some literary significance. In April the *Mercure de France* published the replies given by French and German authors, scholars, and sociologists to the question: 'All politics placed on one side, are you an advocate of stronger intellectual and social ties between France and Germany,

[1] Reported by *Le Coq rouge*, June 1895, p. 107, note.

and what might be, in your opinion, the best means of achieving this?' Most of the authors writing in French agreed, as did Maeterlinck, that nearer relationships were desirable, although some, like Vielé-Griffin, with reservations. Citing the French Romantic movement—'erroneous in itself, but useful in its consequences'—which was stimulated by English and German influences, Maeterlinck affirmed that such cultural relations were always useful. A somewhat superficial knowledge is disclosed, however, when he makes the astounding statement that Goethe and Schiller revealed Shakespeare to England. Possibly referring to Novalis and Schopenhauer, who had deeply affected his personal thinking, he mentioned the profound transformation of the human spirit wrought by German metaphysics. He comes out strongly in favour of each country learning the other's language. But the whole tenor of his reply is moderate in tone and certainly not that of the fervent Germanophile he has been made out to be before 1914. The first contact Maeterlinck had had with German letters was in 1894, when the dramatist Hermann Bahr began sending him copies of his works, although Maeterlinck himself was read beyond the Rhine almost from the outset of his career.

In May 1895 a breakaway group from *La Jeune Belgique* launched a new review, *Le Coq rouge*. Verhaeren and Maeterlinck were on its editorial board, but the latter did not contribute to it and in May 1896 his name was dropped, possibly because of his lack of interest. The review survived two further years.

Meanwhile the friendship between him and Georgette Leblanc was ripening. They continued to correspond regularly. The later essays collected in *Le Trésor des humbles* give some indication of his mood and temper about this time. They are concerned with the mystical discovery of the soul: it awakes, just as Maeterlinck himself is awakening to love for the first time. He is finding within himself hidden depths of goodness and, at long last, a capacity for happiness, for 'the kingdom of love is above all the great kingdom of certainty'.[1] He was as yet unable to rid himself entirely of what might be described as his *bourgeois* prejudices and so, perhaps to rationalize his liaison with a person already

[1] *Le Trésor des humbles*, p. 79.

married, he attacked accepted moral standards. He postulated love as the supreme justification; this is in effect the argument no less of *Pelléas et Mélisande* than of his later play, *Monna Vanna*. The essays reveal an upsurge of optimism, of faith in the future, directly ascribable to his own personal feelings.

By good fortune, Georgette Leblanc was able to remain in Brussels. After *Carmen* she began her second season with *Thaïs* and *Fidelio*. She saw her lover frequently—at least twice a week in the spring of 1896. Finally, in the Bois de la Cambre, a favourite picnic haunt outside Brussels, Maeterlinck proposed to her. Georgette Leblanc's reaction is interesting: 'How could one descend from Paradise to call at the registry office! ... The idea of a marriage never occurred to me for one moment until the day when Maeterlinck spoke of it. ... At the first word, he saw me in such a perfect bewilderment that he did not insist.'[1] Her previous marriage still subsisted, and her Spanish husband and she were irrevocably joined, because no divorce laws existed in Spain. Only by recourse to the Pope might it have been possible to have the union annulled. (Much later Raymond Poincaré indeed offered to intervene with the Holy See on her behalf, but she and Maeterlinck refused.)

In February 1896 Maeterlinck attended a banquet in honour of Verhaeren, who was leaving Belgium for good to establish himself in Paris. Perhaps it was this occasion that also gave Maeterlinck the idea of taking the same step. Such a move would undoubtedly please Georgette Leblanc, for in Paris the opportunities to further her career would be more numerous. Moreover, it would provide a solution to the social impasse in which the couple found themselves. They could settle in peace far from the scandal that would undoubtedly attach itself to their union if continued openly in Brussels. As has been seen, the author felt no particular love or gratitude to Belgium. In the freer intellectual climate of Paris he would be able to breathe more easily.

It was therefore with the resolve to leave Belgium that they entered into a 'union of the left hand', an unlegalized companionship that was to last until 1918, although the ties of affection that

[1] Georgette Leblanc, *Souvenirs*, p. 53.

bound it had been strained beyond repair long before that year. The pact between them consisted in each allowing complete freedom to the other to dissolve their union whenever he or she desired. Such an agreement may sometimes prove harder to break than one sealed with due legal formality; and such was the fate of this one.

No immediate necessity arose, however, for an irrevocable decision. In June 1896 Maeterlinck paid another visit to England, probably staying with Sutro. Then also he probably visited George Meredith at Box Hill. He declared that Meredith's genius was on a par with Villiers's, but preferred to *The Egoist* the lesser-known works, such as *The Shaving of Shapgat* and *The Tragic Comedians*.[1] Meanwhile Georgette Leblanc, accompanied by her brother Maurice, travelled to Schinznach in Switzerland for treatment for her throat. Upon Maeterlinck's return they met again at Retournemer, in the Vosges, and then went off to spend a holiday together at a farm-house that had been lent them in the Vendée region. There Maeterlinck made a final revision of a new play, *Aglavaine et Sélysette*.

This play is the dramatic hinge which finally closes the door on Symbolism for Maeterlinck. It is a variation on the theme of the 'eternal triangle'. Aglavaine, a woman of strong determination, comes to stay with Sélysette, the typical Maeterlinckian heroine in the Pre-Raphaelite manner, and Méléandre, her husband. Aglavaine and Méléandre fall in love. Sélysette chooses the way of renunciation and commits suicide, striving to make her death appear an accident. In this drama the characters 'come to consciousness' and exert their will, but in the end disaster in the form of Destiny overtakes them. The end pattern thus does not seem to differ materially from the writer's previous plays. But there are indications that in this 'essay on love in dialogue form' he had not wished to give his work such a tragic denouement: in a letter to Georgette Leblanc dated 1 July 1896 he wrote: 'It is not as I wanted it, this poor drama, and when I review it as a whole in my mind, I don't like it at all. It was to be the triumph, and, all in all, the strength of things has made it almost the defeat, of

[1] F. Lefèvre, *Une heure avec . . . Maeterlinck*, p.232.

Aglavaine.'[1] His dissatisfaction with the way the play was shaping had been manifest even whilst he was still writing it. Georgette Leblanc records that for some time he had refused to discuss the plot with her. One afternoon, on their Vendée holiday, Maeterlinck, not daring to read the final version to her, had thrust the manuscript into her hand and had stalked away. The dramatist's ascent from pessimism was not yet complete.

In the autumn of 1896 another separation was necessary, forced upon the lovers by Georgette Leblanc's theatrical engagements. Maeterlinck remained behind in Belgium whilst she went off to sing first in Nice and then in Bordeaux. The season lasted three months and the actress confesses she lived for his letters. He promised to visit her but then wrote saying he had been delayed by illness. But when he finally arrived he explained that his tardiness was due to 'business reasons' which had obliged him to see a former mistress. This rather casual and dilatory attitude is typical of him throughout their time together. By the close of the year they were separated again, but the actress was consoled by a letter he wrote her on 30 December in which he extravagantly declared that he had passed a year of gentleness, beauty, and love such as perhaps no man had hitherto experienced.

What was the impact of Georgette Leblanc upon the course of his literary career? It is customary to attribute the mellowing of his thought and the cautious growth of optimism about this time entirely to the influence of the actress. Such an explanation is too simple. Among the Symbolists there is a general evolution towards the cult of life. In *Le Domaine des fées* (1895) Gustave Kahn praises married love. In Gide's *Les Nourritures terrestres* (1897) one may discern an exaltation of life. Nor is it only in the Symbolist tradition that there is a lightening of the way. Gustave Cohen has pointed out[2] that in the closing years of the century there was a general renewal of hope, and cites the optimistic endings to Zola's novels *Le docteur Pascal, Les Trois Villes* (1894–8), and *Les Quatre Évangiles*. Moreover, the spread of Socialist

---

[1] J-M. Carré, 'L'Évolution du Théâtre de Maeterlinck', *Revue des cours et conférences*, 31 Dec. 1925, p. 167.

[2] G. Cohen, 'Le Conflit de l'homme et du destin dans le théâtre de Maeterlinck', *Revue du mois*, 10 Jan. 1912, pp. 38–39.

doctrine, with its emphasis on material progress, was not without effect upon writers such as Verhaeren, whose *Les Aubes* (1898) looks forward to a new epoch. Cohen also postulates that the study of the bees and of flowers may have brought Maeterlinck to believe in a happy finality. To such evidence might be added the new vistas opened up to the pessimistic playwright by the study of Emerson, as well as shaking off the oppressive atmosphere of Ghent and the feeling of new beginnings. Love may have been merely the catalyst in a reaction where the essential elements were already present.

In the essays of *Le Trésor des humbles*, as has been shown, the hand of Georgette Leblanc is nevertheless clearly discernible. One day she taxed their author as to why he wrote 'an old philosopher used to say', or 'an old friend', or 'some wise man or another', when all the time he was merely referring to something she had said or written to him. He replied that if he had named her he would not have been taken seriously, as she was only an actress. Doubtless this remark wounded her deeply and impelled her to seek some recognition of what she considered his debt to her. The opportunity came in late 1896 when Maeterlinck had already begun the writing of *Sagesse et destinée*. On 15 December he wrote to her: 'I started work again yesterday and it will progress very well. As always, I have amassed, without realizing it, great treasures in you, and now I spend them, and am happy to do so, without counting them, for all that comes to me from you returns to you in my love.'[1] Such a return did not satisfy her and she sought some acknowledgement of her own creative ability. On her brother's advice she brought the whole matter out into the open in a letter: 'One evening, as you were reading your work to me, you said laughingly to me: "I have stolen from you a little." I said it was of no consequence. I lied (for the moment).'[2] Maeterlinck's reaction to this was extreme: he proposed that for seven years he should publish nothing and meanwhile his companion would have the opportunity of demonstrating her literary talent. Such an offer was obviously preposterous. Living with the author, to all intents and purposes as his wife, yet engaged on a

---

[1] Georgette Leblanc, *Souvenirs*, p. 132.   [2] Ibid., p. 136.

theatrical career, she could not condemn him to silence for so long. Thus the suggestion was rejected and for a while the matter rested.

When, however, the moment arrived for the publication of *Sagesse et destinée* Maurice Leblanc took up the cudgels on his sister's behalf. In September 1898 he proposed to Maeterlinck that the work should appear under joint authorship. The latter objected because he claimed that the public should not be informed of his private life, but put forward the idea of an acknowledgement in a dedication. With much difficulty the following was published at the beginning of the essays:

To Madame Georgette Leblanc

I dedicate to you this book, which is, so to speak, your work. There is a loftier and more real collaboration than that of the pen: it is that of thought and example. I had not laboriously to imagine the resolves and actions of an ideal wise man, or to draw from my own breast the morality of a fine, but necessarily somewhat vague, dream. It was sufficient for me to listen to your words. It was sufficient for my gaze to follow you closely in your life; thereby it followed the movements, gestures, and habits of wisdom itself.

MAETERLINCK

With this somewhat ambiguous and over-careful expression of gratitude the actress had willy-nilly to be content. One of the hardest blows she suffered after their final separation was the suppression of this dedication when a new edition of the book appeared in 1926.

The spring of 1897 saw Maeterlinck and her finally installed in Paris. She had rented for them the Villa Dupont, in the rue Pergolèse, not far from the Seine and in the quiet district of Passy. Their apartments had been furnished in 'Island of Walcheren' style: a Dutch interior of distempered walls enlivened by burnished copper ornaments. She had engaged a servant who bore the outlandish name of Cunégonde. Two days before he arrived she was heartened by a letter in which he declared that they were really marrying now in every sense save the legal one. On the afternoon of the great day she had taken care that a roaring fire, a sumptuous meal, and wine should welcome her lover in fitting fashion. She sallied forth to meet him and bore him back in triumph. But the reception misfired. Upon their arrival the fire was ashes, the dinner a cindery mess, and the wine-bottles empty: Cunégonde was snoring underneath the dining-room table.[1]

Their 'marriage' was placed on a strict financial basis. For the upkeep of the household Maeterlinck would contribute a modest seven francs a day. All was organized to secure his peace and comfort. Since it was plain that Georgette Leblanc's musical practice would disturb the writer, a study was also rented for his use at 4 rue Lalo, near the Bois de Boulogne. Here, perched on the fifth floor, Maeterlinck continued to work steadily at *Sagesse et destinée*. At home, moreover, to preserve the privacy and silence the Belgian loved, stern injunctions were given the servants that usually all callers were to be turned away and they should move as quietly as possible about the house. Thus began Maeterlinck's new life in his self-appointed exile: a gesture had been made to the world. Georgette Leblanc prophesied: 'The significance of this gesture was immense. His glory, which I wished to be world-wide, should start from France, from Paris.'[2]

[1] Georgette Leblanc, *Souvenirs*, p. 112.   [2] Ibid., p. 109.

5

'UNION OF THE LEFT HAND'

MEASURED in terms of fame and success, Maeterlinck's life from 1897 to 1911 was destined to be the most triumphal period of his career. But, although characterized at the outset by a continued strengthening of his faith in life, by the time it ended the dark shadows were beginning to close in once more around his mind. A 'honeymoon' period with Georgette Leblanc was followed by a *bourgeois* serenity which lapsed finally into mere indifference to his companion. The actress was supplanted in his affections by a much younger woman, Mlle Renée Dahon, eventually to become his wife. Surrounded at first by a throng of new acquaintances, Maeterlinck gradually withdrew from society—particularly literary company—and chose to lead a life of retirement.

The summer of 1897 was spent in Normandy. The couple rented a villa, 'La Montjoie', in the Orne department. In the eastern-facing of its two studios the author would continue to work at *Sagesse et destinée*. His method of work was unusual: he would scribble down a thought as it occurred to him and then stick the paper to the wall like a butterfly. Georgette Leblanc would also contribute to this 'collection' of thoughts. From time to time the scraps of paper would be unpinned, the thoughts rewritten, amplified, and arranged in order. This way of writing, employed extensively in his later years, explains the fragmentary and disconnected impression one sometimes gains from his works.

Afternoons were spent in bicycling, a new pastime for the actress, but a favourite distraction for Maeterlinck before he took up motoring, in which he was a pioneer. The actress has described in harrowing terms their excursions awheel.[1] She would set out in a dress trailing an ample train, swathed in scarves that flapped gaily in the breeze. When he criticized her outlandish garb,

[1] Georgette Leblanc, *Souvenirs*, p. 116.

declaring it not very athletic, she was piqued and ordered a boy's suit, which she wore on future expeditions. However, this streamlining availed nothing. She could not keep up with the steady pedalling of her more muscular partner. Eventually, on day outings, he would press on, arranging to meet her at a certain inn for lunch. When she arrived breathless and exhausted, she would more often than not find him, replete and contented, lighting up his pipe. She then tried the expedient of setting out hours before him, but he, cycling swiftly and effortlessly along, would soon catch her up. Such were the trials of love.

By September 1897 the collection of essays was taking final shape and Maeterlinck departed alone to Belgium for a few days. Georgette Leblanc admits her domestic incompetence and possibly the author would return for a spell with relief to the well-ordered household in Ghent, with its creature comforts and love of rich living. In Belgium Maeterlinck met Van Lerberghe. Van Lerberghe records the encounter in a letter to Fernand Severin: 'We have the same ideal of art, almost the same vision. In short, Maeterlinck is myself to the hundredth power. The principal difference between us is that he prefers the twilight and I the dawn—and that he has genius.'[1]

Winter in Paris—Maeterlinck's first since 1885—followed, with a welcome from his fellow expatriates. Mallarmé also visited the couple and Georgette Leblanc's pet lamb, Tintagiles, obligingly inspired him to compose some *vers de circonstance* whose *leitmotiv* was the expressive bleating sound of the animal. Incidentally, in the previous March Maeterlinck had contributed a few lines from one of his plays to the famous *Album Mallarmé*, inspired by Mockel, offered to the Symbolist poet by his admirers. Other French friends and acquaintances that were entertained in the Maeterlinck household were Mirbeau, Paul Adam, Barrès, Jules Renard, Gide, Jean Lorrain, Paul Fort, Huret, Rodin, Jules Gaulthier, Colette, and Rachilde—a representative list of the outstanding artistic personalities of the day. Anatole France came with his mistress and her husband and in turn invited them to the 'Villa Saïd', his home in the same street. Unfortunately Georgette

[1] C. Van Lerberghe, *Lettres à Fernand Severin*, p. 90.

Leblanc incurred the displeasure of France's companion, who forbade her lover to acknowledge her; but one day France plucked up enough courage to explain to her the reason for his rudeness.[1] When Barrès visited Georgette Leblanc he gallantly declared she belonged to the age of Renaissance Venice; this observation, passed on to Maeterlinck, was embroidered into an essay for *Sagesse et destinée*.[2] Another interesting character, Oscar Wilde, dined with the Maeterlincks in May 1898. The dandy and one-time idol of Paris and London was then living quietly in a hotel in the rue des Beaux-Arts. But Maeterlinck did not take to Wilde, summing him up as a superficial personality.

Sagesse et destinée, finally published in 1898, indicates in a lucid but poetic style the development of Maeterlinck's character during his early association with the actress. The book is a meditation upon the connexion between wisdom and destiny, between the sage and his fate. The essential elements for happiness, the joys of love, the place of death, the role of sacrifice and suffering, the paramount importance of the soul—each of these themes is examined and for the first time there is elucidated a hopeful, practical, everyday philosophy,.the chief tenet of which is that wisdom can conquer Destiny or at least protect the soul against its blows. The influence of Marcus Aurelius, whose particular form of Stoicism had been studied intensively by Maeterlinck, is everywhere apparent, although for the Belgian wisdom is above and beyond reason, which the Roman takes as his guide. An eclectic selection of ideas, culled from writers as diverse as Shakespeare, Carlyle, Pascal, Renan, Goethe, and Schopenhauer, as well as from the study of antiquity, furnishes the themes of many of the essays. The portrait of the author that emerges is not entirely dissimilar from that emerging of Montaigne in the first book of the *Essais*: a Stoic (but with a different model) who is striving to live with the idea of death, and who has his dreams of heroism.

The book marks the close of the moral crisis that had begun over a decade before, but which was already on the way to being

---

[1] Georgette Leblanc, *Souvenirs*, p. 116.
[2] Ibid., p. 117, and M. Maeterlinck, *Sagesse et destinée*, pp. 241 et seq.

resolved in *Le Trésor des humbles* and in *Aglavaine et Sélysette*. A tract in favour of a qualified optimism, it points to a salvation, albeit here on earth and without religion. Pagan in its complete acceptance of life, it is mystic in the belief in a power beyond reason. Yet all the great questions, universal in scale and content, with which Maeterlinck was to concern himself once his fatalistic attitude had been virtually abandoned, are, in fact, left unsolved: the riddle of the universe, of space and time, of life, death, and immortality, and of an unknowable or even mythical God. The high plateaux of his thought were not to gleam for long under the bright sun of optimism. Maeterlinck had forsaken Ruysbroek, the Christian guide, for Marcus Aurelius, the pagan, but the ultimate darkness had not been dispersed.

Sagesse et destinée brought Maeterlinck's name to the fore in many countries. The English translations of his works have already been mentioned, and some had also achieved publication in New York. Germans had also translated him, but in February 1898 he first came into contact with Friedrich von Oppeln-Bronikowski, who was to be his faithful interpreter to the German public for over a quarter of a century. The year 1898 marks the real beginning of Maeterlinck's international reputation; as few writers have done in their lifetime, he enjoyed an audience composed of many nations. So great was his popularity abroad that London, New York, or Berlin would often publish his new books before they appeared in France and Belgium. He had a strong business sense and realized that the commercial rewards for both books and articles were sometimes greater by tenfold in New York than in Paris.

The Dreyfus affair, revived by the publication on 13 January 1898 of Zola's letter, *J'accuse*, made little impact upon Maeterlinck. In Belgium Charles Van Lerberghe had organized the *Manifestation Zola* and had drawn up a declaration of support for Zola which was signed by many leading Belgian writers and scholars. Maeterlinck agreed to sign it, as did Verhaeren and Mockel, the other Belgian expatriates, but showed no particular enthusiasm for this demonstration of professional solidarity.

During the spring of 1898 he was occupied in writing either

a rough draft or the first part of a short play entitled *Sœur Béatrice*, intended as a libretto. The plot is a new version of the medieval legend of the wayward nun who elopes with her lover, but is not missed in the convent because her place is taken by the Virgin. In his treatment of the legend the dramatist uses all the devices of Romanticism: whilst he has turned his back upon Symbolism he is only just beginning to exploit a new dramatic vein, in which the plays are written with Georgette Leblanc specifically cast in the leading role.[1]

'La Montjoie' had proved hardly big enough for a summer residence and so a more suitable holiday home was found in an old presbytery at Gruchet Saint-Siméon, near Luneray (Seine-Inférieure). The surroundings were idyllic: encircled by beech trees, the house was approached by a farm-track that led through an orchard. A tiny garden enclosed a white-walled house, with a glass porch and green shutters. A nine-year lease, at an annual rent of 300 francs, was signed, and a negress cook, bearing the name of Bamboula, was later engaged. This remained the country residence of the Maeterlinck household for almost a decade. Following his father's example, the writer always ordered his life about two homes, a *pied-à-terre* in a town for the winter, and a country house for the summer.

In June 1898 he paid another visit to London, this time to see *Pelléas et Mélisande* performed for the first time in English. After reading Professor Mackail's translation, Mrs. Patrick Campbell had persuaded Forbes-Robertson, the famous actor-manager, to stage the play,[2] although he personally had misgivings, thinking it weak and morbid. She took the part of Mélisande, whilst Mr. (later Sir John) Martin Harvey played Pelléas and Forbes-Robertson Golaud. Sir Edward Burne-Jones, whose paintings Maeterlinck had long admired, designed some of the costumes. Gabriel Fauré, who happened to be in London at the time, was commissioned to write the incidental music for the production. Maeterlinck, accompanied by Van Lerberghe, came to London

---

[1] For a study of *Sœur Béatrice* and the other libretto, *Ariane et Barbe-bleue*, cf. W. D. Halls, 'Les Débuts du théâtre nouveau', *Annales de la Fondation Maeterlinck*, vol. iii, 1957.

[2] Mrs. Patrick Campbell, *My Life and Some Letters*, pp. 126–7.

to attend the first of nine performances given at the Prince of Wales Theatre. He was loud in his praises of Mrs. Patrick Campbell, to whom he wrote: 'You have taught me that one must never be afraid of dreaming too beautiful dreams, since one has sometimes the good fortune to encounter a privileged being who can make them visible and real.'[1] Such a eulogy is understandable when one recalls the bitter controversy that *Pelléas* and the earlier plays had aroused in Paris and Brussels. This summer triumph, followed in October by the simultaneous publication in Paris, London, and New York of *Sagesse et destinée*, represents the turn of the tide in his literary career. Paradoxically, however, it may be argued that by then his true significance as a literary figure was already diminishing.

He returned to France in a mood of jubilation. In August he spent a few days on holiday at St-Aubin, a small coastal resort near Dieppe, but in September he and Georgette Leblanc set off for Spain. Accompanied by Albert Carré, the director of the Paris Opéra-Comique, and by the theatre's scenic artist, they had as the object of their journey the acquisition of local colour for a season of *Carmen* to be put on that winter, with Georgette Leblanc singing the title role. In the quest for the ideal gipsy girl they visited Seville, Madrid, and Granada in turn. By October the party was back in Paris.

Disappointingly, Maeterlinck derived little creative stimulus from travel. England, Germany, and Holland he knew already. In later years he was to travel extensively in Italy, revisit Spain, make trips to Egypt, Greece, Palestine, and North Africa, spend some time in Portugal, and live for years in the United States. These journeyings abroad were to bear singularly meagre literary fruit. Even the long essay 'Siciliades Musae', reproduced in *L'Araignée de verre*, and the short monograph he wrote on Ancient Egypt are primarily historical in approach. At the outset of his career Maeterlinck had been deeply susceptible to foreign *literary* influences, but unfortunately travel did not open up new horizons for him.

Before the opening of *Carmen* that December the stormy

[1] Ibid. She reproduced the letter from which an extract is given in facsimile on pp. 131-4.

temperament of Georgette Leblanc clashed, for the first but not the last time, with Albert Carré, who threatened to replace her by the English singer Mary Garden. In a fit of pique the actress threw up the part and poured out her woes on paper to Maeterlinck, then away in Ghent. Only his personal intervention, added to that of Mirbeau and Paul Adam, succeeded in patching matters up. By all accounts the actress was exceedingly difficult to work with, and used Maeterlinck's name freely in order to achieve her ambitions.

During the winter Maeterlinck would seem to have been in poor health[1] and wrote little. He had to refuse an invitation to visit Berlin, where Oppeln-Bronikowski, by articles and translations, was daily enhancing his master's reputation. In April 1899, possibly to convalesce, he made his first journey to the South of France.[2] This first contact with the South probably made him resolve to settle on the Riviera when his financial affairs allowed it. Back from his holiday he contracted influenza, but despite these upsets he put the finishing touches to *Ariane et Barbe-bleue*,[3] which he described as 'a sort of legendary or fairy opera in three acts', written, like *Sœur Béatrice*, for music and with Georgette Leblanc specifically in mind.

The actress claimed indeed to have inspired this latest work. Its sub-title, *La Délivrance inutile*, epitomized the 'useless deliverances' she indulged in by helping lame dogs over stiles, only to find afterwards that they spurned her. Carré interprets the play on a personal plane: Bluebeard's former wives are called Ygraine, Bellangère, Mélisande, Alladine, and Sélysette, all the names of characters in the writer's Symbolist plays. With the possible exception of Ygraine, they symbolize a type of womanhood submissive to Fate, the puppets of Death. Ariane is the first true heroine of the Maeterlinckian drama: she embodies the author's new concept of womankind and reflects his more positive *Weltanschauung*. For a while Georgette Leblanc, whose attitude

---

[1] Unpublished letter to Oppeln-Bronikowski, Maeterlinck's German translator, dated 17 Feb. 1899. The whole series of unpublished letters to Oppeln-Bronikowski (O.-B.) will be cited frequently because they provide invaluable biographical and literary information. The letters are in the Bibliothèque Royale, Brussels, bound in two volumes under the reference MS. II 7004C, and are, with few exceptions, in chronological order.

[2] Unpublished letter to O.-B. dated 22 Apr. 1899. [3] Cf. p. 64, n. 1.

towards Maeterlinck was maternal as well as wifely—her pet name for him was 'Bébé'—exemplified this ideal. Whether wintering in Paris or spending the summer in Normandy, his life revolved around the actress. Only at intervals did he escape for a brief visit to Ghent, and even then he possibly went alone because Georgette Leblanc was disliked by his parents.

In her descriptions of him the actress certainly depicts him as a moody, childish personality. She recounts how he would sometimes sulk for days on end, closeting himself in his study and only emerging for meals. One day she peeped in and found him, his work laid on one side, deeply absorbed in the cutting out of paper soldiers, armies of which were drawn up in battle formation on his study desk. He was also subject to violent dislikes and very strong antipathies even caused fainting-fits.[1] Fortunately his moods and fancies passed as quickly as they came.

On the other hand, a different picture of his personality emerges from reading Harry, his first biographer. The association with Georgette Leblanc had mellowed the author, although he retained a fundamental simplicity of character, shy and reserved as always. His life was orderly and followed a regular routine. He kept early hours. As for writing, the mood had to be upon him and there was never question of a daily stint to be accomplished. Like J. M. Barrie, his great consolation was tobacco. His life was passed in calm and serenity.

According to Georgette Leblanc, meals were sacred to him and he would brook no interruption to them. One meal-time one of Maeterlinck's German translators, a small, dandified creature, shrunken and bilious-looking, had come to see his master on business. Maeterlinck's initial silence exploded in anger and the unwelcome intruder was given one minute to leave. The diminutive individual had not understood one word of this peremptory command, rapped out in impassioned French. Without further ado, Maeterlinck rose from the table, picked him up bodily, and thrust him through the open window on to the pavement outside. The next day the luckless translator wrote pardoning him for this summary treatment!

[1] Georgette Leblanc, *Souvenirs*, p. 157.

Such abasement was a natural consequence of the vogue that Maeterlinck now enjoyed in Germany, particularly since the publication in 1899 of a German translation of *Sagesse et destinée*. 'Unser Maeterlinck', as he came to be known in some literary circles, was extravagantly compared to Nietzsche. Shocked at this comparison, he retorted that he had read little of the German philosopher and what little of his thought he had studied was somewhat antipathetic to him.[1] In reply to a questionnaire, he was at pains to disavow the influence of Goethe to any degree upon his intellectual course.[2] He had certainly never been attracted to German literature as he had to English literature. Apart from one lyrical outburst before 1914, he never professed much interest in Germany, although it proved a very lucrative source of income.

The *bourgeois* in his nature made him appraise realistically the market value of his work. Articles were obviously much more profitable than books, and he was turning more and more to the essay genre. After a short trip to Belgium in June 1899[3] he spent until mid-September at Gruchet Saint-Siméon, where he wrote a long essay for the *Cornhill Magazine* entitled 'Le Drame moderne'. The following winter, spent in Paris, although broken up by trips to Ghent in early November, at Christmas,[4] and the end of March,[5] was also devoted to essay-writing. In April 1900 there occurred another interruption when the household moved from the Rue Pergolèse to 69 Rue Raynouard, a house nearer the Seine, and Maeterlinck groaned in a letter to Oppeln-Bronikowski: 'I have been plunged for a week into the upset and horror of a complete removal.'[6] It was with a sigh of relief that he went off to pass the first summer of the new century at Gruchet. By then he envisaged collecting the series of essays he was engaged upon—some of which had already been published—into a third volume. He meditated calling it *Le Mystère de la justice* (in the

[1] Unpublished letter to O.-B. dated 18 Apr. 1899.
[2] Unpublished letter to O.-B. dated 7 Aug. 1899.
[3] Unpublished letter to O.-B. dated 9 June 1899.
[4] Unpublished letters to O.-B. dated 7 Nov. and 29 Dec. 1899.
[5] Unpublished letter to O.-B. dated 13 Mar. 1900.
[6] Unpublished letter to O.-B. dated 8 Apr. 1900. 'Je suis plongé depuis une semaine dans les tracas et l'horreur d'un déménagement total.'

event it was entitled *Le Temple enseveli* when published in 1902) and of including in it not only the title essay, but also 'La Loyauté du mystère' (later renamed 'L'Évolution du mystère'), 'Le Règne de la matière',[1] and a further essay he was then engaged on.[2]

This latter essay, *La Vie des abeilles*, occupied more than the summer and soon grew to the proportions of a separate volume. It was the result of the interest in bee-keeping that Maeterlinck had maintained since the days of his boyhood at Oostacker. One day, reading the works of Fabre, the great French naturalist, in the garden of Gruchet, he had been struck by the excruciating style. From this reflection his own account of the life of the bee was born.

Gaston Bonnier, the eminent French scientist, has commended this first essay in entomology for its exactness of observation, particularly in those sections of the book where the author records experiments he has undertaken himself.[3] Indeed, upon his return to Paris, not content with his field-work at Gruchet, Maeterlinck set up a glass-plated observation hive in his study and stood saucers filled with honey upon his desk in order to attract the bees.

The work is, however, more than a scientific monograph that sets out to describe the life of the honey-bee through the cycle of the seasons. A skilful but biased comparison is drawn between Man and the insect, interlarded with satirical remarks on human society. The bee is depicted as the epitome of unselfishness and social solidarity, is supremely adaptable to its environment, and has discovered for itself the economic advantage in the division of labour. By contrast, Man is essentially individualistic, alien to his surroundings: he does not possess the same moral drive, the essential unity that sustains the hive. For Maeterlinck, moreover, the apiary represents a state, whose queen is revered, but only as a symbol. In the human sphere is there any polity so faithfully reflecting the general will, any democracy where independence harmonizes so perfectly with the renunciation of individual

---

[1] Unpublished letter to O.-B. dated 24 June 1900.
[2] Unpublished letter to O.-B. dated 21 Sept. 1900.
[3] G. Bonnier, 'La Science chez Maeterlinck', *La Revue*, vol. xlix, 15 Aug. 1907, p. 449.

rights? Thus the creature is idealized and Man diminished: Maeterlinck pushes comparison and analogy too far in his satire of the human condition. Deeply interested as he was about this time in questions of social justice, he had nevertheless thought only superficially about the mildly Socialistic views he held.

Equally superficial is his knowledge of Darwinian theory. Although the poetic prose of the book is enhanced by the personalization of the bee, Maeterlinck runs counter to the most eminent authorities from Buffon onwards in ascribing intelligence to the insect. Natural selection, he maintains, has strengthened its intellect, which is manifested in many diverse ways. He was of course unaware of modern entomological theory, which postulates that the seemingly intelligent behaviour of the bee derives from the scent-glands, each of which exhales a distinctive odour. On the intelligence–instinct controversy, however, Bergson, Maeterlinck's contemporary, may have the last word: whereas Man's consciousness allows him an indefinite number of choices, the animal can only momentarily escape from the grip of its own automatism.[1]

Metaphysically, Maeterlinck has hesitantly progressed beyond the bland near-paganism of *Sagesse et destinée*. He has read Herbert Spencer and half-accepted his agnosticism: the inscrutable power behind the universe is unknowable. But the 'very eminent theologian of atheism'[2] has many backward glances: Man's goal, the 'aim' of life, like that of the insect, may be no more than its own initial impetus. Yet, just as the destiny of the honey-bee is to produce honey, Man's may be that of creating the strange 'fluid' known as thought. We know not where this activity will lead—but the bee is ignorant of why it secretes nectar—nor who will profit from this spiritual substance we introduce into the world, but the process must continue. The final principle—God, Providence, Nature, Chance, Fatality (for Maeterlinck the appellation is of no consequence)—may be good or evil, but the life process must be lived. This is the 'message' of the moralist

---

[1] H. Bergson, *L'Évolution créatrice*, p. 286.
[2] G. Grappe, in *La Revue bleue*, 26 Apr. 1902, quoted by D. Horrent, *Écrivains belges d'aujourd'hui*, 1ère série, p. 33.

that emerges from this book. As Bernardin de Saint-Pierre had allayed the anxieties of the utilitarian moralists and the materialists, whilst refusing to kneel at the altar of Christianity (unlike Chateaubriand), so Maeterlinck comforted those who, a century later, lived in the vacuum created by the collapse of Positivism, nourished vaguely 'progressive' aspirations, but rejected the militant socialist Christianity of Péguy.

La Vie des abeilles, indeed, connotes a new crystallization of Maeterlinck's moral and philosophical ideas. He has by now learned to accept life, to overcome pessimism, although his victory was to be short-lived. He adheres to a not entirely negative faith: Man must continue adding to the sum of thought and intelligence in the world, hoping that one day its secret will be revealed. If secret there be none, as he is half inclined to believe, the very search will have been its own justification.

By March 1901 *La Vie des abeilles* was ready for publication[1] and Maeterlinck, in whom the essayist and the dramatist alternately predominated, turned seriously, after a gap of five years, to the writing of a full-length play.[2] The plot of *Monna Vanna* had already been sketched out the previous summer and, apart from a few modifications in *Ariane et Barbe-bleue* to fit the score of Paul Dukas, he was free again at Gruchet to meditate upon the new drama. By November, after his return to Paris, the play was completed. A theatre had now to be found to stage it. Georgette Leblanc was resolved to make her début in the dramatic theatre with this play. Through Marie Kalff, a young Dutch actress whom Maeterlinck had recommended to L'Œuvre, Lugné-Poë heard of his old friend's latest work. He also learnt of Mme Leblanc's ambition. Curious, he finds out more about her. He sums her up as a mediocre opera singer of apparently little standing in the musical world, of whom the best her closest friends can say of her is that in mime she would be incomparable.[3] But Lugné-Poë has learnt enough to act with circumspection. He casually mentions to Maeterlinck that the Théâtre-Français and

[1] Unpublished letter to O.-B. dated 2 Mar. 1901.
[2] This play, *Monna Vanna*, was first mooted in an unpublished letter to O.-B. dated 24 June 1900.
[3] G. H. Lugné-Poë, *La Parade sous les étoiles (1902–1912)*, p. 47.

Clarétie might be interested. The actress reads the play but does not agree to recommend it. Sarah Bernhardt does likewise. Eventually the impresario realizes that, whilst he has effectively demonstrated that a bigger theatre is unfavourable to the play, he must resign himself to Georgette Leblanc playing the lead if he wishes to stage it himself. By a fortunate chance his office near the Place Pigalle is opposite the premises of Spinnewyn, Maeterlinck's fencing master, and he and the author meet often. He also enlists the aid of Mathilde Deschamps, whom he describes as 'a sort of factotum of gloomy appearance', who ran the domestic side of the Maeterlinck establishment. Simulating extreme reluctance, Georgette Leblanc consented to play the lead and congratulated herself on having 'extracted the play from Maurice' for the Théâtre de l'Œuvre.

Despite coaching and advice sought from Mounet-Sully and the elder Coquelin,[1] Georgette Leblanc, according to the impresario, exhibited little acting ability at rehearsals. She unscrupulously courted personal publicity and even the cast was changed at her whim. But, although a perpetual thorn in the producer's side, she nevertheless achieved a triumph at the first performance, given on 7 May 1902, enabling Lugné-Poë to give the play a further fortnight's run at the Théâtre de la Porte St-Martin. Despite this success, Maeterlinck's increasing boorishness clashed with Lugné-Poë's ever-mercurial temperament and the author wrote somewhat ungraciously: 'It is certain that blunders are being made about [*Monna*] *Vanna*, it is certain that the best possible use has not been made of it; it is certain that you have never liked the play, it is even more certain that you have hated Georgette.'[2] This only partially true indictment exemplifies the aggressive attitude that Maeterlinck, emerging from his shyness and modesty, adopted for a time in his personal relationships.

Perhaps it is no accident that *Monna Vanna* also finally rejects Symbolism. Maeterlinck himself declared: 'It is time that poets recognize it: the symbol suffices in representing provisionally an accepted truth or a truth that one cannot or will not yet gaze

---

[1] Georgette Leblanc, *Souvenirs*, pp. 193–4.
[2] G. H. Lugné-Poë, *La Parade sous les étoiles (1902–1912)*, p. 54.

upon; but as the moment comes when one wishes to see truth itself, it is good for the symbol to disappear.'[1] In another respect, moreover, his ideas have radically changed; in 1901 he wrote: '... it has seemed fair and wise to remove Death from that throne to which it has no certain right. Already in the last [drama], ... in *Aglavaine et Sélysette*, I should have liked it to yield a part of its power to love, to wisdom or to happiness....'[2] Henceforth the drama must treat moral or philosophical problems.

Monna Vanna typifies this new conception of the dramatic art. Vanna, wife of Guido Colonna, the Pisan commander, consents to give herself for one night to Prinzivalle, the general of the Florentine forces besieging Pisa, in order to save the city. Her husband is revolted at the idea, but her ageing father-in-law, Marco, urges her to sacrifice herself. In the event Prinzivalle, a mercenary whose position with the Florentines has become precarious, does not violate her because he recognizes her as one he has secretly loved since childhood. At dawn, in order to save him from the Florentines, she returns with him to the Pisan lines. Only Marco, however, believes the night she has spent to have been guiltless. In despair, she lies to her husband, alleging that Prinzivalle has taken her and she has lured him to Pisa to wreak vengeance upon him. Secretly, shocked by her husband's disbelief and moved by Prinzivalle's constancy, she now reciprocates the latter's love. She intends to liberate him and then flee with him to happiness.

The moral question here posed is: should a woman's chastity, or even a wife's honour, be deemed of more importance than the lives of a whole city? For Maeterlinck the answer is plain: sexual exclusiveness and faithfulness, although estimable, must on occasion be sacrificed to greater issues. In *Le Trésor des humbles* and *Sœur Béatrice* the theory had been advanced that the sins of the body cannot injure the soul, which is inviolable. If her consent is obtained by force, can Monna Vanna be held to offend against any moral standard save the conventional one? Indeed, her attitude is the only truly moral position: the slaughter of thousands of innocent people cannot be justified in order to uphold

---

[1] *Le Temple enseveli*, p. 131.   [2] *Préface* to *Théâtre*, vol. i, p. xxii.

an abstract principle of personal honour. Such casuistry has precedents: medieval legend recounts how the Virgin herself, in like circumstances, sold herself to the ferryman for the price of her fare; and there was also Maupassant's *Boule de suif*.

The other facet of the play concerns the morality of love. Monna Vanna rejects Guido, breaking her marriage vows because love is its own justification and may topple over all conventional barriers. Such a concept essentially destructive of human society does Maeterlinck, the new Maeterlinck revivified by Georgette Leblanc, propound through the lips of Vanna. The parallelism between the circumstances of the actress and the character she portrays is self-evident.

In the drama, as in no previous work, the author at last penetrates to life and reality. Flesh-and-blood characters externalize their passions and emotions. The clearly drawn plot is laid in Renaissance Italy, with its outrageous brutality and cruelty, its shock of arms, its colourfulness and upsurge of new life. The ethereal castles and mist-bound Northern forests that formed the backcloth of the earlier plays have been supplanted by a beleaguered city, encamped around by a hostile army, eager to sack, pillage, and murder the inhabitants.

Despite these sombre notes in the play, Maeterlinck asserts that Love can elude Destiny (which still, however, lurks in the background) and illuminate the whole of life. A lyrical outburst by Prinzivalle epitomizes the effect that Georgette Leblanc may have had upon the dramatist:

It seemed also to me that men were changing, that I had been mistaken about them until this day.... It seemed to me above all that I was changing myself, that I was emerging at last from a long prison, that the doors were opening, that flowers and foliage were pushing aside the bars, that the horizon was removing each stone, that the pure morning air was penetrating my soul and engulfing my love.[1]

Arrangements had been made to take the play on a tour of Europe. In London a performance had been organized by Philip Comyns-Carr when, at the last moment, the censor banned it. Nothing daunted, the organizer hastily founded a Maeterlinck

[1] *Monna Vanna*, p. 127.

Society and gave a 'private' matinée in the Victoria Hall, Bayswater, on 19 June 1902. *The Times* pertinently commented on this subterfuge: '. . . The London Maeterlinck Society seemed to consist chiefly of fashionable ladies wearing hats admirably calculated to hide all view of the stage. If the censor would only veto these hats we should feel more indulgent towards his peccadilloes in the matter of plays.'[1] The Lord Chamberlain's intervention was more sharply criticized in a letter published in the newspaper on 23 June, signed by, among others, William Archer, Richard Garnett, Thomas Hardy, George Meredith, Swinburne, Arthur Symons, and W. B. Yeats. This heavy salvo by the big guns of the English and Irish literary world failed to induce the censor to confess that he had erred.

Lugné-Poë ingeniously asserts that the mistake turned upon a misunderstanding. A stage direction in the second act read: 'Monna Vanna entrait nue sous un manteau.' The Reader of Plays, a certain Mr. Redford, either through bad eyesight or because his schooling in French prepositions had been inadequate, read this as '. . . entrait nue *sans* un manteau'.[2] According, however, to a rumour published in *Le Temps*, the ban was due to a specific objection lodged by no less a person than Queen Alexandra herself, who took exception to the play's thesis that virtue and fidelity cannot count against human lives. Thus this drama, 'written by a distinguished French writer of the highest moral reputation', still lies under the interdict of our antiquated censorship laws.

Not that the play won universal approval: from the literary viewpoint not a few considered that Maeterlinck, in exploring a new dramatic vein, had begun badly. Charles Van Lerberghe, visiting the dramatist in Paris in January 1902, wrote to a friend that he considered the play inferior to the earlier dramas.[3] This judgement was echoed by Shaw when he saw it performed in 1905; he wrote:

> I confess I think *Monna Vanna* a greatly overrated abortion. It

---

[1] *The Times*, 20 June 1902.
[2] G. H. Lugné-Poë, 'Mes confidences sur Maeterlinck', *Conferencia*, 15 Sept. 1933, p. 368.   [3] C. Van Lerberghe, *Lettres à une jeune fille*, p. 206.

seems to me as plain as a pikestaff that he had planned a really interesting play and that Georgette Leblanc insisted on his making it a 'possible' one, so that she might have a Sarah Bernhardt success. The first act is all right: one awaits with great interest the duel of sex in the *condottiere*'s tent. It is clear that the lady is going to get out of the difficulty somehow, like Marina in *Pericles* or Lady Cecily in *Brassbound*: otherwise there will be no play. But when nothing more ingenious comes than 'Don't you remember little Tommy?' 'Bless me! It's little Liza! My! Only fancy!' a defrauded public is entitled to its money back; and the business with the cloak becomes a mere indecency to get a vulgar laugh every time she pretends she is going to open it.[1]

Georgette Leblanc, reciprocating Lugné-Poë's dislike of her, persuaded Maeterlinck to cede the touring rights of the play to another impresario, Schurmann, on condition that she still acted the title role. Maeterlinck let no considerations of friendship stand in his way, and even went so far as to write asking for Marco's costume, which part had been played by Lugné-Poë himself, and ending his letter, 'Thank you in advance ... O regretted Marco.'[2] Despite this, the European tour enjoyed great success.

Lugné-Poë's poor opinion of Georgette Leblanc's talent was confirmed by Debussy, who was involved in a fracas with Maeterlinck in early 1902. After nine years the composer's score for *Pelléas et Mélisande* was at last finished. Half-asleep in his armchair, the author listened to it being played through by Debussy in the flat in the Rue Raynouard and agreed that Carré of the Opéra-Comique should stage the opera in Paris. Georgette Leblanc alleges that it was then understood she was to play Mélisande. In January Maeterlinck learned from his newspaper that Carré and Debussy had invited Mary Garden, the talented but then almost unknown English singer, to play this part.[3] Maeterlinck stormed down to the theatre, but failed to make the impresario and the composer change their minds. Debussy even allowed Georgette Leblanc to sing part of the score to a group of musicians acting as judges; their verdict went against her. Maeterlinck broke off all connexion with the production. He

[1] C. Bax (ed.), *Letters of Florence Farr, Bernard Shaw and W. B. Yeats*, p. 24.
[2] G. H. Lugné-Poë, *La Parade sous les étoiles (1902–1912)*, p. 55.
[3] Cf. Mary Garden and Louis Biancolli, *Mary Garden's Story*, pp. 69–72.

threatened a lawsuit, only to discover that the French civil code gave prior rights to the composer of the score over the librettist. Moreover, in his initial authorization he had expressly declared that the opera could be performed how, when, and where Debussy wished.

A legal revenge being impossible, he brooded over other ways of satisfying his injured pride. A keen swordsman, he challenged Debussy to a duel. The composer declined, but Albert Carré declared his willingness to act as a substitute. (Maeterlinck rather fancied himself as a duellist: a year or two previously he had offered to meet in Berlin, 'sword in hand', George Stockhausen, whom he had accused of 'pirating' his works.) Lugné-Poë recounts how Maeterlinck thrust a sword in his hand and stood him against the garden wall, crying, 'Put yourself there, in the place of Albert Carré.' But this encounter of hard steel never occurred and in the end it was Debussy whom the irate author sought out. He stalked off to the Rue Cardonnet and threatened Debussy in his own house with a good drubbing from his walking-stick. The composer had collapsed weakly into a chair and called for smelling-salts. Before such passivity the aggressor had relented.

However, on 14 April 1902 a letter appeared in *Le Figaro* above Maeterlinck's signature:

> The management of the Opéra-Comique announces the forthcoming production of *Pelléas et Mélisande*. This production will take place in spite of me, for Messrs. Carré and Debussy have failed to recognize the most legitimate of my rights. . . . Indeed, M. Debussy, after having agreed with me as to the actress whom I esteemed alone to be capable of interpreting the part of Mélisande according to my intentions and wishes, in the face of the unjustifiable opposition of M. Carré to this choice, thought fit to refuse me the right to have a say in the casting, by making misuse of a letter I wrote to him nearly six years ago. Thus they succeeded in shutting me out from my own work, which, from then onwards, was treated as conquered territory. Arbitrary and absurd cuts have been made in it. In the libretto just published, it will be seen how far the version adopted by the Opéra-Comique differs from the authentic one. In short, the *Pelléas* in question is a play that has become foreign to me, almost inimical; and, bereft of all control of my work, I am reduced to wish for it to be a prompt and resounding 'flop'.

Many thought this indictment had torpedoed the production and on 15 April it was even rumoured Debussy had committed suicide. But the last shot had not been fired in the 'battle of *Pelléas*'. Preparations went steadily forward and on Saturday, 30 April, a carefully selected audience was invited to the dress rehearsal: Clemenceau, the politician, Charles de Chambrun, the diplomat; writers such as Gide, Valéry, Claudel, de Régnier, even Willy and Colette; Réjane the actress, the composers Dukas and Fauré. Some three hundred people were in the auditorium. Chuckles and suppressed laughter greeted the first act, whilst quips such as 'Pelléas et Médisances' and 'Palisandre et Mêle-Casse' circulated from mouth to mouth. Outside the theatre an allegedly official programme had been hawked, which turned out to consist of sardonic and even obscene parodies of the opera. Fighting even broke out during the intervals at the dress rehearsal. Carré laid these provocations at Maeterlinck's door, although it is doubtful whether he would go so far in attacking what was undoubtedly half his work. On the Monday press criticisms were mainly hostile, but no untoward incidents occurred at the first night and after a week the opera was playing to packed houses. Years later, in 1925, Maeterlinck admitted that in his feud with Debussy all the wrong was on his side.[1]

Georgette Leblanc, in fact, does not seem to have enhanced Maeterlinck's popularity among his acquaintances and friends. Mirbeau, the author's original and ever-faithful champion, openly blamed his friend's troubles upon her. If the actress herself is to be believed, the first rift in the lute in their 'companionship' dated from about this time.[2] The ardour of the one-time passionate lover had cooled and the more *bourgeois* traits in his nature were becoming uppermost. In December 1901 rumours had gone the rounds that they were contemplating marriage. Van Lerberghe,

[1] In an unpublished reply to a questionnaire, now in the possession of the Fondation Maeterlinck, Ghent, sent him by his friend Henry Russell about 1925, when the latter was writing *The Passing Show*, Maeterlinck had this to say about the episode: 'L'histoire de Debussy est à peu près exacte; mais si j'avais eu un gros bâton, ce n'était que ma canne habituelle. Du reste, je n'ai pas eu à menacer d'en faire usage, car Debussy qui me voyait d'assez méchante humeur, pour se débarrasser de moi, s'empressa de me promettre tout ce que je voulais. Je trouve aujourd'hui que tous les torts étaient de mon côté et qu'il eut mille fois raison.'   [2] Georgette Leblanc, *Souvenirs*, pp. 199 et seq.

after visiting the couple in January 1920, writes to a friend and damns the actress with faint praise.

Despite the upheavals occasioned by Georgette Leblanc about then, Maeterlinck's life seemed to be on an even keel. An established and successful writer, only in Belgium was the barometer not set fair for him. July 1902 saw him involved in yet another Belgian dispute. On the occasion of the 500th anniversary of the Battle of the Golden Spurs, where at Groningen Field, near Courtrai, the Flemings had routed the French, Maeterlinck penned an article for *Le Figaro* condemning Flemish nationalism and *flamingantisme* in Belgium. In it he coined the unfortunate phrase, 'Flemish clergy, the most ignorant of clergy'.[1] Great was the indignation in Catholic Flanders, whose greatest nineteenth-century poet had been Guido Gezelle, a priest. An anonymous reply in the *Journal de Bruxelles* (13 July 1902), generally ascribed to the critic Eugène Gilbert, regretted that 'this fine writer of Flemish birth and upbringing' had thus besmirched 'the greatness and nobility of his race'. The rebuke was all the more cutting because deserved.

Nevertheless, in the absence of serious competition, the Belgian authorities could not refuse him in 1903 the award, for the second time, of the Triennial Prize for Dramatic Literature. On this occasion the dramatist made no bones about accepting the honour, which was for *Monna Vanna*.

The play had stimulated again his enthusiasm for the theatre, and by the end of 1902[2] he had completed the fairy-tale drama of *Joyzelle*, for which he confidently predicted his greatest success to date. In point of fact, the play, staged in Paris on 20 May 1903 with Georgette Leblanc in the title role, failed miserably and was a financial disaster. Maeterlinck sought to excuse himself by declaring to Larroumet, the critic of *Le Temps*, that *Joyzelle* was intermediary between *Monna Vanna* and his first plays. Chronologically, this is palpably untrue, and the chief reason for its unpopularity is that it fell between the two stools of the fantasy or fairy-tale and the philosophical piece.

The play is, in fact, the allegory of Love, of love that overcomes

---

[1] Quoted by F. Van den Bosch, *Impressions de littérature contemporaine*, p. 223.
[2] Unpublished letter to O.-B. dated 1 Oct. 1902.

the snares by which Destiny seeks to entrap it. Joyzelle personifies the power of love, demonstrating a purity, a singleness of heart and purpose that brook of no despair. She pardons Lancéor's inconstancy, refuses to succumb to jealousy, clings steadfastly to her chastity, but will commit even murder to clear impediments from her path. She is Monna Vanna as that character appears at the end of the play, a *femme forte* who holds Love to be the supreme justification. Once again, the dominant note is that of optimism. In fact, the play is *The Tempest* rewritten.

At the end of 1902 Maeterlinck was still exploring new dramatic fields and was writing his first, and only true, comedy, *Le Miracle de St-Antoine*.[1] This 'buffoonery' in two acts is one of his few plays not described by the Belgian critic Lecat as 'riddled with debts': no 'sources' have been discovered for it. Its interest is that it exemplifies the other side of the Flemish nature—and of Maeterlinck's—its sensuality, delight in feasting, and stolid, middle-class attributes. (The obverse of the Maeterlinckian medal is of course manifested in his earlier mysticism and sense of the mystery of life.) Again, however, the play met with no success: it was staged in Geneva and Brussels during 1903, but not even published in French until 1919.

Having recovered from a mild illness in December 1902[2] Maeterlinck spent a few days in Ghent with his parents before setting off for Germany, where, on his first visit for over a decade, he received an enthusiastic ovation. In Berlin Georgette Leblanc was playing *Monna Vanna* to packed houses. In grand style the author put up at the Savoy and on 18 January 1903 was fêted at a banquet given by the Deutsches Theater. Otto Brahm, director of the Freie Bühne, eulogized *Monna Vanna*, drawing an extravagant comparison with *A Doll's House*. Maeterlinck's speech in reply was likewise laudatory and contained a sentence that, in the light of his later experience, he must have deeply regretted: 'Germany', he declared, 'is the moral conscience of the world, as France is its aesthetic conscience.'[3]

---

[1] Unpublished letter to O.-B. dated 12 Jan. 1903.
[2] Unpublished letter to O.-B. dated 21 Dec. 1902.
[3] O. Brahm, *Kritische Schriften über Drama und Theater*, 1913.

Maeterlinck did not follow the fortunes of his play in Holland, when the Schurmann company moved from Germany to Amsterdam. Here the drama was not well received. By then, however, its author had been drawn once again to the south of France. Making the Hôtel de Turin at Menton his headquarters, he set out to explore the coast on a motor-cycle, his favourite method of transport at that time. By March *Monna Vanna* was touring Italy and most probably he met Georgette Leblanc again there. It is known that he visited Milan at this time in order to see his old Belgian friend, Charles Doudelet, whom he had commissioned to design the scenery for *Joyzelle*.

Nor was his pen idle. There flowed from it a continuous stream of essays, many of which were first published in England or America before being collected in *Le Double Jardin* (1904). The themes are more trivial than hitherto, and the lightness and deftness of touch demonstrate that their author is more contented with himself and the world. One such piece, *Sur la mort d'un petit chien*, achieved such popularity in the Anglo-Saxon world that it was published in book form in three separate editions.

Maeterlinck's passion for animals was such that rarely during his life was he without a dog. (Cats, however, were his pet aversion: Georgette Leblanc alleges that he shot one particularly annoying feline stone dead.) In the early 1920's he became a patron of the International Anti-Vivisection League founded in Brussels. To the very end of his life he kept a tame blind dove, Virginie, which had to be fed by hand.

His affection for the animal kingdom about this time did not, however, extend to human beings. The change in his character from introvert to extrovert had by now been accomplished. One incident may serve to exemplify this. Schurmann, who had followed up the European tour of *Monna Vanna* by producing the ill-fated *Joyzelle*, had by the end of 1903 incurred the author's wrath. The latter wrote to Oppeln-Bronikowski: 'As for Schurmann, let us speak no more of him. Everything is indeed finished between us. He is a fool and a rogue, but even more of a fool than a rogue. If, moreover, he does not knuckle under and everything is not cleared up between him and me I have in reserve for him a public execution and a resounding one he will remember.'[1] Previously self-effacing, his recent struggles on Georgette Leblanc's behalf would seem to have developed a latent aggressiveness in him. He has become temporarily a man over-sure of himself, possessed with the idea of his own importance, exaggerating his (nevertheless considerable) literary merit, a recluse—little is known of who were his friends about this time—shutting himself off from a world he despised. Perhaps it is indicative that from early 1904 he abandons the modest 'M. Maeterlinck' with which he signed himself, for the lordly, more flowing, one-word appellation 'Maeterlinck'. Despite *L'Oiseau bleu*—still unwritten—it is fair to say that the Maeterlinck of the early period, with his delicate touch and occasional profound insight, is dead, or rather, lies dormant: Prinzivalle has ousted Pelléas, Aglavaine has temporarily captured him from Sélysette.

The late January of 1904 once again found the author and Georgette Leblanc in Italy. *Aglavaine et Sélysette* (staged only once previously, at the Odéon in Paris on 14 December 1896), *L'Intruse*, *Joyzelle*, and *Monna Vanna* were put on in Naples and *Joyzelle* and *L'Intruse* in Rome. They met with only a lukewarm reception and the public were disappointed because Maeterlinck did not think it worth while to be present at the performances. In Rome he met Arthur Symons, the critic who was the principal interpreter to England of French Symbolism.

That spring rumours went the rounds that Maeterlinck and Georgette Leblanc were parting for good. The impression was that they were now legally married, which was untrue. A German newspaper even spread the tale abroad that the couple were seeking a divorce; nevertheless, summer was spent as usual together at Gruchet, where Maeterlinck wrote another three-act drama, *Le Malheur passe*.[2] He was not satisfied with it and upon his return to Paris in the autumn he decided not to publish it. (It

[1] Unpublished letter to O.-B. dated 3 Jan. 1904. 'Quant à Schurmann n'en parlons plus. Tout est bien fini entre nous. C'est un imbécile et un filou, mais encore plus imbécile que filou. Si d'ailleurs il ne met pas les pouces et si tout ne s'arrange pas entre lui et moi je lui réserve une exécution publique et retentissante dont il se souviendra.'

[2] The play is mentioned in the following letters to O.-B.: as 'begun' in a latter dated 12 Aug. 1904; as in three acts in a letter dated 10 Nov. 1904; as finished but not to be published, in a letter dated 18 Nov. 1904.

was eventually published in 1925.) The piece, Ibsenesque in mood, is, in fact, spoilt by an involved plot. It centres round the theme of jealousy, the unrequited love of a woman for a man whose affections lie elsewhere, set against a background of political intrigue carried on by Scandinavian and Finnish Separatists in the Grand Duchy of Finland, then controlled by Russia. Biographically, the drama is interesting because Tatiana, the jealous woman, represents yet another type of *femme forte*, completely amoral as regards her love, but capable ultimately of an act of supreme unselfishness. This was obviously yet another piece written with Georgette Leblanc in mind.

On 4 October 1904 Maeterlinck's father died, in his seventieth year. Ernest, Polydore Maeterlinck's younger son, who had also become a lawyer, took charge of all the legal formalities. Maeterlinck was present at the interment in the family vault at Wondelgem, near Oostacker. He does not appear to have been personally distressed at the event, and certainly he and his father had never been very close. His father's death meant, however, that he was henceforth much less dependent than hitherto on writing for earning his living. He felt no urge to return from exile and enjoy his inheritance in his own country. His attitude towards Belgium remained hostile and unreconciled. When invited, for example, to figure in the celebrations marking the 75th anniversary of Belgian independence, in July 1905, he refused in the most scathing terms: 'I mean to take no part in the celebration of a fallacious independence which at present afflicts us with a government which is the most retrograde, the most inimical to ideas of justice and liberty, subsisting in Europe—Russia and Turkey duly excepted.'[1] The Catholic party, led by reactionaries, were still firmly in the saddle, as they had been since 1886.

The main task of 1905, after he had given a lecture in January in Amsterdam, was undoubtedly the writing of *L'Oiseau bleu*, generally considered as 'the apogee of his dramatic career, the most brilliant moment ... of his inspiration'. The play touches the peak of his optimism and thus the date of its composition,

---

[1] Quoted by H. Kistemaeckers, 'Mes procès littéraires souvenirs d'un éditeur', *Mercure de France*, 15 Sept. 1923, p. 671.

which critics have either ignored or not known, is of supreme importance. In the idyllic surroundings of Gruchet, to which Maeterlinck moved as usual in mid-June, he worked hard, and by the end of August the work was completed save for minor revisions.[1]

What were the springs of imagination that inspired him to write this fairy play? Georgette Leblanc asserts that it was occasioned by a newspaper editor's request for a Christmas story and that 'He had created the two children, then, amused by his idea, he soon announced to me that the little story was to become a great fairy play'.[2] This explains the characters of Tyltyl and Mytyl, but does not shed much light upon the play's deeper origins. One must also recall his schoolboy essay in which human characteristics were attributed to the animals of the farm-yard. André de Poncheville ascribes the work to one of Mme d'Aulnoy's fairy-tales told the author in childhood.[3] Michaud says that Rimbaud's *Illuminations*, no less than *L'Oiseau bleu*, derives from fairy-tales:[4] one remembers the good use to which Maeterlinck put Grimm in the earlier plays, although there is no specific German tale resembling the work. For the English critic, however, the sources of the play are apparent: already in 1911 Léon Bocquet had cited J. M. Barrie.[5] The borrowings are not only from *Peter Pan*, but also from *The Little White Bird*, the novel published in 1902 from which Barrie adapted his fantasy. Moreover, Maeterlinck freely acknowledged this debt. In December 1909, when he came to London to see the Herbert Trench production of *The Blue Bird*, he called upon Barrie in his rooms in the Adelphi and wrote on the wallpaper over the mantelpiece: 'Hommage d'admiration au père de Peter Pan, grand-père de *L'Oiseau bleu*.'[6]

There is no doubt, however, that Maeterlinck's work, in contrast to *Peter Pan*, has a deep allegorical significance. The blue

---

[1] Unpublished letter to O.-B. dated 11 Aug. 1905.
[2] Georgette Leblanc, *Souvenirs*, p. 251.
[3] A. de Poncheville, 'L'Oiseau bleu', *Gand artistique*, 1 Mar. 1923, p. 70.
[4] G. Michaud, *Le Message poétique du symbolisme*, vol. i, p. 146.
[5] L. Bocquet, 'L'Archétype de *L'Oiseau bleu*', *Revue bleue*, 18 Feb. 1911, pp. 208–13.
[6] D. Mackail, *The Story of J. M. B.*, p. 319.

3. 'L'Oiseau bleu': Act II: In the Fairy Palace

bird, the object of the children's quest, is not only happiness, but the great secret of the universe. This accounts for the hostility of Nature, for if Man were to solve the enigma he would become the lord of all things. Lewisohn has catalogued the other allegories that arise in the play as follows: the dead live in our memories (Act II, Scene i); simple pleasures are the best (III. ii); Man is gradually conquering disease (III. i); Man will subdue the forces of Nature (V. iii); happiness is to be found at home (end of the play).[1] Being cognizant with the philosophico-moral tone of the dramatist's 'plays of the second manner', one must assume such allegories are intentional and epitomize beliefs he himself held.

But the dominant note is that of the fairy-tale and, considered as such, it has best claim to immortality. As in *Pelléas et Mélisande*, a play that may also survive the erosion of time, its appeal lies in its simplicity and scenic beauty. If *Pelléas* marks the trough of despair, *L'Oiseau bleu* represents the highest peak of optimism reached by the dramatist. Yet even here the hope is qualified: the children do not find the blue bird and even the one that might be a substitute for it escapes them. Happiness can only be provisional, Maeterlinck would seem to argue, and death remains humanity's great insoluble riddle.

Incidentally, *L'Oiseau bleu* provoked a violent dispute between the author and Oppeln-Bronikowski, his German translator, whose income from his translations was now substantial. In January 1906 Maeterlinck was dumbfounded to learn that the German proposed to read extracts from the play in public, before it had even been published. Reacting swiftly, he signed a contract with the German impresario Reinhardt, assigning over all German rights, including that of translation. Oppeln-Bronikowski, singularly obtuse at realizing the heinousness of his offence, threatened legal action. Maeterlinck, never averse to litigation, told him to go ahead. Eventually the translator climbed down, but he had sacrificed for ever the prospect of royalties from this best of all best sellers.[2]

---

[1] L. Lewisohn, *The Modern Drama*, pp. 234–5.
[2] Unpublished letters to O.-B. dated: 5 Jan. 1906; 6 Jan. 1906; 14 Jan. 1906; 27 Jan. 1906.

Best seller though it was, in some quarters the play did not meet with acclaim. W. B. Yeats's criticism after having seen it in London was trenchant: 'It is possibly another of the gasping things Maeterlinck, struggling well beyond his nature, does to please his wife, who was there last night, in a red turban, looking like Messalina. I amused somebody by saying that Maeterlinck was like a little boy who has jumped up behind a taxi-cab and can't get off.'[1] This, from one who when young had succumbed to the influence of French Symbolism and whose play, *The Countess Cathleen*, has overtones of the early Maeterlinck, is highly significant: once again Georgette Leblanc is taken to task.

Yet it would be wrong to lay the blame entirely at her door. It may be argued that she led him in a direction to which his imagination was already turning. Van Lerberghe, writing in 1901, completely upsets the portrait of the dramatist as a young man, as it emerges from his early plays; he asserts: 'As for Maeterlinck, I don't know whether he has these fits of melancholy of which you speak; I even doubt it, never having known him melancholic for a single moment. He has such a confidence in himself and finds in his work such joy and such rewards that these moments must in any case be rare. . . .'[2] Thus he implies that from the outset Maeterlinck's pessimism was purely literary. But the converse is also true: his optimism may also have been a pose, but less fruitful. After *Joyzelle* Grégoire Le Roy, his other old friend, had reported Mockel as writing to him that 'Maurice talked *theatre and money* so much to him that he told him he had to write a book of superb, unsaleable, verse in order to be forgiven'.[3]

The gradually deteriorating opinion of his work taken by his French literary contemporaries may be demonstrated by studying Gide. The author of the *Cahiers d'André Walter*, an early work that bears the impress of Maeterlinck's influence, had once proclaimed: 'Donc, Mallarmé pour la poésie, Maeterlinck pour le drame.' His approval of *Aglavaine et Sélysette* had been qualified, even ambiguous. Apart from a brief encounter at the banquet for

[1] A. Wade (ed.), *Letters of W. B. Yeats*, p. 541.
[2] C. Van Lerberghe, *Lettres à une jeune fille*, p. 198.
[3] Letter by Grégoire Le Roy, quoted in *Épîtres*, Ghent, Fascicule No. 28, Apr. 1949.

Edmund Gosse in 1904 they did not meet again until 1906 in Paris, when Gide describes the occasion as follows:

1906
    5 January.
    Yesterday, end of the afternoon at the Mathurins [theatre]. Georgette Leblanc in *La Mort de Tintagiles*. The little auditorium was packed. Maeterlinck offers me the hospitality of his box. Opposite us, Mary Garden; on our right, the Duse. . . . Complete uninterestedness on Maeterlinck's face; materialism of his features; a man of the North, very positive, very practical, with whom mysticism is a mode of psychic exoticism.[1]

But the final disillusionment came with Maeterlinck's *Intelligence des fleurs*, about which Gide scathingly remarked: 'When I see Maeterlinck so enraptured, I have some difficulty in finding him as intelligent as his flowers.'[2]

Such strictures, however, seem to have affected the Belgian little: hermit-like, he sought to shut himself from his fellows. The dream of settling in the south of France, along the shores of the Mediterranean, still obsessed him. Early in February 1906 he again left Paris for the South, from where he wrote: 'I am continuing to explore the Riviera, from Toulon to Menton, by motor-cycle, to look for an unpretentious villa in which to spend a few weeks each winter. Up to now I have still not found exactly what might suit me.'[3] The inheritance he had had from his father probably made his plan realizable for the first time. He finally settled on the 'Villa des Quatre Chemins' at Grasse, 'the town of perfume'. A house of shimmering white, it was shut off from the road by a garden where flourished the rose, the olive, and the cypress, and ornamented with a trellised pergola beneath whose shade he was to take many a siesta. The property, which had once belonged to Fernand Xau, editor of the *Journal*, was to be his winter home for the next five years. As he had previously

[1] A. Gide, *Journal*, vol. i, p. 163, Rio de Janeiro edition, 1943.
[2] Quoted by H. Perruchot, *Maurice Maeterlinck et la poursuite de L'Oiseau bleu*, p. 7.
[3] Unpublished letter to O.-B. dated 20 Feb. 1906. 'Je continue à explorer la Côte d'Azur, depuis Toulon jusqu'à Menton, à motocyclette, afin d'y chercher une modeste villa où passer quelques semaines chaque hiver. Jusqu'ici je n'ai pas encore trouvé exactement ce qui me conviendrait.'

forsaken Ghent and Brussels, he now escaped from Paris, in which he made only short stays on his way to Belgium or Normandy, where he spent the summer.

The removal must have been distasteful to Georgette Leblanc, whose professional engagements often kept her in the capital. Henceforth her life was a perpetual journeying between Paris and the South. Neither partner suggested she should abandon her acting career, although in 1913 she made preparations to do so. Maeterlinck may have secretly rejoiced that she was not continually present: Georgette Leblanc hints that he was never entirely faithful to her, even during this nominally harmonious period of their life together.[1]

[1] Georgette Leblanc, *Souvenirs*, p. 219.

6

THE NOBEL PRIZEWINNER

THE spiritual partnership between dramatist and actress henceforth subsisted in name only. There is no doubt that this represented a liberation for Maeterlinck. With one exception, the plays he wrote were no longer intended specifically as vehicles for Georgette Leblanc's art. Nevertheless, this almost complete dissolution of their artistic collaboration, this freeing of his mind from the tyranny of a strong female personality, left a gap not easily filled. Thus 1906 and 1907 were years of crisis for the author, in which, despairing of the dramatic form, he turned again to prose.

The year 1906 was in fact taken up with the writing of essays, which were collected in *L'Intelligence des fleurs*. The title essay reflects the interest in flowers one would expect from a native of the horticultural city of Ghent, stimulated by his new residence in Grasse. Previous essays had also been collected in *Le Temple enseveli* (1902); they contrast with the more light-hearted vein struck in those collected in *Le Double Jardin*. They strike a serious, although mildly hopeful, note. Once again the moralist predominates, but disparate themes, such as politics, social justice, and occultism, are also touched upon. All these later volumes of essays lack the vigour of *La Vie des abeilles*, with prettiness rather than beauty characterizing their style: the best period of Maeterlinckian prose already lay behind.

One discerns in them a renewed interest in the esoteric tradition. From the East Maeterlinck drew his attraction to theosophy and Hinduism, from the West his passion for such phenomena as sorcery, soothsaying, magnetism, and spiritualism. Villiers and Huysmans are his predecessors, but the study of the occult had found continuers in Schuré (his foreword to *Les Grands Initiés* was widely read) and 'Sâr' Péladan, whose 'salons' in 1891 had been the centre of Rosicrucianism. Maeterlinck uses occultism in his unceasing attempts to probe the mystery of life.

For him the decline of Christianity signified a new dawn: a fresh basis had to be found for morality. Neither a moral code based on common sense, utilitarian and egotistical, nor one founded on 'good sense', likewise selfish, is sufficient. The third morality will be one of mystic reason, partly intuitional: the volition to formulate a moral ideal of justice and love within oneself. One notes the non-transcendental basis of such a concept: Una Taylor has said that whereas the older mystics were content to seek God in God, or God in Nature, Maeterlinck sought God in Man.

This 'mystic morality' leads inevitably to a deepened sense of justice, expressed by the framing of a new code in which the greatest wrongdoing will consist of offences against the liberty, integrity, and supremacy of the intelligence. Humanity's chief weapon in the struggle to progress is, in fact, the intelligence. Advances can only be made by a more enlightened mode of personal living. Too materialist at present, men must strike the just mean between the claims of the body and of the mind.

New moral rules presuppose a new social order: equality is the goal, to be reached by iconoclastic, even revolutionary, means. Egalitarian in outlook, Maeterlinck is moving towards the support for Socialism openly expressed in 1913. He thought a new dispensation possible, for both the individual and society. This kind of expectation was not uncommon at the beginning of the twentieth century. Zola's *Évangiles* had already elaborated similar principles to those of Maeterlinck: love, work as a duty incumbent upon all, brotherhood, and justice. Such a hope was not to be sustained.

By the beginning of May 1906 the move to Grasse had been completed,[1] and the early summer was spent in writing the long title-essay of *L'Intelligence des fleurs*.[2] Its central theme is that flowers, like bees, possess intelligence. The aim of plants, argues

[1] Unpublished letter No. 26 to Charles Doudelet, dated Paris, 22 Apr. 1906, quoted in *Annales de la Fondation Maeterlinck*, vol. i, 1955, p. 111, gives, for the first time, an indication that he is moving to Grasse. Letter No. 27 is actually shown as written from Grasse on 4 May 19(06).   [2] Unpublished letter to O.-B., 5 June 1906.

Maeterlinck, is the safeguarding and propagation of the species, for which their methods attest to a high degree of intelligence. Again the comparison is drawn with Man, who is imbued with an intelligence that is a manifestation of a supreme intelligence, which may be conceived of as a kind of 'fluid' that has found in men its best conductor. Such a higher intelligence has probably the same motivation as Man: the drive towards happiness and perfection, the conquest of evil and death. Theologically, such a conjecture is to lower the Creator to the status of the creature. But the status of Man has changed: he is no longer the puppet of what Maeterlinck termed in *Sagesse et destinée* an external destiny, but a vehicle for the communication of universal thought.

The amateur botanist in this volume achieves less success than did the entomologist. For personal observation he has substituted the study of Darwin and Schopenhauer. Moreover, the apparently inanimate flower hardly lends itself to the same poeticization as the bee. But the genre was not entirely exhausted, for a score of years later Maeterlinck was to explore once again the microcosm of the insect world. By then, however, his inspiration had vanished and those volumes dealing with the ants and the termites may be classified as mere 'popular science'.

The summer of 1906 was singularly unfruitful. A few days spent with his mother in Ghent at the end of June were followed by the usual summer holiday at Gruchet, where he remained until mid-September, before departing to winter again at Grasse.[1] There he set to work on another play, concerned with the French Revolution. The exact dates of writing *Marie-Victoire* are not known, although it was finished by May 1907.[2] Again Maeterlinck did not feel it came up to standard, and it was not even published until 1927. The plot centres round the legal fight of a woman to save the life of her husband, an aristocrat caught in France in 1799. Apart from the first act, no less than a third of the remaining dialogue is lifted verbatim from the *Mémoires de la Comtesse de la Villirouët*, published in 1902.[3] The sole biographical

[1] Unpublished letters to O.-B. dated 16 June 1906 and 18 July 1906.
[2] Unpublished letters to O.-B. dated 31 Mar. 1907, 28 Apr. 1907, and 23 June 1907.
[3] The full title of the work is: *Mémoires de la Comtesse de la Villirouët née de Lambilly (1767–1813). Une femme avocat. Épisodes de la Révolution à Lamballe et à Paris,*

interest of the play is that its heroine, Marie-Victoire, is of the same mettle as the other heroines of the plays of the 'second manner': inspired by love, her courage touches supreme heights of sacrifice.

The year 1907 was to be an inauspicious one for Maeterlinck. It opened with the death of Charles Van Lerberghe, who had been ill since the previous October. Maeterlinck had been so convinced that he would recover that he had even made arrangements for him to convalesce at Grasse.[1] In December 1906 hope of saving him had been virtually abandoned; Maeterlinck wrote to an inquirer: 'It is unfortunately only too true that my poor friend Van Lerberghe is very ill, not mad, but stricken by a general paralysis. According to the doctors, there is perhaps no hope of saving him, but, we, his old friends, still hope against hope.'[2] Doubtless the death of the poet of *Ève*, at the age of forty-six, shocked Maeterlinck far more than that of his father had. His attitude towards him had been for many years that of a rather condescending elder brother, but he was certainly one of his closest friends. In May 1926, when a memorial was proposed to Van Lerberghe, he sent a cheque to Mockel for no less than 10,000 Belgian francs.

Their Paris home having by now degenerated into a mere stopping-off place, Maeterlinck and Georgette Leblanc looked round for a smaller apartment, suitable either for the actress when she was working in the capital or when Maeterlinck was obliged to go there on business. Eventually a flat was found in Neuilly, at 32 boulevard Maillot.

At the same time the author had grown tired of Gruchet as a summer residence. The Belgian author, André Fontainas, who had also settled in France, informed him that the great Benedictine abbey of St-Wandrille in Normandy was up for sale. This huge

published by her grandson, the Comte de Bellevue. Pages 62–146 contain in essence the plot and some of the dialogue of *Marie-Victoire*.

[1] Unpublished letter No. 17 to Mockel, dated 21 Oct. 1906, quoted in *Annales de la Fondation Maeterlinck*, vol. i, 1955, p. 101.

[2] Unpublished letter to O.-B. dated 17 Dec. 1906. 'Il n'est malheureusement que trop vrai que mon pauvre ami Van Lerberghe est très malade, non pas fou, mais frappé d'une paralysie générale. Au dire des médecins, il n'y aurait nul espoir de le sauver, mais nous, ses vieux amis, espérons encore, contre tout espoir.'

Gothic religious house, dating from the fourteenth century, had been destroyed during the Wars of Religion and rebuilt in the seventeenth century. Huysmans had interested himself in the work of its Benedictine monks after the resettlement in 1894. Then the 'Loi Combes' had forced its community, numbering some 400 religious, to abandon it. At the time when Maeterlinck heard it was up for sale, a chemical syndicate interested in the manufacture of armaments was negotiating for it.[1]

Georgette Leblanc was eager to make the abbey their new home. As a child, holidaying at Jumièges, she had visited it and been entranced by its beauty. Through the extensive estate in which it stood ran the river Fontenelle, renowned for its trout-fishing, a pastime that Maeterlinck revelled in. Although the once splendid abbey church lay in ruins, its magnificent refectory and superb cloisters imparted the atmosphere of decaying grandeur to it that was bound to delight one whose early plays had been set in tumbledown castles, with crumbling walls enclosing vast wooded parks.

On the point of buying it outright for 100,000 francs, Maeterlinck was approached by representatives of the Benedictine Order, who requested that they be allowed to purchase it in his stead. They guaranteed him a 99-year lease in exchange for a rent of 3 per cent. of the agreed purchase price. He accepted this not ungenerous offer and there, in these Arcadian surroundings, spent every summer until 1914, when he decided that the war made evacuation essential. Georgette Leblanc, with her sense of the dramatic if not of the fitting, would sometimes sweep along its interminable corridors garbed in the habit of an abbess. The author, in moments of distraction, donned a pair of roller-skates and, intent on exercise, glided along the cloisters. So vast were the buildings that the new occupants would sometimes lose themselves, and to warn each other of their whereabouts they devised a special call of distress.

Despite the inspiration to be drawn from this unique residence, where he spent the summer of 1907 after the usual brief visit to Ghent, it was the most sterile season Maeterlinck had ever passed.

[1] M. Lecat, *Le Maeterlinckisme*, vol, i, p. 16, note 2.

After a few weeks in the abbey Georgette Leblanc reported to her brother that he could not concentrate on work: 'I feel he is at a difficult turning-point. I fancy also he needs a new inspiration. Ten years ago I was the first turning-point, my arrival by his side occurred at a favourable time, it marked the second phase of his life.'[1] The exactness of this judgement as regards the decline of her influence is irrefutable. Maeterlinck himself felt that in his recent books and plays he had done nothing but repeat himself. He frittered the months away in trivial occupations such as fishing, gardening, fruit-picking, furniture-painting, and other odd jobs. He was bored, and confided to Oppeln-Bronikowski that he was passing through a difficult stage:

> Alas, I have been able to write nothing this summer. I have suffered from an onset of neurasthenia, and the doctor has strictly forbidden me all intellectual work, so that I have lived like an animal, in the open air. Happily, as I caught it in time, I am now much better and am only waiting now for the doctor's authorization to begin work once more. But for me, who have never had the habit of laziness, this forced inactivity—I am scarcely allowed to read—is the hardest of cures. Moreover, apart from this nervous depression, all my organs are in perfect condition.[2]

But the impetus that his companion had hitherto supplied was now exhausted, and his complete recovery did not really occur until 1911.

In 1907 *L'Intelligence des fleurs* was at length published and Paul Dukas also finished the score of *Ariane et Barbe-bleue*. Since she claimed to have inspired the play Georgette Leblanc felt she had the right to sing the title role. This contention was resisted by her old enemy, Albert Carré of the Opéra-Comique, where Dukas had arranged for his work to be staged. However,

---

[1] Georgette Leblanc, *Souvenirs*, p. 184.
[2] Unpublished letter to O.-B. dated 4 Oct. 1907. 'Je n'ai, hélas, pu rien écrire cet été. J'ai souffert d'un commencement de neurasthénie, et le médecin m'a strictement interdit tout travail intellectuel, de sorte que j'ai vécu comme une brute, en plein air. Heureusement, comme je m'y suis pris à temps, je vais en ce moment beaucoup mieux et je n'attends plus que l'autorisation du docteur pour me remettre au travail. Mais pour moi, qui n'ai jamais eu l'habitude de la paresse, cette inaction forcée — à peine m'est-il permis de lire — est le plus dur des traitements. Du reste, à part cette dépression nerveuse, tous mes organes sont en parfait état.'

with the composer's backing she eventually had her way and the opera was successfully launched on 10 May 1907. The actress asserts that her personal triumph was so overwhelming that a thousand or more opera-goers petitioned for her to sing *Pelléas et Mélisande*. Furthermore a few score of devotees formed 'The Knights of Ariane', a club for which the sole membership qualification was to have seen the opera a certain number of times. One day the noble 'knights' were even entertained to a party at St-Wandrille at which their 'lady' sang and Maeterlinck dispensed champagne.[1] Despite this elaborate publicity, Dukas's work failed to achieve the same popularity as Debussy's *Pelléas*.

Slowly Maeterlinck emerged from the depths of his depression and by January 1908 began meditating a new play, *Marie-Magdeleine*. After reading an account of Paul Heyse's *Maria Magdalena* he claimed to perceive dramatic possibilities that the Munich playwright had not exploited. Envisaging his own play as a free adaptation of Heyse, he was willing to share the royalties with him. The German author refused to consent to what, in short, was tantamount to plagiarism. Despite this setback Maeterlinck continued throughout the year to work on his own version. To his credit, he did not pass over his debt to Heyse, despite contrary advice tendered by his German translator, to whom he wrote:

I venture not to share completely your opinion regarding the attitude to adopt towards Heyse. I have never had and never will have the intention of denying the borrowings I have made from him. It seems therefore preferable to me, fairer and more elegant, to forestall any claims by a statement beforehand. If not, whatever I do, I shall always have seemed to desire to conceal what I wished to proclaim loudly.[2]

When his work was finished it was accepted by the Odéon, but, hearing that the theatre was on the verge of bankruptcy,

---

[1] Georgette Leblanc, *Souvenirs*, pp. 175–8.
[2] Unpublished letter to O.-B. dated 24 Jan. 1909. 'Je me permets de ne pas être toutà fait de votre avis au sujet de l'attitude à prendre vis-a-vis de Heyse. Je n'ai jamais eu et n'aurai jamais l'intention de nier les emprunts que je lui ai faits. Il me semble donc préférable, plus loyal et plus élégant, d'aller au devant de toute réclamation, par une déclaration préalable. Sinon, quoi qu'on fasse, j'aurai toujours un peu l'air d'avoir voulu dissembler ce que j'ai toujours voulu affirmer hautement.'

Maeterlinck withdrew their option. Eventually the play first reached the stage in Leipzig at the Neue Stadttheater on 12 March 1910. But it was neither performed nor published in France until 1913.

Nevertheless, it is one of the more interesting of Maeterlinck's attempts to create a philosophical and moral theatre. Hitherto his *femmes fortes* had been set in legendary, historical, or even contemporary surroundings. In *Marie-Magdeleine* the biblical courtesan moves in the most difficult historical times, during the life of Christ, for a dramatist to depict. If this play may be termed religious, it is, however, marked by a continual dialectic between the Christian and Stoic ideals, between the followers of the Way and those of the world, represented by Rome. The great defect of the drama is that only in the last act does the real dramatic action begin. Jesus has been arrested. Verus, a young blackguard of a Roman soldier who is in love with Marie-Magdeleine, has the power to save Christ. In return for his letting his prisoner escape, he proposes that she should give herself utterly to him. Fully aware of the tragic consequences that will ensue, she refuses, and Christ passes on to the judgement of Pilate.

The dynamic of the play thus lies in the character of the courtesan and in the impact of Jesus upon it. If she is 'in love' with her new-found Master, ultimately she realizes that her love has become part of the Divine Love to which all things, her own human affections as well as the earthly body of Christ, must be sacrificed. Unlike Monna Vanna she does not maintain that sexual love is the highest morality; instead, her will becomes dissociated from passion. The shameful surrender of her body, not to save a mere city, but the very person of the Saviour of the world, cannot be justified. She reasons that she holds two deaths in her hand: the first is that of the physical body of Jesus; the other is undoubtedly His work, all that He came to establish on earth. Her rejection of Verus, on moral grounds, is therefore the supreme act of the will, the highest act of love.

In contrast to this ignoble Roman officer there stands Silanus, a nobler Roman, whose sentiments are those of the Stoic. Maeterlinck, it would appear, has now come to accept Stoicism even more unreservedly than in *Sagesse et destinée*. But it is Seneca, quoted verbatim in the play, rather than Marcus Aurelius, who has convinced him that death must be accepted and that passion must wither away.

For Maeterlinck's own career this play was also, after the event, to have deep significance. It is the last drama written specifically for Georgette Leblanc. Thus finally peters out their long dramatic collaboration and with it is brought to a close his 'theatre of the second manner'. The plays that compose it, written from 1898 onwards, indeed resemble each other. Although great philosophical and moral themes run through them, the central motif is always the concept of love. Its claims are absolute, its power, if of no avail against the might of Death, is capable of turning aside the blows of Destiny. The arbiter of human happiness, love, demands energy, action, and even sacrifice. It is epitomized in the *femmes fortes*, whose types are many and complex. Monna Vanna is portrayed as the sensuous, Joyzelle as the beautiful; whereas Tatiana is an admixture of wickedness and abnegation, Marie-Victoire is the exemplar of married happiness. Finally, Marie-Magdeleine, physically voluptuous, develops into the personification of spiritual self-sacrifice. In creating such a diverse array of female characters, whose dominant characteristics are strength of will and purpose, as a vehicle solely for Georgette Leblanc, there is no doubt that Maeterlinck exhibits a certain submissiveness in his nature. One cannot also fail to note that with the passage of the years there is a weakened emphasis on the physical aspects of love and an increasing stressing of its spirituality.

After his first disastrous summer at St-Wandrille, Maeterlinck's gloom was dispelled by the triumph of *L'Oiseau bleu* in Moscow, where the world première took place at the Arts Theatre. Despite this success, the play had still no takers in Paris. The winter of 1907 passed uneventfully. In November he again moved his *pied-à-terre* in Paris, this time to 32 rue Perronet, still in the suburb of Neuilly. The winter in Grasse was disturbed the following February, when he returned to Paris for a month's treatment by an eye specialist.[1] The infection had hampered his writing, and even after his return to the South he had to be careful of his eyes.

[1] Unpublished letter to O.-B. dated 6 Feb. 1909.

This would account for the first six months of 1908 again being a time when he produced little.

Before his usual summer trip to Ghent he paid a flying visit to London, where on 21 June a matinée of *Pelléas* was given, using for the first time the incidental music of Gabriel Fauré. As in the original London production, Forbes-Robertson played Golaud, but Sir John Martin Harvey acted Pelléas. After the show Maeterlinck had tea on the stage; Sarah Bernhardt was also present.[1]

Although Georgette Leblanc indicates that from 1908 onwards she remained with Maeterlinck merely from habit and convenience, another decade was to pass before their partnership was formally dissolved. True intellectual collaboration between them had ceased, but they still worked together on a lower plane. That summer at St-Wandrille was spent in devising a new translation of *Macbeth*. Maeterlinck, whilst upholding that all translations were bad, resembling the originals only as monkeys do men, asserted that this particular one required doing again, because that of Jean-François-Victor Hugo was so poor. In a letter to her brother Georgette Leblanc describes his method of tackling the task:

... Maeterlinck follows the English text, whilst I read aloud the different interpretations made by translators. ... At first he says the sentence, constructing it almost according to the French form, then he says it again, tearing away its French garb, which does not fit it—he repeats it, splitting up more and more the first meaning proposed; and then, above a pile of words dropping at random, like empty husks, the true thought of the poet spurts forth, enormous, immense, untranslatable.[2]

On several occasions the opinion of Gérard Harry, Maeterlinck's bilingual friend, was sought.[3]

The actress then conceived the grandiose idea of presenting the play, in its new translation, at St-Wandrille itself. The rambling abbey and parkland would constitute an ideal setting, and the various changes of scene could be accomplished by merely

---

[1] The Enthoven Collection, in the Victoria and Albert Museum, London, possesses a programme of the first matinée on which Mme Enthoven has written: 'Went with Mme. Sarah Bernhardt and M. Maeterlinck. Had tea on stage after. Gabrielle Enthoven.'

[2] Georgette Leblanc, *Souvenirs*, p. 237.

[3] G. Harry, *Mes mémoires*, vol. iii, p. 261.

moving cast and audience to suitable natural spots. She won her first victory when Maeterlinck agreed, for he clung to his privacy, and when rehearsals started they irritated him considerably. The conditions of the performance caused a sensation: it was agreed that only some sixty spectators should be allowed, at a cost per ticket of 200 francs—about £8. Any profits would go to the village poor. Gaston Calmette, editor of the *Figaro*, gave the venture wide publicity. Thus, on the evening of 28 August 1909, a distinguished company assembled. In the audience were Harry and his wife, Princess Murat, Calmette, Adolphe Brisson, Octave Uzanne, and Iwan Gilkin, who had travelled especially from Belgium. Britain was represented by no less a person than Mr. McKenna, the First Lord of the Admiralty. These guests had been received by Lady Macbeth's ladies-in-waiting, already dressed for the part, and Georgette Leblanc's ever-faithful 'Knights of Ariane', likewise in costume. Burning braziers and moonlight cast fittingly sombre shadows over the scene. Maeterlinck walked among his visitors, also appropriately clad—Georgette Leblanc had taken the precaution of sending a costume to his room and he had been the first dressed for the performance. The enthusiastic notices of the play made the actress resolve to repeat the venture as soon as possible.

An autumn visit to Ghent was followed by retirement for the winter to Grasse. But in December 1909 Maeterlinck was again back in London, accompanied by Georgette Leblanc, for the première of Trench's production of *The Blue Bird*, which ran until the following June. Meanwhile the play had also been published in Paris and a copy had come into the hands of the actress Réjane when she was touring the Argentine.[1] Upon her return to Paris she arranged for its production in Paris in the spring of 1911.

But in 1910, when his dramatic career was touching the highest pinnacle of fame, Maeterlinck's mind was already deeply occupied with philosophical matters. Perhaps, with the final flickering out of the immediate incentive to write for the stage, his thoughts had caused him to turn back to the fundamental problem of death,

---

[1] G. H. Lugné-Poë, *La Parade sous les étoiles (1902–1912)*, p. 247.

whose solution he saw as the key to all existence. *La Mort*, beginning as an essay, lengthened into a volume and was complete by about May 1911.[1] It was then published in English, but did not appear in French until 1913.

The work is significant because it marks 'the point of departure for the grand inquiry' concerning Man and the universe, an investigation that was now to occupy Maeterlinck until his life's end and whose provisional conclusions were to be embodied in many books. It is indeed strange that the starting-point for such an enterprise should be not life, but death. This almost pathological obsession with the close of life had been apparent in the early plays, where death is perceived in fear and terror. Its roots lie deeply embedded in his schooldays in Flanders itself. Natives of Ghent, such as Pierre Maes and Franz Hellens, have emphasized the dreary atmosphere of the brooding city, whose gabled rooftops reach out like ghostly hands to embrace the spectre of its cathedral, shrouded in mist. Ghent, Bruges-la-Morte—these 'still cities' of Flanders inspire even today melancholy and pessimism. Personal circumstances conspired to strengthen Maeterlinck's neurosis. For a while Georgette Leblanc had dispelled the lurking shadows, but now her power to charm away despair was all but spent. Van Lerberghe, whose *Flaireurs* had been the precursors of Death, had told his old friend he would return from beyond the grave to greet him. *La Mort* represents the author's inevitable attempt to analyse and explain this greatest enigma of life.

Of the possible explanations as to what happens after death Maeterlinck can accept only one: survival in the universal consciousness. This steers a middle course between total annihilation and the survival of personality. He rejects, incidentally, the theories of metempsychosis and reincarnation. But one can divine little of what continuation in the universal consciousness is meant to imply. Maeterlinck asserts, however, that the state would be a happy one, because it is impossible to imagine an infinite entity, of which human survival would inevitably form a part, as existing for its own unhappiness. Although this conclusion is partly

---

[1] Unpublished letters to O.-B. dated 10 Nov. 1910, 28 Jan. 1911, and 19 May (1911).

negative, in effect, in all the later works he wrote he never advanced beyond this point. Whereas previous essays had demonstrated his evolution from pessimism to optimism, by now the lines of his thought have crystallized back into pessimism, a qualified despair. He considered that no final conclusions were possible. Although he sought continually to discover the unknown, ultimately all his explorations lead him back to his starting-point—and to a confession of ignorance: We do not know.

If 1910 was remarkable only for the writing of *La Mort* and a short article on Fabre, by contrast 1911 was another year of destiny for Maeterlinck. In January rehearsals of *L'Oiseau bleu* started in Paris under the supervision of Georgette Leblanc, who had had the opportunity of studying Stanislawski's Moscow production. Usually Maeterlinck stayed away from rehearsals of his plays—and often from performances as well—but these he attended. At one of them he met Renée Dahon, whom some eight years later he was to marry. She was then a young girl of eighteen, who had been given two parts in the play: Rhume du Cerveau and Bonheur du Printemps. A slight, boyish figure, she had large dark eyes and a well-shaped mouth; *petite*, fair, and slim, she was the very epitome of youth. She sprang from a typical French middle-class family—her father, M. Joseph Dahon, a rich merchant, had recently moved from Nice to Paris. By the rest of the cast his diminutive daughter had been nicknamed Gland d'Argent, because of the silver tassel on the cap she wore. One day she summoned up courage enough to ask the famous author to sign her autograph book. This simple gesture of hero-worship brought her to his notice and that very evening she was invited to dinner with him and Georgette Leblanc. Thus began a friendship that continued long after the first performance of *L'Oiseau bleu* at the Théâtre Réjane on 2 March 1911. It culminated in a mutual esteem that gradually ripened into love, which was followed by marriage.

On 22 May 1910 Maeterlinck received an urgent summons to Ghent: his mother, whose health had been failing for some time, was dying. On 6 June she still lingered on and he was able to write: 'My mother is a little better and there remains some hope of saving her.'[1] But on 12 June the ineluctable arrived and once again the family stood round the family vault at Wondelghem. This time his sense of personal loss was deeper, for it had been his mother who, contrary to his father's wishes, had always encouraged him, even surreptitiously helping him financially in the publication of his early works. By a stroke of Fate, she was just to miss seeing the crowning honour of the Nobel Prize for literature being awarded to her son.

At St-Wandrille that summer Georgette Leblanc, who had had dreams of converting the abbey into a French Bayreuth, triumphed again in a production of *Pelléas et Mélisande*. Among the audience were Sacha Guitry and the actress Réjane, as well as Iwan Gilkin, this time representing the Belgian government. His presence stirred up a hornets' nest in Belgium: the right-wing Brussels newspapers launched a diatribe against the responsible minister, Baron Descamp-David, for according official recognition to a secular play performed on consecrated ground. This attack did not deter the government from again awarding him the Triennial Prize for dramatic literature, thus honouring *L'Oiseau bleu*. There was no doubt that an enterprise such as that at St-Wandrille contributed to Belgium's cultural fame. That Maeterlinck did not view the performance in this light was apparent when, on the night of the dress rehearsal, he grew so exasperated at his lack of privacy that he fired a warning shot into the air to indicate that the cast should quickly get off to bed. His lukewarmness to the whole undertaking prevented Georgette Leblanc from proceeding further with plans for staging *Hamlet* and *La Princesse Maleine* at the abbey.[2]

His general irritability, possibly ascribable in part to his mother's death, gave way in the autumn to another onset of neurasthenia. The doctors recommended that efforts should be made to distract him. Renée Dahon, with her gay and zestful outlook on life, was admirably suited to the task. It may well have been Mlle Dahon who persuaded him that a change of scene was

---

[1] Unpublished letter to O.-B. dated 6 June 1911. 'Ma mère va un peu mieux et il reste un peu d'espoir de la sauver.'
[2] Georgette Leblanc, *Souvenirs*, p. 249.

indicated, with the result that, after the usual winter move to the South, the author decided to leave Grasse for Nice. Such a removal had much to commend it. The nights in Grasse were cold, because it was perched so high above sea-level, and snow and ice occasionally made an unwelcome appearance. It was not, the author felt, the true South, the land of the mimosa and the palm-tree.[1] On the other hand, the 'Villa Ibrahim', on the Colline des Baumettes overlooking Nice, to which he moved, was flanked by eucalyptus trees, and its luxurious garden contained an orange grove. In this one-time place of retreat for Italian nuns, with its Moorish architecture, Maeterlinck installed his southern home for the next score of years. He rechristened it the 'Villa des Abeilles'.

There had been rumours all summer of his candidature for the Nobel Prize.[2] Paul Spaak had proposed that Belgium put forward jointly the names of Maeterlinck and Verhaeren, and Maeterlinck, consulted by Harry, had agreed. Verhaeren, then very poor, would doubtless have welcomed the award for financial reasons alone. Accordingly, Baron Descamp-David, Belgian Minister for Sciences and Arts, canvassed the members of the Nobel Prize committee with both names. But the joint honour was not to be and on 9 November the Swedish Academy decided to confer the distinction on Maeterlinck alone. The text of their citation ran: 'To Maurice Maeterlinck, on account of his diverse literary activity and especially his dramatic works, which are outstanding for their richness of imagination and for poetic realism, which sometimes in the dim form of the play of legend display a deep intimacy of feeling, and also in a mysterious way appeal to the reader's sentiment and sense of foreboding.' Maeterlinck accepted the award with equanimity but, allegedly suffering from influenza, did not make the journey to Stockholm to receive his prize. Instead, he was represented at the ceremony on 10 December by M. Wauters, the Belgian Minister to Sweden. The author detested such official occasions, which, for one so timid before an audience, were an ordeal.

---

[1] Cf. C. Buysse, 'Bij de Maeterlinck's te Nizza', *Groot Nederland*, 1913, p. 730.
[2] Letter from Maeterlinck to Marie Kalff, one of 'Quatre lettres inédites de Maeterlinck', *Opéra*, 8 June 1949, pp. 1–2.

His selection as the Nobel prizewinner aroused conflicting views. The elder Rosny, a founder member of the Goncourt Academy and a fellow Belgian writer who had also settled in the south of France, spoke for many when he wrote: 'I think that his crowning has no significance or use. It is water poured into the river. I should have much preferred them to crown Lemonnier or... Verhaeren or even Georges Eekhoud.'[1] For this comment Maeterlinck bore no grudge and in 1932 even promised to intercede with the King of Sweden to secure Rosny's own nomination for the prize! On the other hand innumerable congratulations were showered on the new laureate, including even those of the Ghent Bar, in whose list of members his name still stood.

About this time representations were made to persuade him to seek election to the French Academy, if he would renounce his Belgian nationality. Raymond Poincaré and Paul Hervieu assured him that if he stood for election he would be dispensed from the usual courtesy visits to the other 'Forty Immortals'.[2] Nevertheless, some quirk of national pride restrained him from taking the indispensable initial step, and the plan fell through. When reapproached in 1914, he also held back. He told Hervieu that the obligatory eulogy on his dead predecessor would seriously embarrass him: the only one he would revel in making would be on his would-be sponsor and '... really, I couldn't accept this supreme sacrifice on your part!'

In the summer of 1911 Henry Russell, the English impresario, who was destined to become Maeterlinck's closest friend, approached both him and Debussy with the aim of producing the opera of *Pelléas et Mélisande* at the Boston Grand Opera House, of which he was then director. By the use of models of elaborate stage sets and by tempting Georgette Leblanc with the opportunity of at last singing Mélisande, he persuaded both author and composer to fall in with his plan. The actress immediately started rehearsing with André Caplet, who was to conduct the orchestra in Boston. Hiding away in secluded corners of St-Wandrille, she conned the score of the opera once forbidden her by Debussy.

---

[1] (Various opinions on) 'Le Prix Nobel', *Le Thyrse*, Brussels, 5 Jan. 1912, p. 162.
[2] O. Milhe, 'Maurice Maeterlinck', *Synthèses*, Brussels, No. 3 of 1949, p. 329.

Russell did his best to induce author and composer to come to America for the production, but Debussy had reluctantly to refuse and Maeterlinck categorically declined, perhaps glad for a while to be free of his companion. Thus, in December 1911, she sailed alone to New York.

The impresario was, however, a resourceful man. A week before the opening, advance booking for the opera was negligible and to stimulate publicity was obviously desirable. He began by persuading Maeterlinck to write a letter to him forecasting a triumph for the production.[1] He then informed reporters that the author might have arranged to travel incognito aboard the *Olympic*, with Georgette Leblanc, and alleged that he had bet Maeterlinck he could not land without being spotted by journalists. These stunts assured that all seats for the opening night were sold. He even went to the length of spreading the rumour that Maeterlinck would be present in disguise. The hoax was carried so far as to have a mysterious gentleman—in reality a minor member of the company—book in at a Boston hotel, attend the performance, and then slip quietly away. Despite this advertising the opera proved to be a damp squib: at the first night, on 10 January 1912, the takings grossed $5,000, but by the third performance they had dropped to $200.[2]

Whilst in New England Georgette Leblanc was invited to meet Helen Keller, the celebrated deaf, dumb, and blind lady, who wrote: 'We look forward to the pleasure of . . . knowing Madame Maeterlinck, who is endeared to us by her gracious talents, and by the name of the poet who has sent light into our darkness.'[3] From their meeting sprang the actress's essay on Helen Keller, published in New York under the not inappropriate title, *The Girl who found the Blue Bird*. Before returning to France the actress was also invited to sing in many fashionable drawing-rooms, including those of the Vanderbilts and the Duke of Connaught.

---

[1] Unpublished letter to Henry Russell, dated 3 Sept. 1911, now in the Fonds Russell, Fondation Maeterlinck, Ghent.
[2] H. Russell, *The Passing Show*, pp. 160–5.
[3] Unpublished letter from Helen Keller to Mrs. Alice Russell, then the wife of Henry Russell, the impresario, dated 1 Feb. 1912, Wrentham, Mass. The letter is now in the Fonds Russell, Fondation Maeterlinck.

After two months' absence, however, she was anxious to return home: throughout, she had not heard a word from Maeterlinck.

For him, 1911 had ended in a paean of glory. The crowning honour of the Nobel Prize represents the apotheosis of his world-wide fame, but it came when his peak of excellence in literature was long past. To this universal acclaim was added the joy of his meeting with Renée Dahon, or Sélysette, as he came significantly to call her. Henceforth, with mind and spirit renewed, his life was to flow along fresh channels.

7

FAME IS THE SPUR

PARADOXICALLY, it might be argued that Maeterlinck's reputation would have remained undimmed if he had died in 1912, at the age of fifty, at the acme of success, rather than linger on till 1949, a neglected star of the literary firmament, forsaken or forgotten by those who had enthused over *Pelléas et Mélisande* and *L'Oiseau bleu*. The works as yet unwritten—three volumes of 'popular science', a dozen collections of essays turning on moral, philosophical, and religious themes, almost as many plays —these unfortunately added nothing to the brilliance of his fame, but rather diminished it. For a while his personal affairs were to be smeared in gigantic headlines across the yellow Press and his dream of a leisurely, retired existence smashed. Opinion was that he had become a literary curiosity rather than an elder statesman of letters. His ascent to glory had been sudden, swift, and meteoric; his decline into obscurity was henceforth to be gradual, steady, and unrelenting. The succession of disappointments and tribulations he was to endure set the seal of bitterness and sorrow upon him. All this was not yet, but lay in that impenetrable future he was for ever straining to see. In 1912 the Nobel Prize invested him with the aureole of glory and his name was honoured everywhere.

Somewhat tardily, Belgium decided that a special celebration should mark the first occasion that this highest award for literature had ever gone to one of its sons. In May 1912 the Brussels municipality approved a proposal that, in conjunction with the capital's Cercle artistique et littéraire, a gala should be held at the Théâtre de la Monnaie. Harry, sent as emissary to Nice, persuaded the author to come and receive this homage in person. Ten days before the event Maeterlinck contracted bronchitis, but this time recovered sufficiently to attend the festivities.

It was a triumphant official welcome back to the land of his birth. Met by the Burgomaster, he was conducted to luncheon at the Town Hall. In the evening King Albert and Queen Élisabeth attended the crowded gala performance. The first act of *Pelléas* was presented and 'Le Vol nuptial' from *La Vie des abeilles* was read by Mme Bartet. An excruciatingly bad poem, composed by Harry for the occasion, was recited, one verse of which ran:

> Nous saluons ce soir un noble enfant prodigue
> Qui de Flandre en allé vers de plus bleus climats
> Nous revient pour un jour, souriant de fatigue
> Sous le fardeau de gloire accumulé là-bas.[1]

The 'prodigal son' sat ill at ease until, at the interval, accompanied by the Burgomaster and aldermen, he went to the royal box to be presented. After the Grand Marshal of the Court had effected the usual introductions an awkward silence ensued, which Maeterlinck, throwing etiquette and protocol to the winds, broke by putting a banal question to the King about his recent trip to the south of France. Unoffended by this lack of ceremony, the monarch invited him to attend at the palace the next day. According to Harry, King Albert admitted to Maeterlinck that he had looked forward to their meeting with some trepidation, 'for you had only before you for the first time a King of the Belgians, whereas I had a King of universal Thought'.[2] This anecdote, although it has an apocryphal ring, would at least explain their mutual embarrassment. At the palace the insignia of Grand Officier de l'Ordre de Léopold were conferred upon him. He had come a long way since he had been refused an appointment as justice of the peace!

Belgian writers were disappointed at the 'Festival Maeterlinck'. In a way, his home-coming represented the triumph of the movement begun almost half a century ago. Yet none, not even his earliest friends, were invited to the official functions. Grégoire Le Roy, the third survivor of the Ghent trio, remarked bitterly in an unsigned article that the nation was honouring the man who had been clever enough to win a huge money prize rather than

---

[1] G. Harry, *Mes mémoires*, vol. iii, p. 254. [2] Ibid., p. 255.

the talented writer. Sarcastically he ended his piece with the comment: 'M. Gérard Harry has been appointed vice-consul at St-Wandrille.'[1] Maeterlinck raised no protest against the absence of his contemporaries, but this is explicable by the fact that the whole proceedings meant little to him. About them he wrote to Oppeln-Bronikowski: 'I was indeed sorry not to have been able to meet you in my own country. But, as you were doubtless told there, I fled the day after the celebrations, for those things irritate me beyond measure and I hastened to find again my calm, my silence, and my roses at Nice.'[2] Such timid misanthropy could hardly be carried much farther.

In the years immediately preceding the First World War Maeterlinck laid down his pen and settled down to enjoy life in a way he had never done before. As more and more of his time was spent in the company of the young and pretty Renée Dahon, so did the storms with Georgette Leblanc increase in frequency and intensity. The supplanted middle-aged actress would pour out her troubles to another writer, Lucien Descaves.[3] Her outbursts availed her little, for Maeterlinck seemed to have acquired a greater serenity. He was now wealthy enough to write only when the fancy took him, and so he cultivated a host of other pastimes. For some years he had interested himself in boxing, a sport he had greatly favoured when young, and had even engaged his own instructor, a certain Raymond Bon. The journalist Michel Georges-Michel, in describing a visit to 'Les Abeilles' with Georges Maurevert, says that Maeterlinck, already nursing a beautiful black eye, insisted on sparring with the company, among them Albert Wolff, the future composer of the music of *L'Oiseau bleu*.[4] Other sources report that the author took boxing lessons from Georges Carpentier and even gave an exhibition bout with him in 1912 for charity.[5] To Georges-Michel he also talked of

---

[1] G. Le Roy, 'Le Poète prodigue', *Le Masque*, Brussels, No. 5 of 1912 (unsigned), p. 198.
[2] Unpublished letter to O.-B. dated 10 June 1912. 'J'ai bien regretté de n'avoir pu vous rencontrer dans ma patrie. Mais, comme sans doute on vous l'a dit là-bas, j'ai fui dès le lendemain de la fête, car ces choses m'ennuient outre mesure et j'avais hâte de retrouver mon calme, mon silence et mes roses de Nice.'
[3] P. Descaves, 'Maeterlinck et son inspiratrice', *Le Monde français*, Apr. 1947, p. 32.
[4] Michel Georges-Michel, *En jardinant avec Bergson . . .*, p. 82.
[5] J. Bithell, *Life and Writings of Maeterlinck*, p. 141.

his new motor-cycle, with almost childish enthusiasm: 'A dream. It gets up the hills without my even noticing it. I do 80 [kilometres] an hour in the mountains, if I like.' Such were the typical, if somewhat unusual, occupations of this Nobel Prizewinner.

He then passed for holding Socialist views. Certain essays he had penned, such as 'Le Suffrage universel', and the thinly veiled social satire of *La Vie des abeilles*, encouraged the Belgian labour movement to count on his support in their struggle against the Catholic party. In the spring of 1913, when the Belgian trade unions declared a general strike over the question of votes for all, he did not disappoint them. On 9 April he wrote to Wauters, the editor of the Brussels newspaper *Le Peuple*, offering him free use of his essay on the question, whilst at the same time he wrote to Vandervelde, the strike leader, enclosing a cheque for 1,000 francs.[1] Despite this, his reforming and egalitarian zeal was of comparatively short duration, and with the passage of the years he inclined more and more to a political authoritarianism.

Georgette Leblanc, possibly in a despairing effort to save her relationship with Maeterlinck from shipwreck, declared in 1913 that she would shortly retire from the stage. In March, however, she played the part of Marie-Magdeleine when the drama received its French première at the Nice Casino. Among the cast was a second-rate actor named Roger Karl, with whom she surreptitiously formed a liaison which was later to be the ostensible cause of the final rupture with Maeterlinck. The play enjoyed a short run in Paris and then the actress turned once again to her favourite project of creating a Théâtre Maeterlinck at St-Wandrille and vowed she would settle down to writing. Her gambler's throw to hold the affections and interest of Maeterlinck had failed, and she says that the years from 1912 to the war were sombre ones for her.[2]

At the beginning of October 1913 Maeterlinck again visited England, where Sutro, his English translator, was his host. The reason for this journey across the Channel is not known.[3]

---

[1] A. Pasquier, *Maurice Maeterlinck*, pp. 60–61.
[2] Georgette Leblanc, *Souvenirs*, p. 273.
[3] An unpublished letter to Georges Doudelet, written on 4 Oct. 1913, is headed 'Redlands, Witley, Surrey' (Sutro's home). Cf. *Annales de la Fondation Maeterlinck*, vol. i, 1955, p. 115.

In 1913 a revised and enlarged edition of *La Mort* appeared, published for the first time in French. At long last the Catholic Church decided that it would have to take action against a writer whose works were considered in ecclesiastical circles as being openly heretical and pernicious. Accordingly, on 26 January 1914, his name was formally placed on the Index. The formula used was *omnia opera*, which in point of fact only censures works believed to express ideas contrary to religion and morality. The Brussels newspaper *Le Soir* inquired his reaction to this interdict and on 2 February 1914 printed his telegraphic reply: 'Did not know of excellent piece of news. Publisher will be delighted. For the rest, prehistoric phenomenon of no importance.' But the censure obviously hurt him because, when referring to it again, he wrote: 'I am excommunicated because of my book *La Mort* and with a major excommunication if you please, since all my books, present and to come . . . are on the Index "in odium auctoris", as they say.'[1] His assertion was, however, doubly incorrect, for he was never excommunicated by the Church, nor was the phrase *in odium auctoris*, signifying a total ban on all his works, used in his case.

He was more and more interested in supposedly psychic phenomena and supernatural manifestations. He was also intrigued by the problem of animal intelligence, for he held that if it could be proved that one single creature apart from Man was intelligent, then Man's long isolation in the universe would be ended and vast new vistas of knowledge would be possible. Thus, in September 1913, he went off alone to Germany to investigate the so-called 'intelligent' horses of Elberfeld. In the little Rhineland town he met Herr Krall, a wealthy goldsmith, who had been carrying out experiments with the animals. He formed the opinion that Krall's integrity was above suspicion and that, moreover, he was so rich that trickery for financial gain could not interest him. The German claimed to have successfully trained four horses, but admitted failure in his attempt to 'teach' a baby elephant! The author spent two days subjecting to most rigorous tests of intelligence these animals, who communicated by means of hoof-

[1] F. Lefèvre, *Une Heure avec Maeterlinck*, p. 237.

tapping on the ground. They were set mathematical problems of varying complexity, including even the solution of quadrilinear roots. The answers, in the main the correct ones, were tapped out so promptly that to Maeterlinck this suggested the possession of intuitive knowledge. He came away convinced that the horses were genuinely 'intelligent' and that he had witnessed a kind of mediumistic or telepathic communication that he was at a loss to explain. Unfortunately for him, it was not till later that scientists exposed the German trainer as the skilful illusionist, and charlatan, that he was.

The conclusions reached from this investigation and other more strictly psychical researches were embodied in *L'Hôte inconnu*, written in Normandy during the summer and autumn of 1913 but finished and revised that winter at Nice. The book is a study of the smaller inexplicable phenomena of life rather than the greater mysteries. Apparitions, haunted houses, psychometric manifestations, and Man's foreknowledge of the future are all placed under the microscope. Maeterlinck projected a second volume which would deal with the miracles of Lourdes and elsewhere, with materializations and 'fluidic asepsia', but this was never written. *L'Hôte inconnu* is based largely on accounts and cases culled from the proceedings of such bodies as the English and American Societies for Psychical Research, and consequently generalizations are reached from mainly second-hand sources. All religious explanations are rejected out of hand. Many mysteries can be ascribed to telepathy or suggestion. The spiritualist hypothesis is considered likely to prove false. But, in fact, comparatively few cases can be deemed inexplicable.

Plus est en vous. Long ago Maeterlinck's imagination had been fired by this motto, set above an old patrician house in Bruges. *L'Hôte inconnu*, 'the unknown guest', is the faculty inherent in all men, capable of linking them with the forces of the future and of the dead. That this faculty is not a free agent is demonstrated by the fact that only rarely do its warnings of disaster penetrate to the consciousness. In the obscure realm of metaphysics, 'As one progresses thus, with slow and circumspect steps . . . one is forced to recognize that there must exist somewhere, in this world or in others, a place where all is known, where all is possible, whither all goes, whence all comes, which belongs to all, to which all have free access, but whose ways, too long forgotten, we have to learn again, like lost children.'[1] If this 'unknown guest' can foresee the future, it must follow that what is to be is predetermined. Occasionally, however, a premonition can avert an impending disaster. This apparent incompatibility can only be reconciled by abolishing the conventional divisions of time.

Such theories smack of Bergson, who also believed that ultimate reality can be attained only by the intuition. But whereas the Belgian postulated a fundamental opposition between the subconscious faculty and the intelligence, the anti-intellectualist philosopher believed that the intelligence has a very practical use. An obscurantist mysticism and a vague pantheism lie at the end of the path that Maeterlinck would fain have us tread.

From essays he turned once more back to the drama: at the end of 1913 it is known that he was working on a play, but no further details are available as to whether it was ever finished or reached a publisher's desk.[2]

The First World War burst upon a frightened Europe like the thunderclap of doom. To many *La Mort* appeared to be a prophetic title. Its author registered his horror at the imminent catastrophe when, in July 1914, he finished a letter, his last to Oppeln-Bronikowski for over a score of years, with the words: 'May, when this letter reaches you, the horrible scourge not be unleashed!'[3] Unexorcized, however, the demon of war strode ruthlessly across Belgium and swept on into France. Maeterlinck judged it prudent to evacuate St-Wandrille, where he was staying at that time with Georgette Leblanc. Fearing a German occupation, he went round the estate sedulously stowing away in safety his valuables—incidentally, particular precautions were taken with the cellar contents! Then, saying a sad farewell to St-Wandrille, where he was destined never to live again, he drove

---
[1] *L'Hôte inconnu*, p. 76.
[2] Unpublished letter to O.-B. dated 26 Dec. 1913.
[3] 'Puisse, quand vous parviendra cette lettre, l'horrible fléau n'être pas déchaîné.'

first to Verneuil, to the home of Georgette Leblanc's sister; in October they removed to Neuilly, and finally settled for the duration of the war in 'Les Abeilles' at Nice.

Maeterlinck had distinguished himself from his contemporaries by his belief in Germany's esteem of cultural values. The tales of atrocities and vandalism by the invading army that reached him from Belgium brought about a complete reversal of his attitude. Germany became anathema to him, he became the champion of his country's cause and its most bellicose and distinguished literary ambassador. Already, on 2 August 1914, he had made the journey to Rouen to inquire if he could enlist in the French Foreign Legion. Considered too old at the age of fifty-two, he wrote off to Harry in Brussels pleading with him to intervene in his favour, 'for, cost what it may, we must struggle against the enemy of the human race, the great scourge of the world'.[1] When the long-awaited call to the colours—or recall, for had he not drilled with the Ghent Civic Guard?—did not arrive, he reiterated his appeal. But Harry was informed by the authorities: 'Say to him that his inspired pen, put to our service during this war, will be worth as much to us as the rifles and guns of a whole division.' A visit paid later to the refugee Belgian administration, then installed at Sainte-Adresse, near Le Havre, confirmed this condemnation to military inactivity.

In the initial confusion of the war Maeterlinck did not forget Harry, one of the few old friends left in Belgium. When the journalist, having fled with his family to England, was destitute, he wrote offering to share half his fortune with him. He himself had also suffered financial loss, because much of his money was in a Brussels bank and at the outbreak of war the funds he held in Russia had been blocked.

The second initiative was now taken to have Maeterlinck elected to the French Academy, but this time to allow him to retain his Belgian nationality. Raymond Poincaré, an Academician himself, thought the candidature would be a popular one, but was told by Ernest Lavisse, the historian, that some of their colleagues were hostile to the proposal because the Belgian author

[1] Quoted by G. Harry, *La Vie et l'œuvre de Maeterlinck*, 1932, p. 104.

epitomized the German rather than the French spirit, and moreover, some of his works were on the Index. Poincaré records in his *Memoirs* for October 1914 that he also received Lamy, the secretary to the Academy, at the Élysée, where he had called to object to the idea because it would be imprudent to irritate the strongly Catholic Belgian government. Because of this lack of unanimity the proposal was again dropped.[1]

Meanwhile, however, Maeterlinck had already set about determinedly to make propaganda for the Allied cause. As early as 14 September 1914 he wrote an article for the *Daily Mail* in which he emphasized that 'war guilt' must be borne not only by the Prussian militarist but by the German people as a whole. In a pamphlet he lauded Belgium's stand against 'the most filthy invader that the earth has ever borne'.[2] He riposted violently when the German Max Brewer attempted to deny the charge of barbarism, by specifying the 'atrocities' committed by the Germans at Louvain and Aarschot.[3] His indignation was so great that, despite his loathing for public speaking, he consented to appear on the platform. On 10 October 1914 he visited England and spoke at Newcastle upon Tyne against the violation of Belgian neutrality.

His obvious success with an English-speaking public induced the Belgian government to invite him, in November 1914, to plead his country's cause in Italy, then still neutral. His colleagues were both members of the Belgian Parliament: Georges Lorand and Jules Destrée, the friend of Henry Carton de Wiart, and whom Maeterlinck had known in the days of *La Jeune Belgique*. With them, he spoke at the Scala in Milan. He termed this first Italian propaganda tour a 'nightmare'[4] and judged his speeches severely as being devoid of rhetoric, unspontaneous, and ineffectual.

He nevertheless consented to go again. Before undertaking the

[1] R. Poincaré, *Memoirs* (tr. by Sir George Arthur), vol. i, pp. 219 and 221.
[2] M. Maeterlinck, *Le Roi Albert*, p. 4 (no date or place; 1914?).
[3] M. Brewer, *Lettre ouverte de Max Brewer de Dresde à Maurice Maeterlinck*, Düsseldorf, 20 Oct. 1914, and M. Maeterlinck, *Réponse de Maurice Maeterlinck au Sieur Max Brewer*, p. 12. These two pamphlets, together with *Le Roi Albert*, are bound in *Le Roi et la famille royale, varia*, Bibliothèque Royale, Brussels (B.R. III. 49.984 IA).
[4] J. Destrée, *En Italie avant la guerre*, p. 77.

journey Jules Destrée spent a pleasant interlude with him at 'Les Abeilles' and commented enthusiastically on the superb surroundings of the villa, on one side of which was visible the sparkling blue Mediterranean and on the other the wild mountain-side, capped by snow. From Maeterlinck's study, whose windows reached to the ground and in which a mirror reflected the garden, he could contemplate the exotic vegetation of the South: the scented mimosa, the palms, the eucalyptus and cypress trees. On one wall hung a reproduction of the Van Eyck triptych, *The Adoration of the Lamb*. In the grounds Golaud, a ginger bull mastiff, roamed unchecked. The war had upset Maeterlinck's regular habits of work. Georgette Leblanc, honorary president of a war charity organization for English soldiers, was busy with charity performances.[1]

In March, however, she accompanied Maeterlinck and Destrée to Italy. Maeterlinck remarked on the changed atmosphere they encountered: 'healthy hatred [for the Germans], necessary hatred, which is here only a magnificent love of justice and humanity, had flooded in over everything'.[2] The prestige that surrounded his name ensured official tolerance of the meetings he addressed in Naples and Florence, although Italy remained neutral until May 1915. Georgette Leblanc contributed to the successful tour by giving recitals of extracts from Maeterlinck's works in Florence. In Rome the author scored his biggest triumph, when he was given a tumultuous welcome by the Press association.

Two incidents on this journey exemplify Maeterlinck's distaste for the limelight. In Rome he brusquely refused his signature to autograph-hunters, confiding to Destrée: 'When I attained what is called glory, I had to choose between tranquillity and politeness. I chose rudeness; I had to do so to preserve my work.'[3] In Florence, where he left Destrée to return to Nice, he found the train had no restaurant car, a circumstance sufficient in itself to upset him, for he was a great lover of food. Buying provisions in the station buffet, he was buttonholed by an Englishwoman who,

---

[1] J. Destrée, *En Italie avant la guerre*, p. 73.
[2] M. Maeterlinck, *Préface* to *En Italie avant la guerre*, p. (xi).
[3] J. Destrée, 'Maeterlinck en Italie', *Gand artistique*, 1 Mar. 1923, p. 45.

without further ado, begged him to explain to her a passage in *Sagesse et destinée*, at which the exasperated author replied: 'You can see, Madam, I am buying sandwiches. That's all I can say for the moment.'[1] Such were the penalties of fame.

On 7 July 1915 he was again in England, this time to speak at a meeting in the Queen's Hall, London, on the theme, 'A Homage to England'. Sutro again entertained him at his home in Witley, Surrey.

Not that his pen was idle. An international public eagerly read the articles he published in the newspapers and periodicals of France, England, and America. These were collected in 1916 into a volume entitled *Les Débris de la guerre*. In a foreword to the book he attempted to explain the intense hatred he now felt for Germany. He who had admired and loved Germany, whose audience there had always been wide, whose hospitality he had enjoyed, would have betrayed love, he maintained, if he had set his hatred at naught. In a pointed reference to Romain Rolland he wrote: 'I have tried to raise myself above the struggle; but the more I raised myself, the more I heard its [Germany's] ravings, and the better I perceived its dementia and horror, the justice of our cause and the infamy of the other.'[2] It is true that in an epilogue he somewhat modifies this rigorous attitude and goes so far as to say that the onus of exculpating themselves from the crimes committed by their masters lies upon the German people. But this, to a second post-war generation, is a familiar argument.

Occasionally, however, the war became pushed into the background. In January 1916, for example, Maeterlinck entertained Verhaeren, who records his visit as follows: 'My two days spent at Maeterlinck's home were delightful: he is a simple friend, reliable, and charming company.'[3] As Maeterlinck's war-time visits to Paris were rare, this may well have been the last occasion on which these two most outstanding Belgian authors saw each other.

That winter Maeterlinck consented to undertake one more

[1] Ibid., p. 46.
[2] *Les Débris de la guerre*, pp. 2–3.
[3] *Lettres inédites de Verhaeren à Marthe Verhaeren*, Letter CCXVII, written at Nice, 31 Jan. 1916.

propaganda mission, this time to Spain.[1] The tour was beset with difficulty because the authorities interpreted neutrality more strictly than the Italians had done. Nevertheless, the writer Gomez Carrillo contrived that he should address the principal literary club of Madrid on the subject of the mass deportations of Belgian workers to Germany. Fearing Germans might create disturbances at the meeting, the Spaniard arranged for his friends to pack the front rows near the speaker, ready to help in case of need. As an additional precaution Maeterlinck carried a Browning pocket revolver. The talk was successful, but Maeterlinck had been worried by the conduct of one tall, fair-haired individual, typically Teutonic in physique. At the end, however, this man approached and tearfully embraced him: he was a fellow Belgian.

Nevertheless, his denunciation had been reported to the authorities by a German agent and so the next morning Maeterlinck and Carrillo were summoned to Senor Romanones, the Spanish Prime Minister. He informed them that the German ambassador had forwarded him a verbatim copy of the speech, protesting at the same time that Germany had never received, on neutral territory, such a potion of vitriol flung in its face. Although Romanones did not forbid a similar meeting arranged for that evening at the Casa del Pueblo, the police were ordered to cordon off all approaches to the building and, despite fighting that broke out, they prevented access to the meeting. Deprived of their audience, Maeterlinck and Carrillo spent the evening toasting the liberation of Belgium in Manzanilla. Thus ended Maeterlinck's last propaganda tour of the war.

He settled down again at Nice, hardly stirring from the south of France until the war was over. In 1917 the writer Franz Hellens succeeded in penetrating the strict isolation in which he lived.[2] A native of Ghent and an ex-pupil also of the Collège Sainte-Barbe, he thus had a special claim to the author's interest. Hellens recalls that the gate of 'Les Abeilles' was kept locked with a rusty padlock.

[1] The account of the tour is based on the highly coloured version by Maeterlinck, 'Comment je suis devenu auteur dramatique' (*sic*), *Conferencia*, No. 11, Jan. 1936, p. 76.
[2] F. Hellens, *Documents secrets*, pp. 71 et seq.

Maeterlinck, who had 'the air of an English lord', lived there like an Epicurean philosopher, steadfastly refusing to receive visitors. (Once, when callers arrived at the gate, the author, working in a green baize apron, was taken for the gardener, and to their inquiry whether his master was at home gave, without lifting his head, a flat denial.) On the contrary, Hellens, who had fallen on hard times, was goodheartedly helped by Maeterlinck.

Both Belgians interested themselves for a while in the reconstitution of an independent Poland. Maeterlinck wrote a pungent article, 'Pour la Pologne', which was, however, badly mutilated by the censor,[1] and also allowed his name to be used by refugee Poles.[2] Because of their support both Hellens and he were inscribed on the roll of honour of the 'Cercle polonais' of Nice.[3]

As the war dragged on, once again Maeterlinck began to write regularly. In 1917 he completed two propaganda pieces, a sketch entitled *Le Sel de la vie* and a full-length play, *Le Bourgmestre de Stilemonde*, both of which were published in 1919. The play, first performed in Buenos Aires in 1918 and subsequently in Spain, England, and America, became known in England as 'the great war play'. So violent were the sentiments expressed in it that after the war the French censorship forbade its performance. Maeterlinck told Frédéric Lefèvre that he had given a number to the German regiment depicted in it and had later been informed by an Allied soldier that a captured German had been found to belong to this self-same regiment and promptly executed as a war criminal!

The piece describes the occupation of a Flemish village by an Uhlan regiment, one of whose officers happens to be the local burgomaster's son-in-law. A brutal Prussian officer is mysteriously shot and an innocent old villager is accused. The mayor refuses to stand by and see the guiltless suffer, and is executed by the local German commander as an example to his fellow citizens.

[1] Reprinted in *Les Débris de la guerre*, p. 259.
[2] Unpublished letter No. 33 to Mockel, dated Nice, 5 Apr. 1917, *Annales de la Fondation Maeterlinck*, vol. i, 1955, p. 103.
[3] F. Hellens, *Documents secrets*, p. 53.

Propaganda purposes have obscured the real moral and philosophical issues that arise in the play: the justification for total war; the value of one human life weighed against another; the limits to which patriotism should go; how far death depends on chance or fate. A circumstantial piece, the drama can now interest only the sociologist investigating the presentation of such problems during wartime.

In another drama, *Les Fiançailles*, written during the winter of 1917, the conflict that is raging in the world is forgotten. A sequel to *L'Oiseau bleu*, there is possibly a symbolism in its title in view of his growing affection for Mlle Dahon. (Its English sub-title, *The Blue Bird chooses*, is perhaps even more symbolical.) The lavishness of the décor required to stage it properly meant that no French producer could be found for the play. It was, however, put on at the Schubert Theatre, New York, on 18 November 1918, and ran for 200 performances before coming to London.

A dramatic allegory in the form of a fairy play, it describes the way in which the woman destined to be his lifelong partner is chosen for every man. The selection depends on neither alone, but on the man's ancestors and future posterity, forces continually working within him. They are, as had already been postulated in *Le Trésor des humbles* a score of years before, 'the power of those who are not yet alive, and, on the other hand, the power of the dead'.[1] Tyltyl, the boy who sought the blue bird, now grown to manhood, goes off to seek his love. Light accompanies him because, Maeterlinck implies, this symbol of the intelligence goes with all men on the solemn occasions of their life, indeed even on the last great pilgrimage of death. Destiny, another companion of Tyltyl, is here a much diminished figure because, as in *Joyzelle*, Love is a force that cannot be commanded and obeys higher laws of heredity and the future. And, on the brink of the definitive break with Georgette Leblanc, it is surely the dramatist's own sentiments that Light speaks almost at the close of the play: 'Our goal is reached; we know now what it is advantageous to know: Man has a right to one sole love; all the others are only sad mistakes that encompass the misfortune of an infinite number of

[1] *Le Trésor des humbles*, p. 199.

existences. We have learnt that the choice of this sole love depends not on us, but on those who precede and those who follow us.'[1] Thus in poetic language are enunciated the Darwinian laws of natural selection.

One further collection of war-time essays, entitled *Les Sentiers dans la montagne*, must be mentioned. In the main they are preliminary sketches of ideas developed more fully in later books. 'La Grande Révélation', 'Karma', and 'Le Silence nécessaire' treat themes elaborated in *Le Grand Secret*. 'La Puissance des Morts' and 'L'Hérédité et la préexistence' not only reflect the views propounded in *Les Fiançailles*, but are dealt with once more in the play *La Puissance des morts*. The trend of Maeterlinck's thought is moving into its final phase.

In recent years Georgette Leblanc had been free to come and go as she pleased at 'Les Abeilles', although she spent much of her time at her sister's house at Tancarville, on the Lower Seine, and at Neuilly. How she had met Roger Karl in 1913 and had fallen in love with him has already been mentioned. She gives few details of their affair, save that he was partly of Russian or Scandinavian origin, became a soldier in 1914 and was wounded more than once. He had admired her from afar as early as 1907. She had tried to give him up, but when he had been wounded a second time she had hastened to see him. Doubtless Maeterlinck was aware of this relationship, but he was certainly by now indifferent to it.

Matters came to a head just after the Armistice. The actress was staying in Paris at the time and helping Henry Russell to arrange a projected American tour for Maeterlinck.[2] She intended to leave for 'Les Abeilles' on 16 December, but three days beforehand a telegram arrived from Nice informing her that Maeterlinck was furious with her and 'knew everything'. He then wired her again telling her she need not bother to come as all was over between them. Georgette Leblanc declares that she was mystified as to why this storm had blown up. In fact, Maeterlinck accused

---

[1] *Les Fiançailles*, p. 174.
[2] Georgette Leblanc, *Souvenirs*, p. 308. Her account is given in some detail.

her of disloyalty and infidelity, not only with Karl, but also with many others. Later he was to write:

> I then [1913] had complete confidence in Georgette. It was not until long afterwards, through letters which were seized and undeniable witnesses, and even public notoriety—so much had their conduct scandalized Nice—that I discovered that a liaison had existed for many years.[1]

He also hinted that she had attempted to steal a will he had made. Despite this, Georgette Leblanc decided to go to Nice, only to find that Maeterlinck refused to see her. He asked Mlle Dahon and her parents, who had been staying at 'Les Abeilles', to go to a hotel because he feared that the jilted woman might take vengeance—he accused her of lurking behind a pillar with a gun in her hand. The spurned actress then repacked her bags and went off to Royat to stay with a Dr. Deschamps, an old family friend.

Her daily letters of entreaty to Maeterlinck remained unanswered. Meanwhile he took the final, irrevocable step: on 15 February 1919 he married Mlle Renée Dahon at Châteauneuf de Contes. News of the wedding eventually reached Georgette Leblanc and, accepting defeat, she paid a last visit to 'Les Abeilles' to collect her belongings. She claims that Maeterlinck, in a note, threw out a half-hearted invitation to her to return, but she felt that all was over.

Thus ended an association that had lasted twenty-three years. Their union of free love had proved a difficult bond to break. As an artistic partnership it had been decidedly to the actress's advantage, but without her the writer's literary course would have been charted across different seas. Yet, in fairness, it must be said that in their early years together he had followed that course of his own free will.

The actress's ultimate fate is not uninteresting. Through her brother-in-law she obtained an annual allowance of 1,000 francs from Maeterlinck, but this was soon stopped. In December 1920, exactly a year after the writer, she landed in New York, accom-

[1] H. Russell, *The Passing Show*, p. 235.

panied only by her great friend, Monique Serrure, a former Brussels schoolteacher. The Hearst newspaper group offered a large sum for her memoirs. One Sunday paper published them under banner headlines and the opening instalment promised to readers 'The Intimate Details of the Most Extraordinary Romance of all History, by the Woman who Fed the Fires of Poet Maeterlinck's Genius'. Living on rare concert engagements, she eventually gave up the attempt to start a new life in the U.S.A. and returned to France in 1924. In 1931 her *Souvenirs* were published in France and great polemics arose around them. Maeterlinck discreetly kept silent and did not bother to refute the allegations against him. Pierre Descaves, the son of Lucien Descaves, the confidant of the actress, has related how a mysterious emissary was sent to negotiate the handing over of the correspondence that had passed between the author and Georgette Leblanc.[1] But she retained possession of the letters, which would have done much not only to clarify their personal relations but also to show the extent of their literary collaboration, and they have still not yet come to light.

The quarrels about her memoirs revolved in reality around their Introduction, written by Bernard Grasset, the publisher. The thread of grievance that runs through the *Souvenirs* is that Maeterlinck refused to recognize how greatly she inspired his work, particularly *Le Trésor des humbles* and *Sagesse et destinée*. Inevitably the partnership of Willy and Colette springs to mind, but the comparison is inexact. Although Maeterlinck may have copied almost verbatim some phrases from her letters and some of the thoughts which, when writing *Sagesse et destinée*, he found pinned to the wall, like butterflies, beside his own, they were placed in their context, transposed, and transmuted by the author. Grasset mentions the feminine streak in Maeterlinck's nature. This in no way conflicts with his strong sexuality, because such men have often the greatest need for tenderness and affection. Georgette Leblanc's role was to supply this psychological deficiency. She helped him to develop, to discover his other self;

---

[1] P. Descaves, 'Maeterlinck et son inspiratrice', *Le Monde français*, Apr. 1947, pp. 32–55.

she brought him out, she fussed over him like a mother. For a while she was the *femme forte*, the dominant partner in their relationship. This is a long way from a literary partnership. Maeterlinck himself answered her charges of plagiarism in a conversation reported by Henry Russell:

> There is this [Maeterlinck said], and does it not apply to all creative artists?—they create because they must. There is that in them—something lent them for a little while—which demands expression. Unless this is found they strangle their spirit. The love of women, or the desire for them, never implanted in a man's soul the ability to create. That love will make the process easier—happier—perhaps more complete, but it is an aid and not a cause. The ability was there first; and, moreover, that ability often finds its voice in spite of love, which is unfruitful in happiness. Believe me, the man who creates does so at the bidding of his soul, and does not owe that soul to any woman.[1]

On the other hand, there is no doubt that Georgette Leblanc possessed some literary ability. Once she handed to Maeterlinck a treatise on *La Morale du bonheur*; the writer read it and remarked: 'You have all the gifts, you only lack the technical skill [*métier*].' Étienne Gilson summed up the rights and wrongs of this whole controversy when he cited an even more illustrious precedent: 'If he met Julius Caesar, Shakespeare could say to him in all truth: "I owe you nothing."'[2]

Georgette Leblanc died in February 1941 at the Chalet Rose, Le Cannet, in the south of France. At the time Maeterlinck, a war-time refugee, was residing in the U.S.A.

The break with Georgette Leblanc, coinciding with the end of the First World War, closes yet another epoch in Maeterlinck's life. For him, both events represented a liberation. Was his marriage to Renée Dahon, signifying his final surrender to social convention, to bring with it a new tranquillity in which he could write the works of maturity the world might expect?

[1] H. Russell, *The Passing Show*, pp. 234–5.
[2] E. Gilson, *L'École des Muses*, p. 178.

8

SÉLYSETTE

MAETERLINCK'S life from 1919 to 1939 is characterized by an increasing withdrawal from humanity and from literature. Although in some respects he becomes more worldly than hitherto, he views the passing show with cynical amusement. The terrible struggle through which mankind had just passed had wrought the final disillusionment. Shattered for ever were the social and humanitarian ideals that had found expression in sympathy for the Belgian strikers in 1913. He continued to write, but in the main his talent for creative, imaginative literature had forsaken him. His unswervingly patriotic stand during the war had somewhat revived his popularity, although he was still wrongly esteemed as the author of *L'Oiseau bleu*, the exponent of a happy optimism that had faded over a decade earlier. His intimate circle of friends became smaller, his connexions with the contemporary stream of literature weaker.

Immediately after the war, however, honours were showered upon him. In 1920 Belgium raised him to the rank of Grand' Croix in the Ordre de Léopold. The University of Brussels awarded him a doctorate *honoris causa*, citing him as one who 'had led us to the limits of knowledge'. A letter from Glasgow University dated 3 July 1919, during the Rectorship of his old friend Raymond Poincaré, offered him the honorary degree of Doctor of Law, 'in view of the conclusion of the war and of your services in it'. The honour was accepted and the Senate conferred the degree upon him *in absentia*. His reputation still stood fairly high.

Through the persuasiveness of Henry Russell, the English impresario, Maeterlinck was finally induced to make a trip to America. During the war Russell owned a farm at La Turbie, a small village perched high in the hills above Monte Carlo, to which Maeterlinck paid frequent visits. Donna, Russell's wife, was American, and as the war dragged on became more and more impatient to get back across the Atlantic. She fired Mme Maeterlinck with a desire to visit the U.S.A. and thus Maeterlinck let himself be persuaded. Mr. Sheridan Russell,[1] Henry Russell's son, at the time a young man of eighteen, describes the writer then as being a kind, rather benevolent person, oldish-looking for his age, somewhat reserved, and deeply in love with his young and pretty wife. Their two families became firm friends and were still on close terms even during the 1930's.

During his Symbolist period (1885–96) Maeterlinck had been greatly attracted to American literature. Like the majority of the writers of the 'generation of 1885' he had read the translations of Edgar Allan Poe made by Baudelaire and Mallarmé. Not only do the settings of his early plays owe much to Poe, but his short story, *Onirologie*, derives almost directly from the *Tales of Mystery and Imagination*. Perhaps it was through Carlyle that Maeterlinck came also to appreciate Emerson. Many essays of *Le Trésor des humbles* bear the stamp of the thought of the 'pastor of Concord'. The technique of some of the poems of *Serres chaudes* may owe something to Whitman's *Leaves of Grass*. On the whole, American literature influenced Maeterlinck more than other Symbolists, Stuart Merrill and Vielé-Griffin possibly excepted. Thus his disappointment at the reality, when he finally came to the American continent, was the more profound.

It was not, however, easy to convince Maeterlinck that the time had come to make the journey, although his agreement to it in theory had been obtained: he clung too much to his daily routine. Russell therefore decided to undertake an exploratory trip first, to examine the possibility of staging Maeterlinck's plays in America, or even of selling them as scenarios to the now rapidly expanding film industry. He bought from Maeterlinck the exclusive rights of *Le Bourgmestre de Stilemonde*, which had achieved outstanding popularity in England and which, if not put on

[1] For many of the facts in this chapter the writer is indebted to Mr. Sheridan Russell, who now lives in London. For a fuller account of Maeterlinck's first American visit cf. W. D. Halls, 'Maeterlinck et l'Amérique: essai biographique', *Annales de la Fondation Maeterlinck*, vol. ii, 1956.

4. The Château de Médan (old print)

quickly in America, would soon lack topicality. At the same time Russell was commissioned to supervise the rehearsals of *Les Fiançailles*, which Winthrop Aimes was preparing for the New York production.

The impresario also suggested to Maeterlinck that a musical version of *L'Oiseau bleu*, the score for which had been written by Albert Wolff, should be given in New York as a benefit performance for French and Belgian war orphans. The writer, with his characteristic generosity towards children, readily agreed to the proposal. A committee was accordingly formed in Paris, of which Mme Edgar Stern and the Comtesse de Berteaux were the principal members, and of which the French President and King Albert of the Belgians were joint patrons. Upon arrival in New York Russell soon aroused the interest of a group of society ladies, presided over by Mrs. Vanderbilt, Jnr., in the charity. The Metropolitan Opera House was hired for *L'Oiseau bleu*. At the same time Russell was approached by the Lyceum Bureau, a lecture agency run by a Major Pond, and asked to use his good offices to arrange a lecture tour for Maeterlinck in America.

In spite of his distaste for public speaking, the author somewhat surprisingly agreed to this last proposal, for he claimed that the war had impoverished him and that he needed the money. Thus the American trip now became definite.

Mr. Sheridan Russell was entrusted with the task of giving the author English pronunciation lessons, for, although he read the language easily, he hardly spoke it at all. This young man, then only nineteen, invented a system of phonetic transcription which was an ingenious imitated pronunciation. Thus a sentence such as, 'I understand that many of you expect me to deliver here some kind of message upon the war', was transcribed as: 'Aï anne de stannde zat mainé ove iou expaikte mi tou délivaire ire same kaïnde ove messidje eponne zi ouar'. The complete text of the lectures was then written out according to this method. The illustrious pupil was put through his paces, but did not manifest much zeal or enthusiasm. The lessons took place after lunch, when both preceptor and pupil were yawning. Maeterlinck repeated the text abominably, but unfortunately Mr. Sheridan

Russell did not always correct his mistakes. Later, to an American journalist, he declared:

> You might as well get me to try to lift an elephant as to try to teach him [Maeterlinck] English. He hated to learn, and although he was receptive and always amiable, he used to dodge my classes like a playful child. I believe, frankly, that he was too old to try to put his mind in a blank, and absorb the new words and the new sounds of what was, to him, a new language.... I commenced his first lesson on October 10th last [1919]. We spent three or more hours a day. I wrote out in euphonious English as many important words as I could. He was thereby able to compare the French pronunciation with that of the English language, and in this way he saw the why and wherefore of the unphonetic spelling of our language.

Accompanied by his wife, Maeterlinck sailed on the liner *Paris*, arriving in New York on Christmas Eve 1919. His landing was the signal for the inauguration of the 'Blue Bird Campaign for Happiness', a title whose irony did not strike the Americans, for whom the poet was still the singer of a facile optimism. From the Statue of Liberty onwards he received a tumultuous welcome. Above the liner wheeled aeroplanes of the Vanderbilt Squadron, with blue-painted wings. Banners strung across the exit from the quayside proclaimed 'Welcome to Maeterlinck'. To the wail of police sirens, escorted by 'traffic cops', he was convoyed as far as the Anderson mansion, where he was to stay first. For a week the capital gave itself over to the 'Blue Bird craze': big department stores featured Blue Bird window displays, and blue favours were even hawked at street corners.

This latest literary idol of New York society was welcomed with open arms. Fashionable hostesses fought to have him grace their luncheon or dinner table. Among the rich industrialists and financiers that fêted him were Otto Kahn, George Blumenthal, and Randolph Hearst. Although a fish out of water in such company, Maeterlinck maintained his simplicity and bluntness. One day, dining with a steel 'king', he was told by a neighbour, whose French was bad, that their host was a 'roi de *style*'. Maeterlinck gazed quizzically around him, observing the vulgar taste and ostentation of the mansion, and murmured, 'Mon Dieu, quel style!' But in general, with a certain good-humoured cheerfulness, the author submitted to such solemnities and even attended a Blue Bird ball.

The musical performance of *L'Oiseau bleu* took place on 27 December. Maeterlinck manfully struggled into full evening dress, a garb he declared he had worn only once before—at his wedding—and which, he avowed, gave him the appearance of a chocolate-seller. Seated in the box of honour with the Belgian ambassador and his wife, Baroness de Cartier, he endured the gala performance, despite his dislike of music.

The lectures got off to a bad start. The first was delivered at Carnegie Hall on 2 January 1920. The platform numbered many notabilities: the Belgian ambassador, a representative of the French Embassy, three American millionaires, some university professors and scholars, and a sprinkling of ministers of religion. He was introduced to an audience 3,000 strong by the Rev. Willard King, a well-known Lutheran clergyman. After he had been speaking for a few minutes there was shuffling and restiveness in the auditorium and finally he was interrupted by cries of 'Louder, louder'. With exemplary patience the orator explained that he could not change his mode of delivery. A French lady in the audience then declared to him that he was speaking loudly enough, but that his English was incomprehensible. She proposed that he should continue in French. This suggestion was not approved by the majority of the audience, who had paid high prices for their seats. The chairman then rose and confessed that he too had the utmost difficulty in following Maeterlinck. To satisfy everybody he ruled that the lecture be delivered in French, but that a translation would be given at intervals as it proceeded.

During this altercation the author preserved a monumental calm. Unfortunately he had brought with him only the phonetic transcription of the English text. Sheridan Russell got up to return to the hotel and fetch the English text proper. Not at all flustered, Maeterlinck even leant over to tell the young man to take Mme Maeterlinck's fur coat with him, as outside the temperature was well below freezing. The whole scene turned to farce when, at the door, the messenger was stopped and questioned about the fur coat by a policeman. Finally, however, the missing text was obtained and the lecture continued.

As the theme of his lectures Maeterlinck had chosen the problem of immortality. The carnage of the recent war had made this subject topical. Lord Dunsany, the late Irish playwright, attended one lecture and told the present writer that Maeterlinck was concerned above all to demonstrate that thought could exist without a physical brain. He cited the example of a plant that had taken root in an old boot. To reach the light it could vary the direction of its tendrils so that they passed through the boot's eyeholes. This rather striking illustration, Maeterlinck alleged, might prove that a kind of intelligence existed in the vegetable kingdom. The abridged text of one lecture, that given at Carnegie Hall on 16 January, was published in English only, under the title: 'Some New Intimations of the Immortality of the Soul'. The author develops ideas already propounded in *L'Hôte inconnu* and outlines the argument of a later book, *Le Grand Secret* (1921): modern science, phenomena such as hypnotism and spiritualism only substantiate the occult tradition that has subsisted since the Vedic doctrines of India, those of the most ancient religion known to mankind.

The morning after his first lecture Maeterlinck was still in bed when three important-looking gentlemen presented themselves at his room to invite him to the annual banquet of their corporation, the biggest bear-hunting company in America. This very American way of honouring him was proposed because of the dexterity he had employed to solve his difficulties of the previous day. Maeterlinck, ever the gourmet, accepted this rather flattering invitation and dined well off reindeer meat, bear's trotters, penguin eggs, and whale steak. The one disappointment was the iced water, because America was already in the grip of Prohibition.

It was apparent, however, that the tour would fail lamentably if each lecture had to be laboriously translated. Pond, whose agency had handled many famous people, from Mark Twain to Conan Doyle, was justifiably indignant. Maeterlinck, for his part, had not deliberately let the agency down. There were, however, threats of legal proceedings. Fortunately, however, Russell's lawyers discovered a technical flaw in the contract and were able to maintain that it was null and void.

Russell's agent, a certain Mr. Macdonald, set about organizing an independent lecture tour. This was too much for Pond, who attempted to prevent Maeterlinck from speaking in New York and neighbouring towns. He tried to serve an injunction to this effect upon the author, but Russell engaged a bodyguard of two private detectives to stop the personal service of a writ that was essential. One day when Maeterlinck arrived at a hotel to give a lecture he was intercepted by the porter who informed him that a process-server was lurking in the lift to await his arrival. The author, not in the least disconcerted, stepped into a service lift and made a dramatic if unconventional entrance at the back of the room in which he was to speak.

On 27 January 1920 Maeterlinck heard for the first time in a theatre the opera of *Pelléas et Mélisande*. Mary Garden was the star. The next day he wrote to the actress: 'I had sworn to myself never to see the lyric drama *Pelléas et Mélisande*. Yesterday I violated my vow and I am a happy man. For the first time I have entirely understood my own play, and because of you.' Thus Time avenged the composer, now dead.

His lecture tour completed in New York, Maeterlinck received an invitation from Sam Goldwyn, the film producer, to settle in California for a while and try his hand at the writing of film scenarios. With his genius for imaginative publicity the American whom Maeterlinck characterized as 'the great organizer and the perfect gentleman' placed at the disposal of the writer, for his journey across the continent, a special railway coach bearing the name of 'Mayflower', an illustrious enough appellation for this new Pilgrim from the Old World—or Innocent Abroad. It had once belonged to President Wilson. In February Maeterlinck and his wife, accompanied by a numerous retinue, set forth; with them were Henry and Donna Russell, an employee of Mr. Goldwyn, a stenographer, a journalist, a Chinese chef, a Japanese butler, a black 'boy', and a quadroon chambermaid. At each stop —and during this long journey there were many—Maeterlinck to his great embarrassment, was heartily cheered by the Campfire Girls, a girl guide organization of which, unbeknown to him personally, he had become an honorary president. The *Toledo Blade*, a local newspaper, reported on 11 February that the director of education had even given permission for the city's schoolchildren to go to the station to acclaim the writer on his triumphal progress.

Thus, through Toledo, Chicago, St. Louis, Kansas City, and all points West, the party finally arrived at Culver City, California. At the time this town was competing with Hollywood as the film hub of the world. Maeterlinck installed himself in a bungalow at nearby Santa Monica. What shocked him about his new mode of living was the complete lack of privacy: he could not understand, for example, why the garden was not enclosed. One evening, while the household were still not abed, the house was burgled. For him, whose delight was in calm and seclusion, this part of the American adventure was a real torture.

Sam Goldwyn, it would seem, was concerned at the low intellectual level of films and relied upon Maeterlinck to set a higher standard. He was thus initiated into the technical mysteries of the art of script-writing, and completed three scenarios. Of two, nothing is known save that the title of one was *The Blue Feathers*, recounted in the form of a fairy story such as *L'Oiseau bleu*. The last, entitled *The Power of the Dead*, took six weeks to write, but like the other two was never filmed. In the summer of 1920, however, he recast it in the form of a play and in 1926 published it. The singularly undramatic plot, which unfolds itself in Flanders, is based upon the idea that the dead may influence the living.

The dramatist failed to adapt his technique to the exigencies of a more popular art. His opinion of this new artistic form was not high, as witness a statement he made to Henry Russell: 'The American cinema appears perfect to me and the best, except for the Scandinavian films, from the point of view of technique; but, apart from one or two films of Charlie Chaplin that are, in their genre, kinds of masterpieces, the others are absurd, primitive or basely sentimental in their scenarios. From this angle they can only interest caretakers, cooks and valets.' Unlike others tempted to California, he was not inclined to temporize in order to attract the multitude.

As relief from this arduous form of writing, Maeterlinck probably almost enjoyed the lectures he gave in San Francisco, Los Angeles, and Berkeley. Nevertheless, it was doubtless with a sigh of satisfaction that after three months he abandoned the unequal struggle and started back on the road that led to the tranquillity of Nice. In Detroit he was honoured by a piano recital given by Cortot, the celebrated French pianist; attending in duty bound, the tone-deaf author's sole comment to Russell, whose prowess on the typewriter was considerable, was: 'I say, Henry, he taps harder and goes more quickly than you!' In New York he was again besieged by reporters and let slip that he had boxed, not only with Carpentier, but also with Kid McCoy, the lightweight champion. The boxer, questioned in his turn about the bout, admitted it, and added: 'He's a good boxer and a mighty good sport. You know, I didn't think much of poetry until recently.'

This final flattery may not have commended itself to the 'poet' in question. But, in any case, he did not care overmuch for America. He admired American generosity, frankness, goodwill, and eagerness to learn. He criticized the lack of graciousness, the disparagement of France and things French, the absence of a cultural tradition, which could not be fostered save by an intellectual élite, for the present numerically too small. American ignorance appalled him. Once, when dining out, an American industrialist had predicted great success for his new invention, which he understood was an agricultural implement; upon inquiring as to what he was supposed to have discovered, the astonished writer was naïvely asked if it was not he who had invented the Blue Bird! Such incidents made him refrain from writing a book about the Americans, because, he maintained, he liked the people too much to be sincere about them. When, in the early May of 1920, Maeterlinck landed at Le Havre from the liner *Touraine*, he certainly had no inkling that from 1940 onwards he would spend seven long years of exile in the country he had just left. From the literary viewpoint also, this first transatlantic visit therefore left no trace upon his work: no doubt Emerson, Poe, and Whitman, his early models, had led him to expect a different kind of America.

However, a month or two in Nice restored his equilibrium, and August found him holidaying in Santander on the Spanish coast.

In 1920 Henry Carton de Wiart, once the protégé of Edmond Picard, had risen to be Prime Minister of Belgium and had appointed Jules Destrée as Minister of Sciences and Arts. Destrée established by royal decree the 'Académie royale de langue et de littérature françaises', the foundation members of which were to be all those writers who had been official prizewinners for literature. These had power to elect others, and Destrée was himself so elected. Maeterlinck, a member as of right, was disgusted to learn that Grégoire Le Roy's candidature had been rejected. To Mockel he wrote: 'I mean to take no part in any act of the Academy so long as it has not remedied the injustice. . . .'[1] In fact, he never attended any of its meetings.

In 1921 he was again concerned with Belgian affairs. Harry had organized a manifesto of '50 disinterested people', exhorting voters at the general election to oppose those candidates favouring the 'de-Frenchifying' of Ghent university. Maeterlinck appended his signature to this document, although his old friend Cyriel Buysse refused to do so.

The same year saw the publication of *Le Grand Secret*, intended as an historical study of occultism and esoteric doctrines from the dawn of history. Maeterlinck examines the Vedic teachings of ancient India, the Osiris cult in Egypt, Zoroaster in Persia, the astrological speculations of the Chaldeans, the welter of ideas current in pre-Socratic Greece, Alexandrine neo-Platonism, the mysteries of the Jewish Kabbala and of the Hermetists of the Middle Ages, nineteenth-century theosophy, and modern metapsychical theory. The principal conclusion, a negative one, that emerges from this comparative study is one insisted on many times before—that God, the Divine principle, is unknowable. Perhaps such negativeness is inevitable, since he dismisses as of

[1] Unpublished letter No. 40 to Mockel dated 7 May 1921, *Annales de la Fondation Maeterlinck*, i, 1955, p. 104.

no account the more recondite aspects of the four major religions that have swept across the world, rejects all 'revelation', and characterizes as sentimental rationalizing all efforts to prove the nature of God by reason.

Nevertheless, he asserts, humanity today has need of a new religion compatible with reason. The sole basis for it would be—and here the premisses are unexpected—'Total agnosticism, with its consequences: divine infiniteness, pantheism, immortality of everything and final optimism.'[1] Existing everywhere, God is partly in man; thus at death the divine part must continue to exist, which gives cause for hope. But the logic of these conclusions is at least dubious. To accept the testimony of medieval alchemists and spiritualist mediums without examining the contrary witness of the saints and of great religious institutions denotes a high degree of prejudice on the part of one who had set out on the quest for the 'great secret'. Terms such as 'immortality' and 'optimism' become meaningless in this context, because they relate only to God and not to Man's personal condition.

From 1921 to 1925 Maeterlinck published nothing. The immediate reason for this lull in his literary output was that he was found to be suffering from heart trouble. He was sent to take the waters at Royat for a fortnight each season; gradually arterial tension was reduced and the danger receded. He was among the eminent *curistes* at the spa who frequented the *salon* of Mme Rouzaud, meeting there such diverse personalities as Gratien Candace, an ex-Minister, Monseigneur Baudrillart of the Institut Catholique in Paris, and the writer Paul Hazard.[2] This more leisurely mode of existence enforced upon him gave him time to travel, a form of relaxation that his young wife also enjoyed. Unlike Georgette Leblanc, she was not disposed to sacrifice their life together on the altar of an acting career.

Not that the author himself felt any great stimulation to work. His sense of disenchantment with humanity led him to retreat into a private world. Various interviews he gave about this time would

---

[1] *Le Grand Secret*, p. 306.
[2] G. Candace, 'Mon souvenir de Maeterlinck', *Revue guadaloupéenne*, July–Aug. 1949. p. 9.

seem to confirm this. To Maurice Martin du Gard he declared: 'I don't do anything, I am taking a rest, I never re-read my own work, it's too sad. . . . Poetry? *Serres chaudes*? It's an illness one must get over, like the measles.'[1] When the flabbergasted interviewer noticed two pet lambs cropping the grass outside the window, Maeterlinck, for whom such creatures had once symbolized purity and innocence, crudely commented: 'Yes, they would be delightful if they didn't flood out my smoking-room.'[2] To Franz Hellens, in September 1923, he confessed that the thought of tasks to be accomplished was anathema to him: 'I get the feeling that I haven't lived up to now. I want merely to enjoy existence.'[3] His puzzled, bewildered attitude is yet another consequence of the war.

On the rare occasions when he did intervene in public life it was to break the idols he had once adored. In 1923 he shocked the Socialists by declaring, on a visit to Belgium, that he now gave his full support to the nationalism of the *Action française*, backing Maurras and his henchman Daudet. He also astounded the literary pundits, then in the first flush of their discovery of Proust and still mourning his death, by decrying the novelist and dubbing 'snobs' the clique of the *Nouvelle Revue Française*.[4] Such gyrations are explicable only in terms of his deep disgruntlement with humanity.

In 1923 the Maeterlincks, accompanied by a friend, set out on an extensive tour of Italy. Setting out in March by car, they followed the coastal route along the Italian Riviera as far as Genoa, and then on through Pisa and Rome to Naples. There they took ship for Palermo and explored Sicily. They returned by sea via Naples and Marseilles. Maeterlinck's account of the expedition is given in an essay entitled 'Siciliades Musae', printed in *L'Araignée de verre*. It is devoid of interest and concerns largely the material discomforts of the journey: bad roads, dirty inns,

[1] M. Martin du Gard, *Impertinences*, pp. 99–100.
[2] This remark is on a par with the (probably apocryphal) story of how an Indian Rajah, hearing that Maeterlinck had written on pigeons, sent him a couple so that the would-be bird-fancier could study their habits. They were promptly eaten for dinner!
[3] F. Hellens, 'Maurice Maeterlinck', *Les Nouvelles littéraires*, 10 July 1926 (*sic*), p. 1.
[4] G. Marlow, 'Chronique de Belgique', *Mercure de France*, 15 Oct. 1923, p. 528.

unappetizing food. He frankly admits that the best part was the passage home by sea: 'On board the well-kept ship, silent and calm, as after an unpleasant exile, we find again at last the appearance and the habits of our country, the order, the cleanliness, the discipline, the obligingness without servility, the kindness and the thousand little things that one only notices and enjoys after having been deprived of them.'[1] His report on his wanderings concludes with the consoling thought, for future travellers, that material conditions, under the 'good and salutary discipline of Fascism', have vastly improved.

(This admiration of Fascism would seem to have continued. During the Italo-Abyssinian war Maeterlinck, in conversation with Gratien Candace, remarked that Italy had acted rightly in attacking 'this essentially primitive nation, which really needed to be regenerated, for an exploitation profitable to all civilized peoples'.)[2]

This Italian journey was followed the same year by a long trip to Egypt, Palestine, Syria, Turkey, and Greece. The circumstances of the journey are not known, but, apart from a short monograph entitled *Ancient Egypt*, it bore no literary fruits. By the winter they were back in France, and in December Lugné-Poë put on a one-act 'bedroom farce', *Berniquel*, in which Mme Maeterlinck played the lead. This burlesque of adultery, which has been compared to Courteline's *Boubouroche*, is remarkable only because, coming from Maeterlinck's pen, it would seem to be a mental aberration of an essentially serious dramatist.

The year 1924 would seem to have been lived in utter privacy, for no details of Maeterlinck's life during it are known, although it was most likely spent in Nice, where he tended the garden he loved and led the life of a retired gentleman.

By contrast, 1925 was a momentous year. On 12 May a disaster happened and Mme Maeterlinck gave birth to a premature, still-born child. This tragedy has only recently become known. If the baby had lived, the whole course of Maeterlinck's closing years

---

[1] *L'Araignée de verre*, p. 125.
[2] Gratien Candace, 'Mon souvenir de Maeterlinck', *Revue guadaloupéenne*, July–Aug. 1949, p. 10.

might have been radically changed. Rarely has any modern dramatist used children so consistently in his plays: their splendid innocence, their capacity for happiness, attracted him profoundly. His characterization of them may well have expressed some deep longing in his own nature for fatherhood. If the child of his love had lived, might it not well have given him cause to hope again? But this was not to be.

When his wife had sufficiently recovered from the worst of her ordeal, she joined him at the Château de Médan, on the edge of the Seine valley, which he acquired in the early summer of 1925. After the war he had not wished to return to St-Wandrille, peopled with memories, now distasteful, of Georgette Leblanc. The Château de Médan had many literary associations. A royal gift to Ronsard, it had once housed the band of Pléiade poets. Torquato Tasso had stayed in it, when accompanying Cardinal d'Este on a ceremonial visit to Charles IX. In its architecture the Middle Ages and the Renaissance were discreetly blended. Its terraced approaches, set in magnificent countryside, permitted a distant prospect of the river. From a first-floor studio Maeterlinck could look out on this new Arcady, in whose setting he was to write his last books in France.

Before taking up his pen again, however, one further long tour was made, this time to Algeria and Tunisia. The trip, which began in January 1926, lasted two months. Nothing is known of it save that he was back in Nice by 18 March.

With *La Vie des termites*, published in 1927, Maeterlinck turns once more to examining the animal kingdom. *La Vie des fourmis* (1930) and *L'Araignée de verre* (1932) complete this second entomological triptych. But a quarter of a century had elapsed since his last excursion into the microcosm, and the ravages of time and experience are only too apparent. The silver thread of optimism that ran through *La Vie des abeilles* has been used up. Into these last scientific monographs is woven in its stead a deep despair. Perhaps an unknowable God, after unsuccessful attempts to fashion an ideal creation in bees, termites, and ants, has failed yet again with Man, the most recent experiment. Indeed, the author postulates a complete *Gleichschaltung*: insects, mankind, the power that moves the world (if one there be)—all are on an equal footing. All hope is an illusion, pessimism the only sane attitude, agnosticism the sole tenable creed.

The intelligence–instinct controversy is reopened, and Man's claim to uniqueness dismissed, for he is similar to the insect in his ecology, his political and social organization, and even his moral codes. The termite, living in perpetual night, the unremitting enemy of the ant, is perhaps the prototype of future Man. In the termitary,

. . . all is shadows, underground oppression, harshness, sordid and filthy greed, the atmosphere of the dungeon, of the convict prison and the sepulchre, but also, at the top, a much more complete sacrifice, more heroic, more reflective and more intelligent, to an idea or an instinct,—the name matters little, the results are similar,—which is disproportionate and almost infinite; which, all in all, compensates for much [mere] seeming beauty, draws the victims closer to us, makes them almost our brothers and, in certain respects, much more than the bees or any other living creatures upon this earth, makes of these unfortunate insects the forerunners and harbingers of our own destinies.[1]

Such is the ultimate form of communism towards which Man is tending.

The study of scientific phenomena occupied him more and more in the years that followed. From 1927 onwards a spate of books poured from him. He envisaged them as a 'methodical and scientific inquiry into all the great enigmas of the universe'. *La Mort* had initiated the series in 1909, and *Le Grand Secret* (1921) had already examined the world's religious beliefs. In 1928 there followed *La Vie de l'espace*, a study of 'the enigma of the dimensions'. *La Grande Féerie* (1929) was concerned with the mysteries of astronomy. In 1933 appeared *La Grande Loi*, 'which is the law of universal attraction on which are grafted the Einstein phantoms of relativity'. Thus the 'grand inquiry' was completed. Once again Maeterlinck's thoughts had turned outwards; he had obeyed the summons of Pascal: 'Let Man then contemplate the whole of Nature in its lofty and full majesty, let him take his gaze from the lowly objects that surround him.'

[1] *La Vie des termites*, pp. 14–15.

Yet, in the end, he arrives at no world-shattering conclusions, for the inquiry resolves itself into the unsuccessful search for God. Space and the problem of a fourth dimension remain unsolved riddles. Maeterlinck compares the parlance of mathematicians with that of the mystics, particularly Plotinus and Ruysbroek: 'Hinton confesses to us that we can never see a four-dimensional figure with our bodily eyes, but only with the help of our interior eye.'[1] This 'interior eye' may be in fact the organ whereby the mystics perceived God. For him both scientist and saint 'seek in truth the same unknown, the same God under other forms and by different methods'.[2] In *La Grande Féerie* he identifies this God with the universe, which possesses the same quality of immobility. Within it, however, all things move; from star to electron, from living creature to inorganic matter, this truth holds good. Moreover, he envisages the law of gravitation as a hidden, mysterious force, a kind of transmuted Destiny, that governs the world and all the stars. But, finally, all remains a mystery: the quest, almost as naïve as Tyltyl's, ends in failure. Pantheism and agnosticism remain the only sure stays of all such speculations which 'end, in fact, where the postulates of an older theology began'.[3]

Thus the 'grand inquiry' is in reality only an interim report, the final conclusions of which are expounded more fully in the 'Pascalian series' written later.

In 1930 Maeterlinck moved from 'Les Abeilles' to 'Orlamonde', on the Basse-Corniche leading from Nice to Villefranche. The Château Castellamare, 30 Boulevard Carnot (now renamed Boulevard Maeterlinck), to give its official designation, was the work of a White Russian architect and originally intended for use as a casino. The building was never completed, although some thirteen million francs had been spent on it, and thus it retained in part a dilapidated, broken-down aspect quite in keeping with the décor of Symbolist drama. In December 1930 it was

[1] *La Vie de l'espace*, p. 123.
[2] Ibid., p. 124.
[3] Anon., 'The Magic of the Stars', *Times Literary Supplement*, 8 May 1930.

SÉLYSETTE

sold to him by auction for 3½ million francs[1] and by January 1931 he and his wife were installed in it.[2] The house, in which Countess Maeterlinck still resides, looks out on to the magnificent Baie des Anges. The garden slopes down to the sea-shore, but the front door is approached from the main road running above it by means of a rusty old gate, from which descends a drive. The interior of the building is adorned with variegated marble. On the ground floor a long corridor runs the whole length of the house. From this lead out the most-used rooms, all facing the sea: Maeterlinck's study, lined with bookshelves and dominated by an immense desk; a small reception room, which adjoins a dining-room with a solid marble table. Leading off from here is a small sitting-room where Maeterlinck and his wife spent most of their time. On the first floor are the bedrooms and a huge drawing-room used on more formal occasions. In such surroundings, apart from the long interlude of the war, the author lived out his life as a recluse. The front gate was not even provided with a doorbell to give warning of the arrival of visitors: unexpected callers were simply not received. Although he possessed a telephone, Maeterlinck would rarely use it and never answer it; he would say that its ring was like that of a master summoning a servant. The number never appeared in the directory. Fierce dogs patrolled the grounds and intruders felt their teeth. If a couple wandered up from the sea-shore, having walked along it at low tide, Maeterlinck would be furiously enraged and once even threatened to fire upon someone who invaded his privacy in this way. As in the days of St-Wandrille he slept with a loaded firearm ready to hand and was always ready to make the rounds of his domain if strange noises were heard at night. His stubborn insistence upon the sanctity of his private life became almost a mania.[3]

During his latter years he was very much a creature of habit, his routine hardly ever varying. He rose between seven-thirty and

---

[1] Michel Georges-Michel, 'De Bruxelles à New-York avec Maeterlinck', *Les Nouvelles littéraires*, 12 May 1949.

[2] Unpublished letter to Henry Russell dated 12 Dec. 1930, Fonds Russell, Fondation Maeterlinck.

[3] Much of the personal detail in this and the following chapter was kindly communicated to the present writer by Countess Maeterlinck.

eight o'clock. Physical jerks would be followed by the recital of poetry while he was dressing—verses from some favourite author, such as La Fontaine, Verlaine, or Baudelaire. He breakfasted on fresh fruit and a glass of water. A walk in the garden would be followed by the reading of the post. At nine o'clock he was already installed in his study ready to start work, although he by no means resented interruptions. He would write until an hour before lunch, when he would stroll in his garden with his wife. Lunch was served punctually at 12.30: punctuality was a fetish with him; all the clocks in the house were always fast; he himself wore two wrist watches; he refused to wait if meals were late. After lunch there followed a siesta. The rest of the afternoon would be spent in reading, walking, or taking a drive along the Riviera coast, where his rather shabby white Fiat was a familiar sight. Dinner was served at seven-thirty, and the time afterwards was spent in reading or talking, although he remained a very uncommunicative person. He himself ran much of the household, a trait that his wife considered sprang from the Belgian side of his nature.

Old age had not diminished his love of life. In *Avant le grand silence* he wrote: 'I try to be bored so that the last hours of my old age may be longer for me; but they pass more quickly than those of my youth and middle life. It is very difficult to cultivate boredom when one takes to it too late.'[1] This will and zest for existence, a permanent facet of his nature, contrasts strangely with the negative philosophy expressed in his writings. But he considered his truly literary career as a thing of the past and for the rest of his days intended merely to enjoy himself.

In 1932 Belgium paid him the highest honour it had to bestow by making him a count. He had idly remarked to the Belgian writer, Maurice des Ombiaux, that he was astonished at the ease with which painters and musicians became barons and deplored the fact that such distinctions were not conferred on men of letters. This observation came to the ears of Count Henri Davignon, the prominent Belgian Academician, and thus to the King himself. Thus, through King Albert, the title of count was duly

[1] *Avant le grand silence*, pp. 14–15.

5. *The Countess Maeterlinck in 'La Princesse Isabelle'*

given to this one-time disdainer of his country's honours. To Cyriel Buysse, elevated to the dignity at the same time, he confided: 'Between ourselves, I don't care at all for being made a count! But I don't see how to refuse without being unmannerly.'

Upon her marriage, Mme Maeterlinck had all but abandoned her acting career. In 1935, however, her husband wrote for her a play, *La Princesse Isabelle*, which has in it a breath of the poetry of his early dramas. It was staged in Paris at the Théâtre de la Renaissance-Cora on 8 October 1935. The plot is based on the fact that the large village of Gheel, situated between Antwerp and Brussels, had since the fourteenth century received a number of harmless mental cases who were boarded out with local families and who, so far as possible, led a normal life. The story centres in a young girl of middle-class family, Isabelle, who has become mentally deranged; she goes to Gheel, falls in love with a young doctor, and is dramatically cured. The humour of the play is rather heavy. What is remarkable is that, after forty years of self-imposed exile, Maeterlinck could still use his native Flanders as a background for his play.

During the 1930's Maeterlinck's contacts with public life were few. He did, however, become firm friends with Dr. Salazar, the dictator of Portugal, whose régime he admired and to whose country he paid several visits. He maintained that he respected the authoritarian ruler's intelligence, courage, lack of extremism, and disinterestedness, a quality which he esteemed was rarer in democracies than intelligence. On one such visit he met François Mauriac, who took the opportunity of telling him how much he liked *Serres chaudes*, to which the one-time poet rejoined: 'What, did you believe all that?' In 1935 he also met Yeats again, when they both attended the Volta Congress arranged in Rome by the Italian Academy.

In 1938 the centenary of the birth of Villiers de l'Isle Adam was commemorated in St-Brieuc and Maeterlinck was invited to the celebrations by Théophile Briant, the Breton poet. Although he had to refuse the invitation, the terms of his letter again reveal that his esteem for his mentor of half a century before had in no way diminished: '. . . Villiers de l'Isle Adam is the greatest admiration, the finest memory and the greatest shock in my life. My life has two mountain slopes, before and after Villiers. On the one side, shadow, on the other, light. On coming into contact with Villiers I understood what the apostles must have felt.'[1] On the other hand, one may divine that his opinion of Mallarmé was not so high, since in April 1936 he refused to succeed Vielé-Griffin as the president of the Académie Mallarmé.

The immediate pre-war years were given over to the writing of what has been termed Maeterlinck's 'Pascalian series': *Avant le grand silence* (1934); *Le Sablier* (1936); *L'Ombre des ailes* (1936); *Devant Dieu* (1937); *La Grande Porte* (1939); and *L'Autre Monde*, which, although not published until 1942, obviously completes the collection.

In 1934, at the age of seventy-two, Maeterlinck considered that the moment had come to sum up: what was his ultimate philosophical position, what were the conclusions of the long search for truth that had obsessed him all his life? He was granted a longer respite than most—fifteen years, before the great silence at last enveloped him—in which to expound the wisdom of his experience. This lingering grace probably accounts for the numerous contradictions to be detected in these successive works, inconsistencies which he justifies by declaring: 'He who does not dare to contradict himself does not go to the extreme limit of his thought and has never seen all sides of an idea.'[2] The incoherence of these books, evolved from notes not logically arranged, he also vindicates by claiming that a sort of 'natural order' will emerge. No philosophical system is outlined, no positive assertions made: if these were possible, Maeterlinck argues, he would no longer be a man, but would stand on a level with God.

The six volumes in the series testify to the diversity of his reading. Bossuet and Pascal are cited very frequently, although he condemns the Christian apologist's celebrated 'wager' as 'that bargaining of an old Jew'.[3] Marcus Aurelius, also quoted, comes in for some criticism. Other typical authorities cited are: Bergson, whose theory of intuition had always attracted Maeterlinck;

---

[1] 'Deux inédits', *Lettres françaises*, 12 May 1949, pp. 1–2.
[2] *Devant Dieu*, p. 11.   [3] *Le Sablier*, pp. 119–20.

Spinoza, for his pantheism; St. Augustine, whose form of Predestination he makes the mistake of confusing with orthodox beliefs; and Shakespeare, a never-failing source of meditation for the thinker whom Mirbeau had once bracketed with that illustrious name. Quotations from lesser and more esoteric authors also testify to the eclecticism of Maeterlinck's reading.

What epistemological theory is here propounded? He had progressed beyond the instinctive ideas implicit in the Symbolist dramas. Indeed, neither intuition nor reason is a sufficient ground for knowledge. The senses deceive, and 'all that one can know, is to know that one exists'.[1] Learning only serves to enlarge the field of our own ignorance. Modern scientific discoveries have revealed no more about the purpose of life than was already known to the sixteenth-century humanist. Even the conquest of space will probably not help to penetrate the secret of the universe. Such a secret is, in fact, unknowable, but because the unknowable may be only provisional and personal every man must seek to find his own solution. This nineteenth-century concept of the possibility of progress is typical of one who regarded his life as an attempt to enlarge the boundaries of knowledge. In *Le Trésor des humbles* he had expressed his hope that one day all would be known, and a spark of that optimism had survived into his old age. Science, for example, may legitimately explore the domain of religion and make useful discoveries. The search for 'the great secret', although a groping in the dark, must nevertheless continue.

God remains the central enigma. With a wave of the hand, religion of 'revelation' is dismissed. Following Freud, he asserts that men make God in their own image. The pagan deities were cruel. The Jewish Jehovah was a God of vengeance. Christians proclaim that God the Father sent his son to redeem the world, but the very sins of mankind were implanted by Himself. If God created Man, His folly exceeds that of His creature. But, in fact, no creative God exists. What possible purpose could there be in Creation? Why, if God fashioned Man, did he perform his task so unsatisfactorily, creating 'monsters and wretches'?[2]

Thus, while admitting the existence of a God, he attacks the

[1] *Devant Dieu*, p. 76.　　[2] *La Grande Porte*, p. 24.

concept of a personal, creative deity. Although agnostic as regards His attributes, he asserts that he has raised up an altar in his heart to the unknown God, who is greater than any mortal conception. Omniscient, omnipotent, such a deity is of necessity incomprehensible. One may seek Him in Man, but, says Maeterlinck, He is perhaps identifiable with the universe or with the concepts of space and time. Thus, since both Man and the universe contain elements of God, it may be concluded that pantheism is the only acceptable religion.

Historically, the religion that most nearly approximates to pantheism and agnosticism is Vedism, the most ancient faith of all, which holds as its first principle: 'man, as long as he lives, will know nothing and . . . God himself does not know what He is.'[1] But, Maeterlinck declares, such a creed can only be that of an *élite*.

The source of all other religions is the fear of death, upon which has been built the edifice of 'revealed' doctrines. These and science are condemned in one breath: 'Religions with their childish stories; too late behind us. Science with its puny solutions: too soon in front of us. There we are between two stools.'[2] 'Revelation' is unnecessary, since illumination comes from within. Thus the saints and martyrs are discarded.

Christianity is bitterly attacked—may not Maeterlinck still be manifesting his adolescent aversion from the Church? Christ's coming was unnecessary, for His life, although sublime, added little to the moral teaching of mankind. Since the nature of God is indeterminable, it is impossible to state whether Jesus was God. Why had the Son to carry the burden of sin for the sake of the Father, who, after all, put sin into the hearts of men: the sacrifice of the Cross was 'insensate' and 'monstrous'.[3] Maeterlinck cannot accept the uniqueness of the Christian religion, as representing the consequences of a single, once-and-for-ever intervention of the Divine in the spatio-temporal process.

Christian beliefs are obviously anathema to him. The doctrine of damnation comes under heavy fire, but on this point his thought had remained constant ever since *Le Trésor des humbles*. Faith he regards as an act of intellectual laziness, the piety of

---

[1] *L'Autre Monde*, p. 15. [2] *Devant Dieu*, p. 95. [3] Ibid., p. 143.

believers, priests, and religious orders as sheer hypocrisy. The theory of prayer, he argues, is untenable, because if God knows our wants it is unnecessary for us to formulate them. Death is the one certainty of life. Persistently quoting Marcus Aurelius's dictum: 'Nothing can fall out of the universe', he affirms again that some part of the human entity may survive, although not in the guise of a personal immortality. The atoms of the body, for example, may be scattered, but will serve again in new creations. Another kind of survival is obviously in the memory of others: every time we evoke the dead they come to life again, and as the remembrance of them finally fades, so they die a second time. Yet another reasonable hypothesis (to him) is that of reincarnation.

Discussing sin, evil, and suffering, he refuses categorically to believe in a Devil or any evil force as such. Sin, for him, consists of 'a few stupidities which do not count'.[1] If intentions are reckoned, all men sin equally. He brings the argument down to a personal level: 'What sins have I committed that merit any other punishment save that of a smack, a flick of the finger, a tap of a ruler on the fingers, or congratulations?'[2] The problem of massive evil, of the suffering of countless numbers in the horror of concentration camps or modern warfare, is not reckoned with. He considers that with the passage of time all sin becomes insignificant.

Such thoughts must inevitably be linked with Man's free will. He is of the opinion that Man is not free to decide his own destiny, that all is preordained, possibly even before birth. He limits the force of Destiny to the stroke of misfortune that comes to a man when he is no longer in a position to resist. Such a blow is ineluctable. Once again the thought of Maeterlinck has come full circle: in the early dramas Fate was unavoidable. In *Sagesse et destinée* he had maintained that wisdom could overcome the greater part of Destiny. His position was now the same as the one he had held in early manhood—a sombre pessimism, but tinged with the darker hue of experience.

Man is the strangest phenomenon on the surface of the globe.

[1] *La Grande Porte*, p. 18. [2] Ibid., p. 21.

Compounded of matter and spirit, he remains profoundly ignorant of the origins of his spiritual nature and of the purpose of his existence. Isolated not only from the universe, but from all other living creatures, he clings tenaciously to his own miserable personality. But this changes in each successive stage of life, and memory is the sole prop of identity. Man is an amalgam of good and evil: heroism, for example, is instinctive with him—but then, it is no less so with the bees and the ants. From men, who may not be the ultimate 'lords of creation', may evolve higher beings. In this lies the only hope of change.

All in all, the record of mankind shows little progress. Maeterlinck imagines how Plato would survey Man's achievements if he returned to earth. Morally, socially, and politically, with the possible exception of the abolition of slavery, he would perceive no difference. Similarly, in the realms of the intellect and of metaphysics he would discern little advance. Undoubtedly the accomplishments of science would at first surprise him, but because of their non-spiritual nature he would not be over-impressed. Such lack of progress, however, is not to be wondered at: if perfection were possible, it would already have been attained, since everything existing or capable of existing must already have done so in the infinity of past time.

The moral nature of mankind is base, but capable of being raised up without the sanction of religion. Christian morality, founded upon the postulate of eternal damnation, is ludicrous, and for any moral justice we must seek within ourselves. Conventional human justice, if founded upon a legal code that assumes all men are good, will only ensure the triumph of the bad.

Maeterlinck's admiration for Fascism and the totalitarian régime of Portugal has already been mentioned. In political theory he starts from the premiss that the masses are stupid and must accept the rule of the intelligent. Monarchies and autocracies are always superior to Parliaments, composed of the second-rate. The ideal political constitution would allow a plurality of votes, allocated according to the degree of intelligence of the voter. Curiously, he deems Communism to be the ideal form of government, but only in a republic of angels. Democracy always ends up as demagogy. These sparks of political dynamite fly off from Maeterlinck's pen almost at random and one gathers the general impression that practical politics do not concern him overmuch.

Thus, finally, one may arrive at a summary of Maeterlinck's philosophical position. It is useful to see first what he rejects. Stoicism he attacks on the ground that its first principle, whereby reason governs the world and we must submit to its behests, is no longer apparent. Marcus Aurelius, his consoler at the turn of the century, is thus left regretfully behind. Happiness is likewise a myth, because it is always the remembrance of things past. Any transcendental basis of life being excluded, only scepticism and pessimism remain. His sad conclusion, 'Count the bad moments and the happy moments of your life. The first fill up cellars and attics, the others are held in the palm of your hand', is reminiscent of Browning's position:

> I must say—or choke in silence—'Howsoever came my fate,
> Sorrow did and joy did no wise,—life well weighed,—preponderate.'

Doubt is the natural climate of mankind. The 'grand inquiry' is a failure, but not entirely despairing: 'all my philosophy ends in saying that I do not know. It's honest, but insufficient.'[1] Neither to hope nor to despair is his watchword, but there is a note of melancholy about this philosophy which shows that he has plumbed the depths: 'I shall leave this life, having sought to know all and having learnt nothing.'

Such a philosophy of necessity lacks originality. All one may say is that Maeterlinck has gone the rounds of all the great thinkers and sought out what most appealed to him in their ideas: his position is thus eclectic. The stages by which he attained his final conclusions are clearly definable: starting from an unrelieved Schopenhauerian pessimism, in which Death and a malevolent Destiny pursued mankind, he gradually thought to perceive that Love could reign as joint monarch with Death. But Love supplanted its consort, bringing with it the development of wisdom and a new dispensation of optimism and happiness. This mood quickly passes, and even before 1914 there is a retrogression. The

[1] *Devant Dieu*, p. 221.

cataclysm of war merely speeded a process whereby what Maeterlinck terms illusions—happiness, love, and confidence—are abandoned. Advancing years bring no comfort. There is a certain intellectual integrity about the way in which he confronts death in his old age: blackness looms up before him and he refuses to avert his head or to deny its reality. From pessimism to pessimism, such is the curve that his reflections on life and death describe, and one can but admire the way in which his life follows the inexorable line of his thought with no less inexorable logic.

Even esotericism, once considered a feasible doctrine likely to add to our explanations of Man and the universe, is now an outworn creed; he writes: 'The secret of Gérard de Nerval, of Villiers de l'Isle Adam and of many others, is that, on the faith of incomplete and apocryphal documents, going back for the most part to the Alexandrine era, they believed themselves initiated into mysteries and revelations which did not exist.'[1] Of these discarded beliefs, he retains only a faith in astrology, and a theory that a 'fluid' or 'ether' regulates all things and is the motive force of the universe.

Whereas Maeterlinck began the compilation of his Pascalian series in the same manner as Montaigne started to write his *Essais*, by meditating on the wisdom of others, he felt unable to advance beyond scepticism. Neither Stoicism nor Epicureanism was acceptable to him. All his reasoning, all his argument reduce themselves to the impossibility of knowing—the *Que sçays-je?* of Montaigne. To this must be added the fear of Death, summed up in Bacon's words: 'Men fear Death as children fear to go in the dark.'

Sicut umbra dies nostra. Once more the darkness of war with Germany was to envelop Europe, and ever longer shadows fell over these last years of Maeterlinck's life. In the early summer of 1939, with war impending, at the invitation of friends he went to stay in Portugal. Just after his seventy-seventh birthday the conflict began.

[1] *L'Autre Monde*, pp. 140–1.

9

THE STRANGER

MAETERLINCK's friendship with Dr. Salazar ensured a welcome for him in Portugal. When the storm clouds finally broke over Europe he was staying near Lisbon with his wife and her parents. In November 1939 the Portuguese government honoured him by conferring upon him the Order of St. James of the Sword. He was then busy upon a new play, *L'Abbé Sétubal*, which was performed at the Theatro Nacional in Lisbon in April 1940 and seen by Dr. Salazar and high dignitaries of the Catholic Church. The setting and atmosphere are faintly Portuguese, but the work is chiefly remarkable for its sympathetic treatment of the Church and, in particular, the author's admiration for the institution of the Confessional. This *drame de conscience* depicts an upright, sincere priest, the Abbé Sétubal, who is striving to reconcile his duty to society with his sacred trust to the Church. On the one hand, he has no moral sanction for allowing an innocent man to expiate a crime of which he is guiltless; on the other, he cannot break his sacerdotal vow to observe the secret of the confessional by revealing the name of a murderer. He seeks to resolve this dilemma by offering himself as a victim; like Bernanos' country priest, his sole care is his flock. At last his ecclesiastical superior realizes his motives for self-accusation and brings off a successful bid to save him at his trial. One is left with the inescapable conclusion that Maeterlinck, whilst, as always, firm in his belief that men are greater than the institutions they represent, has in this play acquired a respect for the Church and for the doctrines of which it is the custodian.

Hitherto, Maeterlinck had not broken his silence concerning the war. The overrunning of the Low Countries stirred him to action. At the end of May, commenting upon the capitulation of Belgium and the accusations of treason levelled at Léopold III, he condemned the King in a broadcast. Speaking of the surrender of the Belgian armies he averred: 'The stupidity of this monstrous act vies only with its baseness, for it can only bring to the one who has committed it eternal shame.'[1] He followed up this virulent outpouring with an article published in the French weekly, *Marianne*, and couched in similar terms.

As the tide of war swirled menacingly nearer Maeterlinck decided that at his great age his wisest course would be to turn his back upon Europe and seek refuge in the United States until the conflict subsided. There was then a distinct possibility that Spain might enter the war on Germany's side and Portugal suffer the same fate as Belgium—for she was England's oldest ally—in which case the Nazis would not forget the Ciceronian denunciations he had made of Germany during the First World War.

As many personal possessions as possible were salvaged from 'Orlamonde' and then, for the second time in his life, he set sail for the New World, this time from Lisbon.[2] On 12 July 1940 the Greek liner *Nea Hellas* arrived in New York, carrying not only him and his wife, but his parents-in-law, M. and Mme Joseph Dahon. A car, thirty-two pieces of luggage, two Pekinese lapdogs and a pair of parakeets accompanied the party. The 'two little birds of happiness', as Mme Maeterlinck described them, were confiscated by the port health authority.

To the reporters who besieged him as he left the ship he sketched his impression of recent events: 'You can't think. What's happened is catastrophic. All you can do is wait. You must wait for history to clarify itself.' He reiterated his condemnation of King Leopold as 'a man of treason'. Personally, he had lost everything. He had left Europe on the advice of the Belgian Minister in Lisbon and, moreover, 'I knew at once that if I was captured by the Germans I should be shot, since I have always been counted as an enemy of Germany, because of my play, *Le Bourgmestre de Stilemonde*.'

Pitchforked once again into the American maelstrom, but this

---

[1] Quoted by M. Lecat, *Le Maeterlinckisme*, vol. ii, p. 82.
[2] For many details of the period 1940-2 the writer is indebted to the files of the *New York Times*.

time in his late seventies, he found it difficult to adjust himself. He settled temporarily at the Esplanade Hotel, on the intersection of 74th Street and West End Avenue. Dr. Saul Colin was engaged to act as a kind of business manager and to run his affairs in the United States. On 29 August, his birthday, a cocktail party was organized for him at the Rockefeller Club, in the R.C.A. Building. Other refugee writers of note that attended were Maurois, Jules Romains, Henri Bernstein, and Robert Goffin, a Belgian destined to become his close friend in America. It was a long time since Maeterlinck had graced with his presence such a distinguished literary gathering. Among his birthday presents was one from a fifteen-year-old American girl, who had sent two blue love-birds, to replace those confiscated upon his arrival. To a reporter he declared, 'At 78 one is not unhappier than at 18.' The blue birds and happiness: it was by these tokens that the septuagenarian was still remembered in the U.S.A.

The cocktail party, that typical social gathering of the Anglo-American world, was not a convivial occasion that he appreciated. His definition, inspired by his American experiences, was: 'Meeting with people whom one does not know, who say things to you that do not interest you, in a language that you do not understand.' A political quip, thrown off after Russia entered the war in 1941, summed up his view of both Nazism and Communism: 'Whilst pestilence and cholera are killing each other off a great hope is rising over the world.' For him America epitomized this hope, for, 'more recently civilized than those it [America] is snatching from death, it is saving thirty centuries of civilization'.[1]

His presence in America continued to attract attention. On 14 October 1940 the Body and Mind Clinic of New York made a formal presentation to him of a scroll commemorating his achievements, paid for, said the presenter, Dr. Edward Spencer Coles, with the pennies donated by the clinic's patients. In the same month he was the guest of honour at a reception given by the Metropolitan Opera Guild, at which Oscar Thompson, the music critic, spoke warmly of *Pelléas et Mélisande*. This was followed

---

[1] Quoted in *La Voix de France* (a war-time French-language newspaper published in New York), 15 May 1942, p. 1.

by the staging of Debussy's opera in Philadelphia on 28 January 1941. Maeterlinck was present at this first American production in English.

Such typically American manifestations of goodwill jarred upon him; other incidents also served to confirm his long-standing impression that the nation lacked culture and *savoir-vivre*. He was short of money and, despite his great age, decided to turn to writing articles again. One such was concerned with happiness in marriage. After he had submitted it to a magazine he was interviewed a few days later by a young American, who in reality came to discuss the translation he had made of it. This rendering in English had unfortunately been embellished with a few sensational touches lacking in the original. Upon reading them Maeterlinck flew into a rage and in no uncertain manner showed his young collaborator the door. On another occasion he was persuaded to visit Harlem, in order to listen to a well-known jazz band, the members of which were later presented to him. Maeterlinck stood the cacophony of sound for about five minutes and then scathingly remarked that he had had enough of watching humanity descending to the level of monkeys. On yet another occasion, when dining with a Walt Whitman society on Long Island, he insisted that a bottle of claret should be served him with his meal, rather than the customary ice-water to wash down the preceding cocktails. He spent long hours in searching out restaurants that pleased him. One such restaurant, opposite the Central Park, where he used to lunch with Robert Goffin and Stefan Zweig, dedicated one of its dining-rooms to *L'Oiseau bleu*. Another discouraging incident concerned *Monna Vanna*, which an American impresario was anxious to produce in a more up-to-date version, in the same way as Bizet's *Carmen* had been rehashed in *Carmen Jones*. Robert Goffin worked to adapt the play for Maeterlinck, but after a month's hard work the whole project ceased abruptly when the American sponsor insisted that 'swing' effects be inserted in the musical score! The octogenarian, the poet, and the moral philosopher had lived too long and was weary of a world and a civilization he could no longer understand.

Yet he continued to write. At the end of 1940 he collaborated with Goffin in a play entitled *L'Impératrice sans couronne*, which was based on a book by Goffin written around Catherine Schratt, one of the mistresses of the Habsburg Emperor Franz Joseph. So far as is known this work has not yet been published or produced. Saul Colin, Maeterlinck's literary manager, made efforts to have *L'Abbé Sétubal* staged in New York, but, as Mme Maeterlinck remarked, 'There was no chance of getting it produced in New York, because the Protestant Americans are ignorant of what the secret of the confessional is and cannot be interested in it.' By December 1940 he had completed already, during his short stay in America, his play *Jeanne d'Arc*, which was, however, not produced and only published in 1948 in France. This work, although it has many effects suitable for the cinema, was not written as a film scenario, but at the especial request of Mme Maeterlinck, who hoped to be able to act in it in 1941. She frankly declares, however, that when negotiating with producers she was told 'Maeterlinck missed the bus . . . he should', &c.

French authors as widely differing as Anatole France, Charles Péguy, and Jean Anouilh have written on the story of the Maid, and foreign dramatists as divergent in outlook as Schiller and Shaw have also attempted it. In the autumn of 1940, when France lay overrun, the thoughts of many Frenchmen in exile, from Bernanos to General de Gaulle, turned back to the French national hero. If an impresario had been found willing to back it there is no doubt that Maeterlinck's play would have been assured of a *succès d'actualité*. Unfortunately his work is no more than a bald recital of the events of Joan's life as the Belgian saw them, lacking in that unconquerable spirit of France, epitomized by Joan, which one might expect of a play written in the circumstances of 1940. The emphasis is not on the superb victories won by the Maid of Orleans, but on the sombre days of her trial and execution. There is neither comfort nor hope, but only an insistence upon the inevitability of death. One can hardly say that the 'dramatic illusion' is established between the playwright and his audience.

Other plays, which were most possibly written originally as film scenarios, were written during this American exile. *Les*

Trois Justiciers, probably dating from 1942, is an elaboration on the theme of the sufferings of Job, here personified in a proud judge, Salomon, whose tribulations lead him finally to a realization of his own misdeeds, a courageous act to save the life of a little boy, and thus to complete redemption. The instrument of Salomon's salvation is his conscience, whose mere presence in men signifies that renunciation of wickedness is possible. The first step along this Damascus road is knowledge of oneself as one really is. With great imaginative power Maeterlinck shows up the sins that flesh is heir to: the corrupting lust for gold, for power, the unending capacity for deception and self-deception. As in his drama of the 'second manner' he is still preoccupied with moral questions, but there is also—and this is novel—an attempt, for the first time, to pose an orthodox solution. Sin, repentance, atonement: expressed in theological language, this is the sense of the play.

Such a surprising movement towards orthodoxy is continued in the second play, *Le Jugement dernier*. Death, expressed in the Symbolist plays as the enemy of mankind, in the essay *La Mort* as near-finality, is here shown to be an illusion. The theme of this play, which probably dates from 1944, is expressed in the words put in the mouth of the Archangel Gabriel, 'On ne meurt qu'une fois pour revivre toujours.' The plot concerns Maeterlinck's vision of what will take place after the Last Trump has sounded. The dead emerge from their graves, realize eventually the fact of their death, and are met by the three Archangels, who explain to them the problems that perplexed them in life. They are exhorted to recall their past joys so that they may fix them in their memory for evermore, and their past sins, so that they may be freed from the burden of them. Led by the archangels, they are then spiritually cleansed in the waters of transfiguration, before, atoned by the blood of Christ, they form a long procession to advance into the presence of God. To the strains of the *Te Deum* the curtain falls.

As in *Le Trésor des humbles*, the conception of God here portrayed is a mystic one. God is in everyone and yet everywhere manifest in space and time. Hell is a reality, but is empty, because sin is unreal. Death is a gateway to optimism. As such the play is a tract for the times. Written in time of war, it offers hope to the bereaved. Soldiers fallen for their country's cause have no need to pass through the waters of transfiguration. They precede all others, closely followed by their sorrowing mothers, for 'un fils qui meurt à vingt ans emporte avec lui tout ce qui restait d'avenir à sa mère'. Was Maeterlinck also thinking of his own brother, Oscar, who, although not killed in battle, died in 1891 at the age of twenty? In the war years many felt—even the most rigorist of Catholics—that some belief in a direct gateway to Heaven, a refusal to consign one fallen soldier to Hell, was part of the divine purpose. The note of sincerity and hope in the play suggests that at the time of writing it Maeterlinck may have been nearer to Christianity than at any time since his childhood.

The last of these plays, *Le Miracle des mères*, also deals with Death. Like *Le Bourgmestre de Stilemonde*, it is remarkable in that the setting is in modern times; in fact, the action takes place during the Second World War, and is therefore contemporaneous with the time of its composition. It concerns an American soldier killed in battle, whose death is concealed from his mother, but who 'returns' and talks to her. Ideas on death, Destiny, and spiritualism are discussed in a way that is difficult to handle in the dramatic medium. Yet, if this play had been published, it would undoubtedly have had popular appeal. It was topical, for it dealt with the anguish of parting, particularly when danger was awaited, and yet it reassured those left behind: the dead, it affirmed, *do* survive. Man's greatest ignorance is of the nature of Death. The fear of it is universal, but such a fear may be half overcome if one lives in company with it: Maeterlinck again puts forward Montaigne's view: '. . . parler de la mort ce n'est pas l'appeler comme on le croit volontiers, c'est apprendre à la connaître et en quelque sorte à l'apprivoiser'. Through the character of the priest Maeterlinck refutes the assertion of the doctor, the man of science, who declares: 'Il n'y a qu'une vérité humaine, la mort, et puis c'est tout. . . . Il n'y a pas scientifiquement autre chose.' To this the priest retorts that life would be too short if there were not 'something else'. Trying to elucidate what this is, the doctor is told laconically by the priest: 'Dieu', and upon this word the play closes. It may be significant that to the very end of his life Maeterlinck was haunted by the mystery of death. It may also be significant that the last word of the last creative work he ever wrote was 'God', that God whom he had sought and never found.

Although the technique and quality of these 'last plays' fall below that of his best work, the development of Maeterlinck's thought that they reveal is noteworthy. Immortality, a personal God, a sympathetic attitude towards the Church—these are outstanding changes in his position. There appears to be no personal circumstance to account for these new attitudes, unless it be his contact with Catholic Portugal in 1940. Perhaps the war years, with their spectacle of suffering, and his own great age, may have moved him to the necessity for a greater tolerance and hope. But this period of lightening gloom did not survive the war years and, according to Mme Maeterlinck, he died in the same fundamental impossibility of belief as he had habitually lived.

During the war years Maeterlinck also wrote a ballet, entitled *The Dance of the Stars*. It depicts the conflict between the stars, protectors of mortals, and a comet, the wreaker of catastrophe. At first the comet claims many victims among mankind, but the stars, led by their leaders Percival and Vera, attack it. 'Suddenly a fearful cry is heard. There is a loud clap of thunder, the comet fades away and there is a sound as of a silken veil being rent asunder. A flaming cross takes the place of the comet.' The meaning of this symbolical ballet might well be that the power of the Cross must eventually destroy the forces of Armageddon.

In New York Maeterlinck found that withdrawal into private life was at first impossible. He had to attend a round of meetings and receptions. Thus in February 1941 he spoke at the opening dinner of the 21st National Drama Week, as did another playwright in exile, Henri Bernstein. The harshness of the northern winter, however, taxed his strength and he was forced to go south to Palm Beach to recuperate. Even here he did not escape public attention. On 24 February 1941 he received the honorary degree of Doctor of Humanities of Rollins Park College. At the same ceremony the pretender to the Habsburg throne, the Archduke Otto of Austria, was similarly honoured. The occasion was noteworthy because Maeterlinck pronounced a speech, entitled 'Les Joies du Soleil', which, since it is the only extant example of a speech made by him during the war in U.S.A., is here reproduced, in the rather inept translation made at the time.[1] He said:

Let us forget for a moment the appalling nightmares reigning in the Old World. And let us look in the more pleasant events. The eye exactly as the heart and soul, needs moments of relaxation, otherwise life would not be possible. Above hell, far above, let's look for Paradise. Why look for it when we have it here? Paradise on earth was always for human beings. A garden, trees, lawns, flowers, fruits, birds, rivers, temperate climate, a blue sky illuminated by the sun which is the father of all human joys. That is the joy, or better the hereditary happiness, simple and naïve, for which the too-refined ones or the snobs have only a disdainful smile, but which over-rules all other joys and remains faithful to us when everything else is lost. I have lived in France under the sun of Nice for thirty-five years. This is in order to let you know how much I am regretting those mild winters, which bring you at Christmas the perfume of Spring. But I don't weep for it any more since I found it back here and since I know that between the winds and snow of New York—this miraculous city, but whose climate is brutal —and yourself, there is only a few hours of distance. No matter what we think or say, the human being will always be a tropical one, or a semi-tropical one. All his happiness will be revolved around the temperature of the primitive oceans and seas which is the same as the temperature of his blood or of his mother's breast. As soon as he keeps away from it, he is an exile who doesn't find any more his country. May he know one day that here is that place. Meanwhile, I don't have to speak to you about the beauties of Florida. You know it better than I because you live here and I, who just arrived, am still dazzled, my eyes have to get accustomed to it. But I intend to get accustomed and to tell you one day the impressions they give me and the joys they make me feel. In conclusion, let me say in a few words my impression. Florida is exactly like Nice, with one-third more of sun and heat, or better, one finds here in February what one finds on the French Riviera in May.

[1] Through the courtesy of the President of Rollins Park College, Florida, U.S.A., the writer obtained a copy of the speech.

There is a certain pathos about this speech made by the octogenarian exile, who longs for home and his familiar way of life.

Much of 1941 was, however, passed in New York. In April Maeterlinck's opinion of America sank lower when his wife, involved in a trivial traffic incident in which right was obviously on her side, obtained from the court a mere apology by the other party involved: the author was furious and promptly wrote an essay, which has never been published, attacking the integrity of judges.[1] The ordeal of another cocktail party of immense dimensions had to be gone through on 15 September 1941, when not only his birthday was honoured but a new bi-weekly periodical, *La Voix de France*, was launched, pro-Free French and anti-Vichy in sentiments. Several hundred members of the French colony, among them André Maurois, assembled at the Rockefeller Center on this occasion. One speaker neatly linked the two-fold purpose of the gathering by declaring that the new publication particularly honoured Maeterlinck because of his 'sympathetic interpretations of the spirit of France's traditional way of life'.

In the early summer of 1942 a sketch written by Maeterlinck entitled *L'Enfant qui ne veut pas naître* was performed at the Carnegie Hall in New York. At the crossroads of humanity appears a mother, played (in English) by Mme Maeterlinck, who feels that the moment of birth of her child is approaching. Behind her looms the cross. The new-born infant is the symbol of all children that have to undergo the ordeal of birth into this unhappy world. Suddenly the mother begins to talk to the child, and from her lips pour the words of pity, love, and mercy that reconcile it to life on earth. One cannot fail once again to note the (for Maeterlinck) unusual symbolism of the Cross.[2]

From 1942 onwards Maeterlinck drops out of the public eye. The war years slowly pass, uneventful for the exile, whose one thought is that he may not live to see his home again. His time is divided between New York and Santa Barbara, in Florida, where

---

[1] R. Goffin, 'Maurice Maeterlinck', *Les Lettres françaises*, 19 May 1949, p. 3.
[2] Reported in *La Voix de France*, 1 July 1942, p. 10. A different version of this sketch is given in *L'Autre Monde*, pp. 178–85.

he has leased a bungalow. He also spends some time on vacation at a country house on an island in Lake Placid, up-country from New York. Peace comes again to Europe, but passages home are restricted and his state of health is precarious. VJ-Day, the final end of World War II, found him living in a cottage on Rhode Island. On that day a visitor to the household found him struggling manfully with the boiler, as the one servant had taken leave of absence to celebrate the victory![1]

In the autumn of 1945 there was a notable encounter with Einstein, when they lunched together in New York. By tacit agreement Einstein did not mention *L'Oiseau bleu* and Maeterlinck refrained from speaking about the Theory of Relativity!

The shadows deepen. Maeterlinck's mind turns to the far-off past, back to childhood days, adolescence, and early manhood. With his wife he reminisces. Both greatly admired such books of memories as Anatole France's *Le Livre de mon ami*. She persuades him to record their conversations, in the form of question and answer. Each evening she presents him with the typescript of their talks together. He revises it with her, polishing up a sentence here, correcting a fact there. Such was the genesis of *Bulles bleues: souvenirs heureux*, first published in 1948, a fascinating if not always reliable recollection of his early years. Maeterlinck then sent a copy of it to Claudel. Although there is little in it to which a fervent Catholic might take exception, the only other truly Symbolist playwright thought fit to send a brusque reply. He reminded Maeterlinck of his religious obligations, declared that the time for repentance was now almost spent and that he must, now or never, accept the 'wager' of Pascal and the authority of Christ. The harsh sincerity of this letter, which might almost have been one of the many the same writer sent to Gide, failed to move its recipient, who sardonically commented: 'He's the church beadle who's drunk the sacramental wine.'

In these last years illness was not to spare him, an affliction hard to bear by one who had enjoyed in the main excellent health. In 1945, at the age of eighty-three, he contracted double

[1] P. Mahoney, 'Chez Maeterlinck le jour anniversaire de ses 80 ans', *Le Littéraire*, 18 Jan. 1947, p. 3.

pneumonia and was only saved by the prompt use of penicillin. Paul Spaak visited him during his convalescence and he was fully restored to health at Palm Beach, where an American admirer gave him free use of an apartment for the winter.[1] But further physical incapacity was to overtake him. In 1947 he broke an arm. Three months later he again fell, this time fracturing his knee. He also suffered acutely from rheumatism. To Louis Piérard, the Belgian author, who wrote asking him to accept nomination for the presidency of the P.E.N. Club International, he replied with a courteous refusal. His physical injuries, he wrote, had so incapacitated him that, 'almost a cripple, I shall limp pitifully to my tomb. This is not becoming, it seems to me, in the honorary president of the lofty association that groups within it the spiritual forces of the earth. It is better that I live out my days in silence in a corner of this world that I have not understood.' As for death, 'I have seen death so closely that I look upon her as a sister I do not fear at all.'[2]

Despite these despairing sentiments, he was destined to see his beloved Nice once more. A passage was secured for him on the Polish liner *Sobieski*, by which he arrived in Marseilles on 10 August 1947. He was formally welcomed back to Europe by M. Lamot, the Belgian Consul-General. His close friend, the historian Eugène Baie, offered him hospitality whilst 'Orlamonde' was made ready for occupation once again. The dilapidations had been immense. Italian, German, and French troops had occupied it in succession. In particular, the library had been ransacked and many original manuscripts[3] or typescripts of the author's works had been stolen. Eventually, however, when repairs had been effected, Maeterlinck prepared to take up the threads of the life he had left some seven years before.

His state of health was still precarious. He had not fully recovered from the bout of bronchial pneumonia nor from the

---

[1] P. Mahoney, *The Magic of Maeterlinck*, p. 164.
[2] Quoted by L. Piérard in his *Préface* to the collected edition of Maeterlinck's *Poèmes*, Ghent, 1949, p. vi.
[3] Maeterlinck had few manuscripts. To O.-B., in a letter dated 11 Oct. 1910, he wrote: 'Je n'ai généralement pas de manuscrit, écrivant un brouillon au crayon et achevant le travail à la machine à écrire.'

6. *'Orlamonde'. Maeterlinck's study*

fracture of the tibia. Above all, 'he felt a great weakness',[1] which took some while to disappear. Gradually, however, he regained some of his old spirit. He now kept a sub-machine-gun under his bed in case of prowlers and was liable to fire warning shots when innocent intruders penetrated into the grounds. In the summer of 1948 he was interviewed by a repellently ugly female journalist who, after a series of particularly stupid questions, asked triumphantly: 'Maestro, do you prefer to sleep in a big bed or a little one?' to which the exasperated octogenarian riposted: 'With you, Madame, I wouldn't like to sleep either in a big bed or a little one!' Of learned assemblies of authors and scholars he was wont to say: 'What would you! They're all old fogies!' And, whimsical to the end, he once counselled Milhe, his doctor: 'My dear friend, a good piece of advice, don't believe a word of what there is in my books.' Such anecdotes are typical of the man.[2]

In 1948 he received a further honour. The French Academy, still unable to elect him to full membership, awarded him the 'Médaille de la langue française'.

Thus the last two years of Maeterlinck's life swiftly flowed by at Nice. From December to March, however, since 'Orlamonde' was impossible to heat adequately, he put up at an hotel at Nice. In February 1949 he twisted his foot whilst getting into his car and was forced to rest in bed. He occupied himself by re-reading the five historical volumes entitled *Le Siècle des gueux*, a brilliant study by Eugène Baie of Renaissance Flanders, and also Thucydides on the Peloponnesian War.

For September 1949 Maeterlinck had already agreed to attend the Congress of the P.E.N. Club International in Venice. It was an engagement he was destined never to fulfil. The end happened suddenly, although during the last few months of his life Maeterlinck talked much of death, particularly with his wife. The moment came when spring had cast its carpet of flowers over the Mediterranean earth. On the 5th of May the author seemed to be

---

[1] Dr. O. Milhe, 'Maurice Maeterlinck, ses dernières années, ses derniers moments', *Synthèses*, Brussels, No. 3 of 1949, pp. 324–35. The article gives an account of Maeterlinck's state of health from his return to France until his death. Milhe had first treated Maeterlinck as a patient just before the war.
[2] The three anecdotes are recounted in Milhe's article.

in good form. After a hearty lunch he spent the afternoon discussing with his gardener the flower arrangement for the summer. In the evening of that day a sudden storm and rain spread over the blueness of the sea. Maeterlinck was invaded by a feeling of lassitude; his legs felt heavy, and his pulse quickened. He was, however, quite calm, and read for some while. At 7.30 he sat down to table as usual and ate a little. About nine o'clock he decided to go to bed. His wife tried to persuade him to sleep downstairs in his study, but he refused. She telephoned Dr. Milhe, who prescribed an injection. For twenty-four hours this produced a calming effect. But about ten o'clock the following evening a new crisis occurred. He had a feeling of oppression in his chest. In the throes of a violent heart attack, he murmured, 'It's all over with me.' Mme Maeterlinck tried to reassure him. He replied in a whisper, 'I have only one regret, that of leaving you.' A half-smile played about his lips and he uttered a few unintelligible words. By eleven o'clock on the night of 6 May he was dead.

Early the following morning Dr. Milhe went, at Mme Maeterlinck's request, to break the news to Eugène Baie, who listened in silence and commented, 'A belfry has fallen.' As executor of the will, in which Maeterlinck bequeathed his whole estate to his wife, it fell to Baie to make the arrangements for his funeral. On 10 May a little procession made its way to the cemetery chapel. Eugène Baie and another friend, Georges Marquet, took their places beside Mme Maeterlinck, and a nephew came from Belgium, but otherwise there were no close friends there to mourn him. The ceremony was organized by the municipality of Nice. To represent the civil authorities there were also present the Prefect of the Department, the Deputy Mayor of Nice, the Belgian Consul, M. Loman, and the Belgian Consul in Monaco, that same M. Lamot who had welcomed Maeterlinck back to Europe two years previously. A detachment of the 159th Regiment rendered military honours. Upon the arrival of the coffin, borne by eight men, a band struck up the 'Brabançonne'. Without speeches and with as little ceremony as possible the body was laid in the chapel. In the last few months of his life Maeterlinck had finally rejected the postulate of any God, loving or merciless.

Death was for him the end of all things, and thus no priest was there to bless his remains.

A week later the body was cremated at Marseilles, in accordance with the author's wishes.

Hundreds of messages of sympathy poured into 'Orlamonde' as the news of his passing spread round the world. Death cancels all debts, and in that solemn hour the epithets of 'charlatan' and 'mountebank' were forgotten. All that was remembered was that he had sought in his own fashion after truth. If the quest had failed, it was not due to his occasional insincerity—for who among us could escape that charge?—but rather that he had wandered in the wrong paths, those ways that were farthest from the light. Thus ended the earthly career of one whose long life and works saw the beginning and end of Symbolism, who survived two world wars, and who died in the same spiritual and intellectual isolation as he had begun his long literary career. Thus lived and died one to whom was not vouchsafed the precious gift of Faith.

10

CONCLUSIONS

THE 'seven ages' into which Maeterlinck's life has been divided from 1890 onwards correspond to the stages of his literary development; in fact, there exists an even closer parallelism than is usual between a writer's biography and his works. The phase of paramount literary importance is undoubtedly that which includes his Symbolist drama (1890–5). These plays are those which will survive to posterity, either as typical of the Symbolist theatre—for example, the 'trilogy of death'—or for their own intrinsic worth, such as *Pelléas et Mélisande*. Yet this period is not that of the writer's greatest popularity, which was attained more by the plays of the 'second manner' and by the essays that reflect the emergence of optimism. In this respect, the most outstanding theatrical work is *L'Oiseau bleu*, although its literary merit is little greater than that of *Monna Vanna*. Of the essays, *Sagesse et destinée* is more significant than *La Vie des abeilles*: Maeterlinck, at grips with his pessimism, is there striving to overcome it. Thus are made possible the plays of the 'second' theatre, which glorifies Love and diminishes the force of Destiny.

After the award of the Nobel Prize in 1911 there are no works that surpass or even reach the standard of earlier ones. Maeterlinck's powers of imagination, never very fully exercised—he probably leans more heavily for his inspiration on external sources than any of his contemporaries—seem to have shrivelled up within him. Perhaps his preoccupation with the great questions of life and death prevented him from giving his inventiveness full rein. Certainly all that follows is an unceasing revolving around the same stock of ideas, examined at every conceivable angle; yet in the end they lead the writer to no firm conclusions. The final deduction, if it may be so termed, is that all remains unknowable.

It requires little psychological knowledge to understand why his literary career followed this course. Beneath the taciturn exterior that Maeterlinck presented to the world in early manhood seethed an emotion that bubbled over in the lyrical outbursts of *Serres chaudes*. The dominant motif of the early plays is terror, most apparent when related to death, so vividly portrayed that it seems personal to the writer. It is succeeded by a calmer mood, when Georgette Leblanc, the personification of *la femme forte*, gave him the courage and the will to live. As Bernard Grasset implies in the Introduction to her *Souvenirs*, she bestowed upon him a comfort and an inspiration almost maternal in nature. This he outgrew, like a child that ceases to depend on his mother. The preference that he then manifested for Sélysette—as against Aglavaine—personifying youth and innocence, signifies a reversion to the 'Pelléas type', infirm of purpose, lacking decision and will-power, and mistrusting the intelligence. The final pessimism was thus inevitable.

Pessimism at the end, as in the beginning. Thus the wheel of his thinking came full circle. In youth he had striven to shake off the shackles of nineteenth-century modes of thought. Positivism, a belief in progress, conventional religion (incompatible though it is with Comtian philosophy): such were the fetters that his spirit had to break asunder. On the material plane his revolt was against Philistinism and *idées reçues*. Once, however, he had rid himself of his chains, he found little solace elsewhere. Idealism was still a possible creed, but it was thwarted by the gross, practical side of his essentially Flemish disposition. Thus, in despair, he turned to the negative concept of agnosticism.

Yet, unfortunately, his belief in the impossibility of knowing was in continual conflict with his yearning for knowledge and certainty. He sought to resolve this fundamental opposition by turning his nature inwards upon itself. This accounts for the introspectiveness of *Le Trésor des humbles*, the constant 'quest' for the 'soul' within him. Such a mystical *voyage intérieur* led to disappointment, just as Rimbaud's had done; it is indeed arguable that the discovery of the soul can only come about through the discovery of God. However, unlike Rimbaud, Maeterlinck was able by material circumstances to come to terms with the world. By 1900, whilst denying the postulate of the supremacy of reason, he was closest to Stoicism and, under the influence of Evolutionism, had accepted the concept of progress. Yet the faint optimism he then reveals is always qualified.

Such a position, however, was difficult to sustain. The 'seekers' in his plays of the 'second manner'—and in this connexion the chronology of these dramas, established here for the first time, is important—could not for ever end their quest unrequited. Thus, as this attitude becomes untenable, so does Maeterlinck relapse again into pessimism. His thoughts turn inward for the second time, to the realms of the subconscious, a process of withdrawal from the world that the catastrophe of 1914 accelerated. He began to examine the corpus of so-called occult knowledge whose tradition reaches back into the dim recesses of time. But in this vortex of esoteric thought he failed to distinguish the mumbo-jumbo of fraud from the genuine mass of scientifically unexplained phenomena. The true and false were accepted, for a time at least, with equal seriousness.

Finding in the occult no answer to his questions, he turned to science. Unfortunately, his scientific background was insufficient for him to evaluate the facts he considered and extract any coherent philosophy from them. His speculations became more and abstruse and incredible as he progressively abandoned the factual approach, blending the scientific with the occult.

The 'soul', Evolutionism, the occult, science: these were the laps of the race that he ran, the stages of a journey that was in essence the search for a faith. Yet his attitude to conventional Christianity, save for a brief period at the close of his life, was always markedly hostile. The unorthodoxy of the Christian mystics attracted him, but their harsh, unremitting pilgrimage was one he was unwilling to make. At the same time, his incapacity to examine dispassionately the validity of any 'revealed' religion is a kink in his psychological make-up.

Two ideas, however, although constantly changing in conception, remain always with him: Destiny and Death. In 1900, as his pessimism had waned, so had also the concept of a malevolent

Fate. Yet the inexplicability of suffering and evil convinced him that, outside the sphere of the human, there existed a force that wittingly or unwittingly, with ill-will or with indifference, brought disaster upon the head of mankind. To the very end, even in his last plays, the figure of Destiny appears as a force to be reckoned with, one that is the ultimate arbiter of human action. Its ally in the early plays was Death, the word and concept that occurs unremittingly, unceasingly, and to satiety in all Maeterlinck's works, from first to last, from *Le Massacre des innocents* to *Le Miracle des mères*. Around the problem of the end of this earthly existence and the speculations on what lay beyond, his mind was exercised without rest. In the end, the difficulties that these two extra-human factors presented were unresolved.

The most abiding impression one is left with after a study of his life and work is the sense of mystery. The mysterious may be clad in the forms of mysticism, or of the occult and the unknown, or of mere mystification. All these are present in Maeterlinck's work, sometimes simultaneously. The source of mysticism lies in the ascetic, spiritual side of the Flemish nature, deeply penetrated by Flemish painting and by the thought of Ruysbroek. The unknown embraces the whole field of unexplained knowledge into which he ventured, from telepathy to ideas on the nature of God. The mystification is all the trappings of charlatanism that invest much so-called occultism. Maeterlinck may have advanced the boundaries of knowledge, but it was in reality the concept of the unknown that fascinated him more than the love of truth. This unknown he magnified, poeticized, and, on occasions, debased.

The vogue for Maeterlinck was never so widespread in France and Belgium as elsewhere, particularly in England and U.S.A. This is partly attributable to the fact that he largely drew his inspiration from sources outside the French tradition. Although deeply influenced initially by Villiers de l'Isle Adam and the French Symbolists—and it must be remembered that the movement assimilated much foreign thought and attracted many non-French writers—he also drew largely upon English literature, particularly upon Shakespeare and the Pre-Raphaelites. His mind was essentially *visual*, and thus the Victorian movement, both literary and artistic, appealed directly to him. At first it provided themes and motifs for his plays, but later it inspired him to tableaux plays such as *Ariane et Barbe-bleue* and *Sœur Béatrice*. His 'foreignness' was, moreover, also accentuated by the fact that he was a Fleming writing in French. Apart from the Symbolist drama, written whilst he was still living in Ghent, he deliberately gives a Flemish setting to another six plays. Unlike Rosny, for example, he never renounced his Belgian nationality. Nor did he forget the Flemish language or countryside: in his last published work, *Bulles bleues*, his memories in the main are of Flanders.

This may also account for his style. In the early dramas the speech, which he once claimed was modelled on that of the Flemish peasant, was repetitive, with only rare lines revealing a hidden beauty. On the other hand, in the early essays he demonstrates a striking richness and facility in language. Although this serves to ornament the subject, the striving after effect often obscures the meaning. Such a technique would irritate the logicality of the French mind, imbued with Classical ideas of thought allied to beauty, precision joined to poetry. Maeterlinck may have recognized the element of truth in the judgement of another foreigner writing in French, Stuart Merrill, who said that the essays of *Le Trésor des humbles* were words embroidered around nothing. After 1913 there is little conscious striving for stylistic effect: the thought is expressed in involved language. The very outlandishness of some of the ideas expressed causes his style to disintegrate: polish and exactness are lacking.

Perhaps more so than any other foreigner writing in French Maeterlinck is difficult to place in literature. With the disintegration of what might be called the Symbolist 'school' (although its unity had never been strong) Maeterlinck drew apart from his contemporaries. Educated in a simulation of the French literary tradition rather than the genuine one, he does not identify himself with it save during the Symbolist period. The other great playwright of Symbolism, Claudel, later joined the great Catholic tradition, linking up with the mysticism of Léon Bloy and even

CONCLUSIONS

the Socialistic Christianity of Charles Péguy. For Maeterlinck there was no similar trend, although later, in the 1920's, writers such as Roger Martin du Gard and Georges Duhamel were occupied also with religious and metaphysical phenomena. By then, however, the Belgian was an isolated figure, engulfed in a solitude that he himself fostered.

Consequently, it is during his Symbolist period that one must seek to place him in French literature. His position is not hard to discern: he it was who first realized in drama the theories and ideas of Symbolism. But, although he was the initiator of a new drama, it was one with little inventiveness and few dramatists. A bigger niche in literature it would be unwise to claim for him. Too many eulogistic judgements had been emitted about him when he was young, by eminent writers such as Mirbeau, Mallarmé, and Gide. These exalted him undeservedly. As for his post-Symbolist works, these can have no claim on future generations. In the field of creative literature, for a French public he lost all significance as early as 1913.

In Belgium also he stands outside the dual traditions that *La Jeune Belgique* and *La Wallonie* succeeded in creating. During the latter half of his life his works were seldom read or performed in his native land. When his death was announced in 1949 it was Valère Gille who pertinently declared: 'Belgium is in mourning ... and doesn't know it.'

His direct influence on French literature has not been great. In the field of poetry *Serres chaudes* may have been studied by the Surrealists, although no positive evidence of this has yet been discovered. In the drama he had a few mediocre imitators, such as Saint-Georges de Bouhélier and François de Curel. Although he was one of the first to acknowledge the genius of Claudel, *Tête d'or*, which, like the Maeterlinckian drama, shows a man a prey to Destiny, with Death as the inevitable end, dates from 1890 and therefore owes nothing to the Belgian. The early Gide, although he enthused over Maeterlinck, did not try consciously to imitate him.

However, the master not acknowledged in France or Belgium was listened to with respect in England. Through the intermediary of Arthur Symons, as well as personal contact, Maeterlinck became widely known. Yeats, Wilde, and, for a while, T. S. Eliot came under his influence, as did also lesser dramatists such as Clifford Bax and Harley Granville-Barker. In England he achieved the rare distinction of gaining universal popularity both among the general public and also among the writers.

If one characterizes Maeterlinck's work as being a *quest*, a seeking to explain life, one can only conclude that he failed. He failed to penetrate the mysteries of Destiny and Death, he did not discover the universal secret of wisdom and truth, nor capture the blue bird of happiness. In all the ways he trod he found no joy, but only ever greater ignorance. And in the end he could only make confession of his own failure. One might well conclude as one began, with Sainte-Beuve's dictum: the tree of Maeterlinck's life bore in the end the only possible fruit.

BIBLIOGRAPHY

THE number of works and articles by and about Maeterlinck is very extensive. The most comprehensive bibliography is that compiled by Lecat (*Le Maeterlinckisme*, vol. ii, Brussels, Ancienne Librairie Castaigne, 1941). Lecat's work is marred by a few false references, misprints, and by the fact that even passing references to Maeterlinck in other works are cited.

Of the 2,118 references cited by Lecat, 845 are to books and articles by Maeterlinck himself, in the various editions and languages in which they were published. Lecat's work is completed by Tome 13 (December 1956) of the *Bibliographie des auteurs modernes*, compiled by H. Talvart and J. Laplace, Paris, 1956. There are a few additions, but in general the editors would seem to have drawn mainly from Lecat. A serious defect is that there are few references after 1949, the year of Maeterlinck's death. For posthumous criticism the scholar must therefore look elsewhere. Probably the most convenient source is the *Bibliography of Critical and Biographical References for the Study of Contemporary French Literature*, published under the auspices of the Modern Languages Association of America annually in New York since 1949.

Listed below are the major works of Maeterlinck, i.e. all those published in book form, with the date of their first publication in French. To these must be added the as yet unpublished play mentioned in the text. There follows a select bibliography of the principal critical works and articles consulted. Many of these appear in Lecat, but to these have been added (signified by an asterisk in the list) some 78 books and 30 articles either omitted from, or published since, Lecat's bibliography. Also appended is a short list of the most important reviews necessary for a general study of the period of literary history, in relation to Maeterlinck.

WORKS OF MAETERLINCK

PLAYS

La Princesse Maleine	1890
L'Intruse	1890
Les Aveugles	1890
Les Sept Princesses	1891
Pelléas et Mélisande	1892
Alladine et Palomides	1894
Intérieur	1894
La Mort de Tintagiles	1894
Aglavaine et Sélysette	1896
Ariane et Barbe-bleue	1902

WORKS OF MAETERLINCK: PLAYS (contd.)

Sœur Béatrice	1902
Monna Vanna	1902
Joyzelle	1903
L'Oiseau bleu	1908
Marie-Magdeleine	1913
Le Miracle de Saint-Antoine	1919
Le Bourgmestre de Stilemonde	1919
Les Fiançailles	1922
Le Malheur passe	1925
La Puissance des morts	1926
Berniquel	1926
Marie-Victoire	1927
Juda de Kérioth [fragment]	1929
La Princesse Isabelle	1935
Jeanne d'Arc	1948
*L'Abbé Sétubal	1959
*Les Trois Justiciers	1959
*Le Jugement dernier	1959
*Le Miracle des mères	Unpublished

POEMS

Serres chaudes	1889
Quinze chansons (first published as Douze chansons)	1900
Serres chaudes, Quinze chansons, Vers la fin (collected edition)	1947

ESSAYS

Le Trésor des humbles	1896
La Sagesse et la Destinée	1898
La Vie des abeilles	1901
Le Temple enseveli	1902
Le Double Jardin	1904
L'Intelligence des fleurs	1907
La Mort	1913
Les Débris de la guerre	1916
L'Hôte inconnu	1917
Les Sentiers dans la montagne	1919
Le Grand Secret	1921
La Vie des termites	1927
La Vie de l'espace	1928
La Grande Féerie	1929
La Vie des fourmis	1930
L'Araignée de verre	1932

La Grande Loi	1933
Avant le grand silence	1934
Le Sablier	1936
L'Ombre des ailes	1936
Devant Dieu	1937
La Grande Porte	1939
L'Autre Monde ou le Cadran stellaire	1942

SHORT STORIES

Le Massacre des innocents, Onirologie	1918

MEMOIRS

Bulles bleues	1948

WORKS OF CRITICISM

IMPORTANT REVIEWS

La Jeune Belgique, Brussels, December 1880–98.
La Pléiade, Paris, 1886.
La Wallonie, Liége, 1886–92.
L'Art moderne, Brussels, especially the years 1889–91.
Le Réveil, Ghent, 1894.
Gand artistique, Ghent, 1 March 1923 (number devoted to Maeterlinck).
Visages du monde, Paris, 15 April 1936 (number devoted to Symbolism).
Épîtres, Ghent, No. XXIV, 1949 (number devoted to Grégoire Le Roy).
Annales de la Fondation Maeterlinck, Ghent, T. I, 1955, T. II, 1956, T. III, 1957, T. IV, 1958.

GENERAL WORKS

BARRE, A., *Le Symbolisme*, Paris, 1911.
BEAUNIER, A., *La Poésie nouvelle*, Paris, 1902.
*BÉGUIN, A., *L'Ame romantique et le rêve*, 2 vols., Marseilles, 1937.
BITHELL, J., *Contemporary Belgian Poetry*, London, 1911.
—— *Contemporary Belgian Literature*, London, 1915.
BRUNETIÈRE, F., *Essais sur la littérature contemporaine*, Paris, 1892.
CHARLIER, G., *Les Lettres françaises en Belgique*, Brussels, 1938.
*CHARPENTIER, J., *Le Symbolisme*, Paris, 1927.
CHOT, J. and DÉTHIER, R., *Histoire des lettres françaises de Belgique*, Charleroi, 1910.
DOUTREPONT, G., *Histoire illustrée de la littérature française en Belgique*, Paris, 1939.
GOËMANS, L. and DEMEUR, L., *La Littérature française en Belgique*, Brussels, 1922.
*HANLET, C., *Les Écrivains belges contemporains*, 2 vols., Liège, 1946.

HEUMANN, A., *Le Mouvement littéraire belge d'expression française depuis 1880*, Paris, 1913.
*JOHANSEN, S., *Le Symbolisme*, Copenhagen, 1945.
LALOU, R., *Histoire de la littérature française contemporaine*, Paris, 1922.
LIEBRECHT and RENCY, *Histoire de la littérature belge de langue française*, Brussels, 1926.
*MARTINO, P., *Parnasse et Symbolisme*, Paris, 1954.
*—— *Le Naturalisme français*, Paris, 1945.
*MATHEWS, A. J., *La Wallonie, The Symbolist Movement in Belgium*, New York, 1947.
*MENDÈS, C., *Le Mouvement poétique français de 1867 à 1900*, Paris, 1902.
*MICHAUD, G., *Le Message poétique du Symbolisme*, 3 vols., Paris, 1947.
*—— *La Doctrine symboliste* (documents), Paris, 1947.
POIZAT, A., *Le Symbolisme*, Paris, 1920.
*RAYMOND, M., *De Baudelaire au Surréalisme*, Paris, 1933.
*RAYNAUD, E., *La Mêlée symboliste*, 3 vols., Paris, 1920.
*RETTÉ, A., *Le Symbolisme, anecdotes et souvenirs*, Paris, 1903.
*SCHMIDT, A., *La Littérature symboliste*, Paris, 1950.
*STECHER, J., *La Littérature néerlandaise en Belgique*, Brussels, 1886.
*VAN BEVER, A., and LÉAUTAUD, P., *Poètes d'aujourd'hui*, 2 vols., Paris, 1900.
WILMOTTE, M., *La Culture française en Belgique*, Paris, 1911.

OTHER WORKS

*ANIANTE, A., *La Double Vie de Maeterlinck*, Paris, 1949.
*ANTOINE, A., *Mes souvenirs sur le Théâtre Libre*, Paris, 1921.
*—— *Le Théâtre. La Troisième République de 1870 à nos jours*, Paris, 2 vols., 1932–3.
BAILLY, A., *Maurice Maeterlinck*, Paris, 1931.
*BAX, C. (ed.), *Letters of Florence Farr, Bernard Shaw and W. B. Yeats*, London, 1942.
*BEACHBOARD, R., *Le Théâtre de Maeterlinck aux États-Unis*, Paris, 1951.
*BERGSON, H., *L'Évolution créatrice*, Paris, 1907.
*BILLY, A., *L'Époque 1900*, Paris, 1951.
BITHELL, J., *Life and Writings of Maeterlinck*, London, 1913.
DE BOER, J., *Mannen en Vrouwen van Beteekenis: Maurice Maeterlinck*, Haarlem, 1908.
*BOUQUET, A. C., *Comparative Religion*, 3rd ed., London, 1951.
BRAHM, O., *Kritische Schriften über Drama und Theater*, Berlin, 1913.
BRISSON, A., *La Comédie littéraire*, Paris, 1895.
—— *Portraits intimes*, vol. iii, Paris, 1897.
*BRUNSCHVICG, L., *La Philosophie morale au XIXe siècle*, Paris, 1904.
*CAMPBELL, Mrs. PATRICK, *My Life and Some Letters*, New York, 1922.
CARTON DE WIART, H., *Souvenirs littéraires*, Brussels, 1939.

BIBLIOGRAPHY

CARTWRIGHT, FRANÇOISE D., *Maeterlinck und Amerika*, Berlin, 1935.
*CHARLIER, G., ' "Sœur Béatrice" et "Beatrijs" ', *Mélanges d'histoire littéraire offerts à V. Tille*, Prague, 1927.
CLARK, M., *Maurice Maeterlinck, Poet and Philosopher*, London, 1915.
*COHEN, G., *Ceux que j'ai connus*, Montreal, 1946.
*COMPEYRE, G., *Le Théâtre de Maeterlinck*, Brussels, 1955.
*DANIELS, MAY, *The French Drama of the Unspoken*, Edinburgh, 1953.
*DAVIGNON, H., *Souvenirs d'un écrivain belge, 1879–1945*, Paris, 1954.
—— *Le Visage de mon pays*, Paris, 1921.
DESTRÉE, J., *En Italie avant la guerre*, Paris, 1915.
DOUMIC, R., *Les Jeunes*, Paris, 1896.
DUMONT-WILDEN, L., *L'Esprit européen*, Paris, 1914.
DUTHIE, ENID, *L'Influence du Symbolisme français dans le renouveau poétique de l'Allemagne*, Paris, 1933.
ESCH, M., *L'Œuvre de Maurice Maeterlinck*, Paris, 1912.
ÉVRARD, É., *Nos mandarins*, Tourcoing, 1920.
*FALK, E. H., *Renunciation as a Tragic Focus*, Minneapolis, 1954.
FIDLER, FLORENCE G., *The Bird that is Blue*, London, 1928.
*FONTAINAS, A., *Mes souvenirs du Symbolisme*, Paris, 1928.
*FOUILLÉE, A., *Le Mouvement idéaliste et la réaction contre la science positive*, Paris, 1896.
FRÉDÉRIX, G., *Trente ans de critique*, Paris, 1900.
GARDEN, MARY and BIANCOLLI, L., *Mary Garden's Story*, London, 1951.
GAUCHEZ, M., *Le Livre des masques belges*, 3ᵉ série, Paris, 1911.
*—— *Camille Lemonnier*, Brussels, 1943.
GEORGES-MICHEL, M., *En jardinant avec Bergson*, &c., Paris, 1926.
GERARDINO, ADELA, *Le Théâtre de Maeterlinck*, Paris, 1934.
*GIDE, A., and VALÉRY, P., *Correspondance, 1890–1942*, Paris, 1955.
*—— *Journal*, vol. i, Rio de Janeiro ed., 1943.
GILBERT, E., *France et Belgique*, Paris, 1905.
—— *Les Lettres françaises dans la Belgique d'aujourd'hui*, Paris, 1906.
*GILSON, É., *L'École des Muses*, Paris, 1951.
*GOFFIN, R., *Entrer en poésie*, Ghent, 1948.
*GOURMONT, R. DE, *Le Latin mystique* (Preface by J.-K. Huysmans), 2nd ed., Paris, 1892.
—— *Promenades littéraires*, v, Paris, 1913.
*GRIMM, *Household Stories*, translated by Lucy Crane, illustrated by W. Crane, London, 1882.
HALFLANTS, P., *Maurice Maeterlinck*, Brussels, 1937.
*HANLET, C., *Maurice Maeterlinck, les dangers d'une œuvre littéraire*, Liège, 1942.
HARRY, G., *Maurice Maeterlinck* (English ed.), London, 1910.
—— *Mes mémoires*, vols. i–iv, Brussels, 1927–30.

HARRY, G., *La Vie et l'œuvre de Maeterlinck*, Paris, 1932.
HEINE, A., *Maeterlinck*, Berlin, 1905.
*HELLENS, F., *En ville morte*, Ghent, 1906.
*—— *Documents secrets*, Brussels, 1932.
*HERTRICH, C., *Maurice Maeterlinck, poète, dramaturge et philosophe du subconscient*, St-Étienne, 1946.
*HIND, C. L., *Authors and I*, New York, 1921.
HORRENT, D., *Écrivains belges d'aujourd'hui*, 1ère série, Brussels, 1904.
HUNEKER, J., *Iconoclasts*, New York, 1905.
HURET, J., *Enquête sur l'évolution littéraire*, Paris, 1913 ed.
*INGE, W. R., *Christian Mysticism*, 8th ed., London, 1948.
JACOBS, M., *Maeterlinck, eine kritische Studie*, Leipzig, 1902.
*KEMP, R., *Lectures dramatiques*, Brussels, 1947.
*KNOWLES, DOROTHY, *La Réaction idéaliste au théâtre*, Geneva, 1934.
LEBLANC, GEORGETTE, Introduction to *Morceaux choisis de Maurice Maeterlinck*, Paris, 1910.
—— *Maeterlinck's Dogs*, London, 1919.
—— *Souvenirs*, Paris, 1931.
*—— *La Machine à courage*, Paris, 1947.
LECAT, M., *Le Maeterlinckisme*, 2 vols., Brussels, 1941.
LEMONNIER, C., *La Vie belge*, Paris, 1905.
LEMONNIER, L., *Edgar Poe et les poètes français*, Paris, 1932.
LENEVEU, G., *Ibsen et Maeterlinck*, Paris, 1902.
LE SIDANER, L., *Maurice Maeterlinck*, Paris, 1929.
LEWISOHN, L., *Modern Drama*, New York, 1916.
*LUGNÉ-POË, G. H., *Souvenirs de théâtre, La Parade sous les étoiles, 1902–1912*, Paris, 1933.
*—— *Souvenirs de théâtre, La Parade, Acrobaties, 1894–1902*, Paris, 1931.
*MACKAIL, D., *The Story of J. M. B.*, London, 1941.
*MAHONEY, P., *The Magic of Maeterlinck*, Hollywood, Calif., 1951.
MAINOR, Y., *Maurice Maeterlinck, moraliste*, Angers, 1902.
*MALLARMÉ, S., *Divagations*, Paris, 1897.
MARTIN DU GARD, M., *Impertinences*, Paris, 1924.
*MAUCLAIR, C., *Servitude et grandeur littéraires*, Paris, 1922.
*—— *Mallarmé chez lui*, Paris, 1935.
MIRBEAU, O., *Gens de théâtre*, Paris, 1924.
*MONDOR, H., *Vie de Mallarmé*, Paris, 1941.
NORDAU, M., *Dégénérescences* (tr. by A. Dietrich), Paris, 1894.
PALLESKE, O., *Maurice Maeterlinck en Allemagne*, Paris, 1938.
*PASQUIER, A., *Maurice Maeterlinck*, Brussels, 1950.
*PERRUCHOT, H., *Maurice Maeterlinck et la poursuite de l'oiseau bleu*. No date or place (reprint in pamphlet form of article appearing in *Synthèses*, Brussels, No. 2 of 1949).

PHELPS, W. L., *Essays on Modern Dramatists*, New York, 1921.
PIÉRARD, L., *Maurice Maeterlinck*, Brussels, 1938.
*POINCARÉ, R., *Memoirs* (tr. by Sir George Arthur), London, 1929.
REBOUX, P., and MULLER, C., *A la manière de . . .*, 1ère série, Paris, 1920.
*ROBICHEZ, J., *Le Symbolisme au théâtre*, Paris, 1957.
*RODENBACH, G., *Bruges-la-morte*, Paris, 1892.
*—— *Le Rouet des brumes*, Paris, 1900.
*—— *Évocations*, Brussels, 1924.
ROSE, H., *Maeterlinck's Symbolism*, London, 1910.
*RUCHON, F., *L'Amitié de Mallarmé et de Rodenbach*, Geneva, 1949.
*RUSSELL, H., *The Passing Show*, London, 1926.
SARCEY, F., *Quarante ans de théâtre*, vol. viii, Paris, 1902.
*SCHURÉ, É., *Précurseurs et révoltés*, Paris, 1904.
SERRE, J., *Maeterlinck philosophe*, Paris, 1914.
*SHANNON, C., and WHITE, J. W., *The Pageant*, London, 1896.
*SHERARD, R., *Twenty Years in Paris*, London, 1905.
*STAPLES, L., *An Interpretation of Maeterlinck's Blue Bird*, San Francisco, 1914.
STURGIS, G. F., *The Psychology of Maeterlinck*, Boston, U.S.A., 1914.
TIMMERMANS, B., *L'Évolution de Maeterlinck*, Brussels, 1912.
VAN DEN BOSCH, F., *Impressions de littérature contemporaine*, Brussels, 1905.
*VAN LERBERGHE, C., *Lettres à Fernand Séverin*, Brussels, 1924.
*—— *Lettres à une jeune fille*, Brussels, 1954.
*VERHAEREN, É., *Lettres inédites de Verhaeren à Marthe Verhaeren (1889–1916)*, Paris, 1937.
VISAN, T. DE, *L'Attitude du lyrisme contemporain*, 2nd ed., Paris, 1911.
*WADE, A. (ed.), *Letters of W. B. Yeats*, London, 1954.
WATENPUHL, H., *Die Geschichte der Marienlegende von Beatrix der Küsterin*, Neuwied, 1904.

ARTICLES

*ANON. (various opinions on), 'Le Prix Nobel', *Le Thyrse*, Brussels, 5 Jan. 1912.
*—— 'The Magic of the Stars', *Times Literary Supplement*, London, 8 May 1930.
*—— 'Deux inédits', *Les Lettres françaises*, Paris, 12 May 1949.
*BAIE, E., 'La dernière page de Maeterlinck', *Les Nouvelles littéraires*, Paris, 12 May 1949.
BEAUNIER, A., 'Une philosophie de la mort', *Revue des Deux Mondes*, tome xiv, Apr. 1913.
BOCQUET, L., 'L'archétype de "L'Oiseau bleu" ', *Revue bleue*, 18 Feb. 1911.
BONNIER, G., 'La science chez Maeterlinck', *La Revue*, Paris, 15 Aug. 1907.

BUYSSE, C., 'Bij de Maeterlinck's te Nizza', *Groot Nederland*, Amsterdam, 1913, vol. i, p. 279.
*CANDACE, G., 'Mon souvenir de Maeterlinck', *Revue guadaloupéenne*, July–Aug. 1949.
CARRÉ, J.-M., 'L'Évolution du théâtre de Maeterlinck', *Revue des cours et conférences*, Paris, Dec. 1925, p. 154.
—— 'Maeterlinck et les littératures étrangères', *Revue de littérature comparée*, Paris, 1926, p. 449.
*CHARPENTIER, H., 'L'Époque symboliste', *Visages du monde*, Paris, 15 Apr. 1936.
COHEN, G., 'Le Conflit de l'homme et du destin dans le théâtre de Maeterlinck', *La Revue du mois*, Paris, 10 Jan. 1912.
*DECREUS, JULIETTE, 'L'Enfant dans le théâtre de Maeterlinck', *Comparative Literature Studies*, xiv and xv, Cardiff, 1944.
*DESCAVES, P., 'Maeterlinck et son inspiratrice', *Le Monde français*, Paris, Apr. 1947.
DESTRÉE, J., 'Maeterlinck en Italie', *Gand artistique*, Ghent, 1 Mar. 1923.
DUMONT-WILDEN, L., 'L'Oiseau bleu', *Nouvelle Revue Française*, Paris, Feb. 1910.
*—— 'Souvenirs sur le Symbolisme', *Bulletin de l'Académie royale*, Brussels, Fascicule No. 2 of 1952.
FORTEBUS, T., 'Maeterlinck as Thinker', *Argosy Magazine*, London, No. 75 of 1901.
GEORGES-MICHEL, M., 'De Bruxelles à New-York avec Maeterlinck', *Les Nouvelles littéraires*, Paris, 12 May 1949.
GILKIN, I., 'Chronique', *La Jeune Belgique*, 1889, p. 399.
GIRAUD, A., 'Chronique littéraire', *La Jeune Belgique*, No. 1, May 1888.
*GOFFIN, R., 'Maurice Maeterlinck', *Les Lettres françaises*, Paris, 19 May 1949.
HAMEL, M., 'Deux heures au château de Médan avec Maurice Maeterlinck', *Revue belge*, Brussels, 15 Aug. 1929, pp. 313–26.
HARRIS, F., 'Maurice Maeterlinck', *The Academy*, London, 15 and 22 June 1912.
HELLENS, F., 'Maurice Maeterlinck', *Les Nouvelles littéraires*, Paris, 10 July 1926.
KEMP, R., 'Les Maeterlinck', *Les Nouvelles littéraires*, 22 Aug. 1931.
*—— 'Maurice Maeterlinck', *Le Monde*, Paris, 9 May 1949.
KISTEMAECKERS, H., 'Mes procès littéraires, souvenirs d'un éditeur', *Mercure de France*, 15 Sept. 1923.
LANG, A., 'Le sage: Maurice Maeterlinck', *Les Annales politiques et littéraires*, 15 Nov. 1929.
*LARROUMET, G., 'Chronique théâtrale', *Le Temps*, 25 May 1903.
LEBLANC, GEORGETTE, 'Maeterlinck's Methods of Life and Work', *Contemporary Review*, London, Nov. 1910.

*LEES, F., 'The Forbidden Play', *Pall Mall Magazine*, vol. xxviii, Sept.–Dec. 1902, p. 108.

LEFÈVRE, F., 'Maurice Maeterlinck', *Les Nouvelles littéraires*, Paris, 7 Apr. 1928.

LELONG, G., 'Maurice Maeterlinck', *Le Magazine littéraire*, Ghent, 1891, p. 4.

LEMONNIER, C., 'Réponse à une enquête', *Le Thyrse*, Brussels, 5 Jan. 1912.

LE ROY, G., 'Le Poète prodigue', *Le Masque*, Brussels, No. 5 of 1912.

—— 'A l'aube de sa gloire', *Gand artistique*, Ghent, 1 Mar. 1923.

*LUGNÉ-POË, G. H., 'Mes confidences sur Maeterlinck', *Conférencia*, Paris, 15 Sept. 1933.

*MAES, P., 'Hommage à Maeterlinck', *Épîtres*, Fascicule No. 28, Ghent, Apr. 1949.

*MAHONEY, P., 'Chez Maeterlinck le jour anniversaire de ses 80 ans', *Le Littéraire*, Paris, 18 Jan. 1947.

MARLOW, G., 'Chronique de Belgique', *Mercure de France*, Paris, 15 Oct. 1923.

*MAUROIS, A., 'Maurice Maeterlinck', *Les Nouvelles littéraires*, Paris, 12 May 1949.

MERRILL, S., 'Commentaires sur une polémique', *Le Masque*, Brussels, 1912, p. 346.

*MILHE, O., 'Maurice Maeterlinck', *Synthèses*, Brussels, No. 3 of 1949.

MIRBEAU, O., 'Maurice Maeterlinck', *Le Figaro*, Paris, 24 Aug. 1890.

MOCKEL, A., 'Chronique littéraire', *La Wallonie*, Liège, 1891, p. 94.

—— 'Le Symbolisme en Belgique', *Visages du monde*, Paris, 15 Apr. 1936.

*PICARD, E. (?), 'A propos des *Sept Princesses* de Maurice Maeterlinck', *L'Art moderne*, Brussels, 29 Nov. 1891.

PONCHEVILLE, A. DE, 'L'Oiseau bleu', *Gand artistique*, Ghent, 1 Mar. 1923.

*RODENBACH, G., 'Trois nouveaux', *La Jeune Belgique*, Brussels, 5 July 1886.

*ROLAND, M., 'Maeterlinck et la Nature', *Mercure de France*, Paris, July 1949.

*SAILLET, M., 'Maurice Maeterlinck', *Mercure de France*, Paris, June 1949.

SAINT-POL-ROUX, 'Autour d'une conférence de Mauclair', *Mercure de France*, Paris, June 1892.

*—— 'Souvenirs', *Visages du monde*, Paris, 15 Apr. 1936.

SCHURÉ, É., 'Maeterlinck philosophe: le grand secret', *Revue bleue*, Paris, 15 Sept. 1923.

SCHWAB, R., 'Maurice Maeterlinck: le sage des jours ordinaires', *Mercure de France*, Paris, 16 Mar. 1911.

SÉVERIN, F., 'Maeterlinck et Van Lerberghe', *Gand artistique*, Ghent, 1 Mar. 1923.

*SIMONSON, R., 'La Princesse Maleine', *Bulletin du bibliophile*, Paris, No. 3 of 1953.

*SMET, F. DE, 'Maeterlinck et Doudelet', *Gand artistique*, Ghent, 1 Mar. 1923.
STODDART, JANE, 'An Interview with Maeterlinck', *The Bookman*, New York, May 1895.
UZANNE, O., 'La Thébaïde de Maeterlinck', *Écho de Paris*, 7 Sept. 1900.
VALETTE, A., 'Maurice Maeterlinck et Charles Van Lerberghe', *Mercure de France*, Paris, Oct. 1890.
—— ' "Pelléas et Mélisande" et la critique officielle', *Mercure de France*, Paris, July 1893.
*VAN HALL, J., 'Dramatisch Overzicht', *De Gids*, Amsterdam, Mar. 1903.
*VAN LERBERGHE, C., 'Quelques lettres de Charles Van Lerberghe', *Vers et prose*, Paris, Jan.–Mar. 1914, pp. 7–16.
VAN ROOSBROECK, G., letter in *Modern Language Notes*, Baltimore, Nov. 1919, pp. 439–41.
*VAUTHIER, É., 'Maeterlinck traducteur', *Hommage à Maurice Maeterlinck* (brochure programme of the Belgian Radio Service), Brussels, 1949.
*VISAN, T. DE, 'Sur l'œuvre de Maurice Maeterlinck', *Vers et prose*, tome vii, Oct.–Nov. 1906.
WEEKES, C., 'Maeterlinck as Artist', *Argosy Magazine*, London, 1901, p. 77.
WOODBRIDGE, B. M., 'Two Studies of Maeterlinck', *The Dial*, vol. lxi, Chicago, 1916.
*YEATS, W. B., 'A Symbolical Drama in Paris', *The Bookman*, London, Apr. 1894.

INDEX

Aarschot, 115.
Abbé Sétubal, L', 151, 155.
Adam, Paul, 37, 61.
Aglavaine et Sélysette, 55, 63, 73, 82, 86.
Agnosticism, 70, 135, 146, 167.
Aimes, Winthrop, 127.
Ajalbert, Jean, 14.
Akëdysseril, 14.
Alba, Duke of, 1.
Albert, King of the Belgians, 108, 127, 142.
Algeria, 138.
Alhaiza, M., 39.
Alladine et Palomides, 41.
Amsterdam, 81, 83.
Ancient Egypt (monograph), 137.
Anouilh, Jean, 155.
Antoine, A., 27.
Antwerp, 1, 36, 143.
Araignée de verre, L', 65, 136, 138.
Archer, William, 51, 52, 75.
Ariane et Barbe-bleue, 66, 71, 94, 95, 170.
Armistice of 1918, 211.
Armistice—VJ Day, 161.
Art moderne, L', 11, 30.
Aulnoy, Mme d', 84.
Autre Monde, L', 144–50 *passim*.
Avant le grand silence, 142, 144.
Aveugles, Les, 25, 32–33, 44, 45.
Axël, 14, 28, 43.

Bacon, Francis, 150.
Bady, Berthe, 34.
Bahr, Hermann, 53.
Baie, Eugène, 162, 163, 164.
Baie des Anges, 141.
Baltia, Herman, 8.
Banville, Théodore de, 15.
Barbey d'Aurevilly, Jules-Amédée, 25.
Barrès, Maurice, 61, 62.
Barrie, J. M., 52, 67, 84.
Baudelaire, 29, 32, 126; translation of Poe, 26; opinion of Belgium, 30.
Baudrillart, Monseigneur, 135.
Bauer, Henry, 27.
Bax, Clifford, 172.
Béguinages, the, 4.
Belgium, 25, 27, 42, 48, 56, 61, 63, 68, 88, 99, 118, 125, 136, 169, 171; literary revival, 11; literary prizes, 12, 30, 31, 102; political and social changes, 12; materialism, 19; hostility to writers, 28; critics of Maeterlinck, 40; Flemish nationalism, 79; Maeterlinck's attitude to the government, 83; nominations for Nobel Prize, 103; invasion of, 1914, 113–15; foundation of Academy, 134; surrender of Belgian Army, 151–2.
Benedictines, Order of, 93.
Bergson, Henri, 70, 113, 144.
Berkeley, California, 133.
Berlin, 63, 66.
Bernanos, Georges, 151, 155.
Bernard, Tristan, 37, 51.
Bernhardt, Sarah, 72, 76, 98.
Berniquel, 137.
Bernstein, Henri, 153, 158.
Bloy, Léon, 170.
Blumenthal, George, 128.
Bocquet, Léon, 84.
Body and Mind Clinic, New York, 153.
Boehme, Jakob, 21.
Bon, Raymond, 109.
Bonnier, Gaston, 69.
Bordeaux, 56.
Bossuet, 144.
Boston, Mass., 104, 105.
Bourgmestre de Stilemonde, Le, 119–20, 126, 152, 157.
Brahm, Otto, 80.
Brasserie des Culs de Bouteille, 14.
Breughel, 6.
Brewer, Max, 115.
Briant, Théophile, 143.
Brisson, Adolphe, 99.
Browning, 25, 149.
Bruges, 1, 100, 112.
Bruneau, Alfred, 48.
Brussels, 1, 11, 12, 18, 19, 22, 24, 25, 27, 28, 30, 49, 50, 54, 80, 81, 88, 111, 114, 123, 125, 143; performance of *Les Aveugles*, 32; performance of *L'Intruse*, 33–34; visit of Verlaine, 36; performance of *Pelléas et Mélisande*, 39; reception for Maeterlinck, 107–9.
Buenos Aires, 119.
Buffon, 70.
Bulles bleues, 5, 161, 170.
Burne-Jones, Sir Edward, 27, 64.
Busscher, Lucien de, 35, 36.
Buysse, Cyriel, 35, 134, 143.

Calabresi, 48.
Calamus, M., 6.
California, 131, 133.
Calmette, Gaston, 99.
Campbell, Mrs. Patrick, 64, 65.
Campfire Girls, 132.
Candace, Gratien, 135, 137.
Caplet, André, 104.

INDEX

Carlyle, 25, 46, 62, 126.
Carnegie Hall, New York, 129, 130.
Carpentier, Georges, 109, 133.
Carré, Albert, 27, 37, 94; accompanied by Maeterlinck to Spain, 65; quarrel with Georgette Leblanc, 66; stages Debussy's *Pelléas et Mélisande*, 76–78.
Carré, Jéan-Marie, 66.
Carrillo, Gomez, 118.
Carton de Wiart, Henry, 12, 36, 115, 134.
Carvalho, 48.
Casier, Jean, 36.
Caudheil, 34.
Charleroi, 36.
Château de Médan, 138.
Chateaubriand, 71.
Châteauneuf de Contes, 122.
Chavannes, Puvis de, 29.
Chicago, 132.
Clarétie, 72.
Claudel, Paul, 78; urges Maeterlinck to repent, 161; as a Symbolist playwright, 170–1.
Clemenceau, Georges, 78.
Cohen, Gustave, 56.
Coleridge, 21, 25.
Coles, Edward Spencer, 153.
Colette, 61, 78.
Colin, Saul, 153, 155.
Comte, Auguste, 167.
Comyns-Carr, Philip, 74.
Coq rouge, Le, 53.
Coquelin, the elder, 72.
Cortot, 133.
Coster, Charles de, 11.
Courteline, Georges, 137.
Courtrai, 79.
Crane, Walter, 25, 31, 39.
Crocq, Dr., 34.
Culver City, 132.
Curel, François de, 171.

Dahon, Joseph, 101, 152.
Dahon, Mlle Renée, *see* Maeterlinck, Countess Renée.
Daily Mail, the, 52, 115.
Dance of the Stars (ballet), 158.
Darwin, 70, 91, 121.
Darzens, Rodolphe, 14.
Daudet, Léon, 136.
Davignon, Henri, 142.
Death: as a dramatic theme, 19, 26, 29, 30, 32, 38, 41, 42, 44, 55, 66, 73, 97, 155, 156, 157, 167, 171; place in human existence, 62, 63, 85, 100–1, 135, 146, 149, 150, 158, 162, 168, 169, 172.
Débris de la guerre, Les, 117.
Debussy, 95, 154; given operatic rights of *Pelléas et Mélisande*, 41; quarrel with Maeterlinck, 76–78; his opera staged in Boston, 104–5.
Déprès, Suzanne, 33.
Descamp-David, Baron, 102, 103.
Descaves, Lucien, 109, 123.
Descaves, Pierre, 123.
Deschamps, Mathilde, 72.
Destiny, 91, 147, 149, 166, 171, 172; in *Le Massacre des Innocents*, 16; in *La Princesse Maleine*, 26; in *Les Aveugles*, 33; in *Pelléas et Mélisande*, 38; in *Trois drames pour marionnettes*, 41–42; inimical to mankind, 43–44; in *Aglavaine et Sélysette*, 55; in *Sagesse et destinée*, 62; in *Ariane et Barbe-bleue*, 66; in *Monna Vanna*, 74; in *Joyzelle*, 80; in the 'theatre of the second manner', 97; in *Les Fiançailles*, 120; in *Le Miracle des mères*, 157; an unchanging concept, 168–9.
Destrée, Jules, 115, 116, 134.
Detroit, 133.
Deutsches Theater, 80.
Devant Dieu, 144–50 *passim*.
Dommartin, Léon, 25.
Double Jardin, Le, 81, 89.
Doudelet, Charles, 35, 36, 81.
Dramas for puppets, 41.
Dreyfus, 63.
Duhamel, Georges, 171.
Dukas, Paul, 71, 78, 94, 95.
Dunsany, Lord, 130.

Écho de Paris, L', 40.
Eekhoud, Georges, 31, 104.
Egypt, 137.
Einstein, 139, 161.
Elberfeld, 111.
Eliot, T. S., 172.
Élisabeth, Queen of the Belgians, 108.
Emerson, 21, 25, 48, 57, 134; influence on Maeterlinck, 42, 126.
Enfant qui ne veut pas naître, L' (sketch), 160.
Enthoven, Gabrielle, 98 n.
Epistemology, 145.
Esplanade Hotel, New York, 153.
Ève future, L', 14.

Fabre, Gabriel, 48, 50.
Fabre, Jean-Henri, 69, 101.
Fabulet, 28.
Fascism, 137, 148.
Fate, *see* Destiny.
Fauré, Gabriel, 64, 78.
Fiançailles, Les, 120–1, 127.
Figaro, Le, 23, 24, 42, 77, 79, 99.
Flanders and the Flemish, 167; Flemish nationalism, 1; as setting for Maeterlinck's plays, 26, 29, 35; Flemish element in his works, 52; battle of Golden

INDEX

Spurs, 79; bivalency of Flemish nature, 80, 169; melancholy atmosphere of towns, 100; in *Le Bourgmestre de Stilemonde*, 119; in *La Puissance des morts*, 132; in *La Princesse Isabelle*, 143; 'peasant' dialogue in plays, 170.
Florence, 116.
Florida, 159, 160.
Flushing, 50, 51.
Fondation Maeterlinck, 7 n., 13 n., 29 n., 32 n., 40 n., 64 n., 78 n., 90 n., 92 n., 105 n., 110 n., 119 n., 126 n., 134 n.
Fontainas, André, 92.
Forbes-Robertson, J., 64, 98.
Fort, Paul, 27, 29, 32, 37, 61.
France, Anatole, 61, 62, 155, 161.
Frédérix, Gustave, 24, 30, 40.
French Academy, 104, 114–15, 163.
Freud, Sigmund, 145.

Garden, Mary, 66, 76, 87, 131.
Garnett, Richard, 75.
Gauguin, Paul, 29.
Geneva, 80.
Genoa, 136.
Germany, 162; Maeterlinck visits Cologne, 29; his vogue in Germany, 68; visit to Berlin, 80; his attitude during First World War, 114–19; Second World War, 150, 152.
Gezelle, Guido, 79.
Gheel, 143.
Ghent, 16, 28, 33, 34, 50, 66, 67, 68, 80, 88, 91, 93, 98, 99, 101, 104, 118, 170; Flemish character of town, 1; birthplace of Maeterlinck, 2; home of his relatives, 3; his family move to Boulevard Frère-Orban, 4; convent school, 5; Institut Central, 6; atmosphere of town, 9, 57, 100; university, 11, 134; Maeterlinck admitted to Ghent bar, 13; visit of Villiers de l'Isle Adam, 17; Maeterlinck's life there, 18; reaction to Mirbeau's article, 24–25; Civic Guard, 27, 114; *Le Réveil*, 35; Verlaine's visit, 36.
Gide, André, 56, 78, 161, 171; contributor to *La Wallonie*, 11; meetings with Maeterlinck, 29, 61; opinion of Maeterlinck's work, 86, 87.
Gilbert, Eugène, 79.
Gilkin, Iwan, 11, 22, 26, 28, 99, 102.
Gille, Valère, 171.
Gilson, Étienne, 124.
Giraud, Albert, 11.
Glasgow University, 125.
Goethe, 53, 62.
Goffin, Robert, 153, 154, 155.
Goldwyn, Sam, 131, 132.
Goncourt Academy, 104.

Gosse, Edmund, 51, 87.
Gourmont, Rémy de, 21, 39.
Grande Féerie, La, **139–40**.
Grande Loi, La, 139.
Grande Porte, La, **144–50** *passim*.
Grand Secret, Le, 121, 130, **134–5**, 139.
Granville-Barker, Harley, 52, 172.
Grasse, 87, 89, 90, 91, 92, 97, 99, 103.
Grasset, Bernard, 123, 167.
Greece, 137.
Grein, J. T., 51.
Grimm, 84.
Gruchet Saint-Siméon, 64, 68, 69, 71, 84, 91, 92.
Guéquier, Albert, 36.
Guitry, Sacha, 102.

Hague, The, 41, 51.
Hardy, Thomas, 75.
Harlem, 154.
Harry, Gérard, 26, 51, 67, 99, 103, 114; first contact with Maeterlinck, 3; helps with *Macbeth*, 98; arranges Brussels reception for Maeterlinck, 107–9.
Harvey, Sir John Martin, 64, 98.
Havre, Le, 114, 133.
Hazard, Paul, 135.
Hearst, Randolph, 123, 128.
Hellens, Franz, 100, 118, 119, 136.
Hermetists, the, 134.
Hervieu, Paul, 22–23, 37, 104.
Heyse, Paul, 95.
Hinton, 140.
Hollywood, Calif., 132.
Hôte inconnu, L', **112–13**, 130.
Hugo, Jean-François-Victor, 98.
Hugo, Victor, 13.
Huret, Jules, 28, 31, 61.
Huysmans, Joris-Karl, 17, 21, 28, 89, 93.

Ibsen, 38, 51, 52, 80, 83.
Idealism, 43.
Impératrice sans couronne, L', 154.
Indépendance, L', 40.
Independent Theatre, 51, 52.
Institut Central, 6.
Intelligence des fleurs, L', 87, **89–91**, 94.
Intérieur, L', 41, 45, 51.
Intruse, L', 11, 25, **29–30**, 33, 44, 45, 52.
Italy, 81, 115, 136, 137, 143, 162.

Jeanne d'Arc, 155.
Jeune Belgique, La, 11, 12, 13, 27, 53, 115, 171.
Job, 156.
Joncs, Les, 12.
Journal de Bruxelles, 79.
Joyzelle, 35, **79–80**, 81, 86, 120.
Jugement dernier, Le, 156.
Jumièges, 93.

INDEX

Kabbala, the, 134.
Kahn, Gustave, 56.
Kahn, Otto, 128.
Kalff, Marie, 71.
Kansas City, 132.
Karl, Roger, 110, 121–2.
Keller, Helen, 105.
King, Rev. Willard, 129.
Kipling, 48.
Krall, 111.

Lacomblez, Paul, 22, 34.
La Fontaine, 142.
Laforgue, Jules, 29.
Lake Placid, 161.
Lamot, M., 162, 164.
Lamy, 115.
Larroumet, Gustave, 79.
La Turbie, 125.
Lavisse, Ernest, 114.
Leblanc, Bianconi, 47.
Leblanc, Georgette, 6, 42, 53, 54, 55, 60, 61, 65, 66, 67, 71, 76, 78, 80, 81, 83, 84, 87, 88, 92, 93, 95, 109, 113, 116, 120, 135, 138, 167; family and general background, 47–48; first meeting with Maeterlinck, 49–50; effect on Maeterlinck's literary career, 56; claims part-authorship of *Le Trésor des humbles* and *Sagesse et destinée*, 57–58; she and Maeterlinck settle in Paris, 58–59; Maeterlinck writes plays for her, 64; plays the lead in *Monna Vanna*, 72; first rift in relationship with Maeterlinck, 78; plays title role in *Joyzelle*, 79; rumours that she and Maeterlinck are to part, 82; end of artistic collaboration with Maeterlinck, 89, 98; realizes Maeterlinck needs new inspiration, 94; the personification of the *femme forte*, 97; *Macbeth* at St-Wandrille, 98–99, 100, 101, 102; trip to Boston, 104–5; announces impending retirement, 110; liaison with Roger Karl, 110; break with Maeterlinck, 121–2; subsequent career, 122–3; her part in Maeterlinck's success, 123–4.
Leblanc, Maurice, 47, 55, 58, 94.
Le Cannet, 124.
Lecat, Maurice, 80.
Ledeganck, 1.
Lefèvre, Frédéric, 119.
Leighton, Dorothy, 52.
Leipzig, 96.
Lelong, Gérard, 21.
Lemaître, Jules, 33.
Lemonnier, Camille, 11, 12, 30, 104.
Léopold III, King of the Belgians, 151–2.
Le Roy, Grégoire, 7, 10, 13, 19, 35, 36, 38, 86, 108, 134; *L'Annonciatrice*, 11; in Paris, 14.
Le Sidaner, 48.
Lewisohn, L., 85.
Liége, 11, 12, 51.
Lisbon, 151, 152.
Loman, M., 164.
London, 62, 63, 65, 84, 86; first visit of Maeterlinck, 25; visit of *L'Œuvre*, 51; visit of Maeterlinck for *Pelléas et Mélisande*, 64; performance of *Monna Vanna*, 74–75; other visits of Maeterlinck, 98, 99, 117.
Long Island, 154.
Lorand, Georges, 115.
Lorrain, Jean, 61.
Los Angeles, Calif., 133.
Lourdes, 112.
Louvain, 115.
Love, as a dramatic theme, 26, 32, 38, 41, 42, 43, 44, 73, 74, 79–80, 96, 97, 120, 149, 166.
Lugné-Poë, G., 29, 32, 34, 35, 40, 51, 76, 77; becomes friend of Maeterlinck, 33; produces *Pelléas et Mélisande*, 39; in London, 52; produces *Monna Vanna*, 71–72; produces *Berniquel*, 137.
Luneray, 64.
Lyceum Lecture Bureau, 127.

McCoy, Kid, 133.
Macdonald, 131.
Mackail, J. W., 64.
McKenna, R., First Lord of the Admiralty, 99.
Madrid, 118.
Maes, Pierre, 100.
Maeterlinck, Bernard, 3.
Maeterlinck, Ernest, 2, 83.
Maeterlinck, Mme Mathilde, 2, 101–2.
Maeterlinck, Marie, 3.
Maeterlinck, Oscar, 28, 29, 157.
Maeterlinck, Polydore, 2, 4, 21, 83.
Maeterlinck, Countess Renée, 60, 102, 124, 126, 129, 135, 136–7, 163–4; meeting with Maeterlinck, 101; growing friendship with Maeterlinck, 106, 109, 120; marriage to Maeterlinck, 122; acts in *Berniquel*, 137; life at 'Orlamonde' with Maeterlinck, 141; acts in *La Princesse Isabelle*, 143; in U.S.A., 152, 155, 160; helps in compiling *Bulles bleues*, 161.
Malheur passe, Le, 82–83
Mali, Mlle, 42, 48.
Malines, 50.
Mallarmé, 24, 26, 39, 61, 86, 126, 144, 171; contributor to *La Wallonie*, 11; visits Ghent, 22; lectures on Villiers de l'Isle Adam, 28; attends performance of

INDEX

Pelléas et Mélisande, 37; visited by Maeterlinck, 40.
Marcus Aurelius, 62, 63, 147, 149.
Marie-Magdeleine, **95–97**.
Marie-Victoire, 91–92.
Marquet, Georges, 164.
Marseilles, 162, 165.
Martin du Gard, Roger, 171.
Massacre des Innocents, Le, 6, 15, 16, 169.
Master Builder, The, 52.
Mauclair, Camille, 37, 41.
Maupassant, 74.
Maurevert, Georges, 109.
Mauriac, François, 143.
Maurois, André, 153, 160.
Maurras, Charles, 136.
Maus, Octave, 11, 49, 50.
Memlinc, 39.
Mémoires de la Comtesse de la Villirouët, 91.
Mendès, Catulle, 14.
Menton, 81, 87.
Mercure de France, 52.
Meredith, George, 55, 75.
Merrill, Stuart, 126, 170.
Metropolitan Opera House, 127, 153.
Michaud, Guy, 84.
Middelburg, 50.
Mikhael, Éphraïm, 14.
Milan, 115.
Milhe, O., 163, 164.
Minne, Georges, 19, 36.
Miracle de Saint-Antoine, Le, 80.
Miracle des mères, Le, 157, 169.
Mirbeau, Octave, 22, 24, 26, 27, 28, 37, 40, 61, 78, 171; 'discovery' of Maeterlinck, 23.
Mockel, Albert, 18, 38–39, 40, 61, 63, 86, 92, 134; opinion of Collège Ste-Barbe, 6; founder of *La Wallonie*, 11.
Molière, 5.
Monna Vanna, 54, **71–76**, 79, 80, 81, 154, 166.
Montaigne, 47, 62, 150, 157.
Monte Carlo, 125.
Mort, La, **100–1**, 111, 113, 139, 156.
Mort de Tintagiles, La, **41–42**, 87.
Moscow, 97, 101.
Mounet-Sully, 72.
Mysticism, 16, 21, 43, 63, 80, 90, 113, 156, 167, 168, 169, 170.

Naples, 116, 136.
Naturalism, 26, 38.
Nea Hellas (liner), 152.
Neo-Platonism, 134.
Nerval, Gérard de, 150.
Neuilly, 92, 97, 114, 121.
Newcastle upon Tyne, 115.
New York, 63, 65, 133, 155–61 *passim*; production of *Les Fiançailles*, 120; Georgette Leblanc there, 122; performance of *L'Oiseau bleu*, 127; arrival of Maeterlinck (1919), 128; lectures, 129, 131; arrival of Maeterlinck (1940), 152; Maeterlinck's residence there, 153.
Nice, 56, 101, 103, 109, 112, 114, 116, 118, 119, 121, 133, 134, 137, 138, 140, 159, 162, 163, 164.
Nietzsche, 68.
Nobel Prize for Literature, 102, 103–4, 106, 107, 166.
Nordau, Max, 51.
Nouveau-Bois, Sisters of the, 5.
Nouveaux Contes cruels, 14.
Nouvelle Revue Française, 136.
Novalis, 21, 53.

Occultism, 43, 90, 111, 112, 168, 169.
Oiseau bleu, L', 8, 35, 82, **83–86**, 97, 99, 101, 102, 107, 120, 125, 127, 129, 132, 154, 161, 166.
Ombiaux, Maurice des, 142.
Ombre des ailes, L', **144–50** *passim*.
Onirologie, 18, 126.
Oostacker, 4, 10, 18, 27, 33, 69, 83.
Opéra-Comique, the, 48, 65, 76, 77, 94.
Oppeln-Bronikowski, Friedrich von, 63, 66, 68, 81, 85, 94, 109, 113.
Optimism, 63, 100, 125, 128, 135, 145, 149, 157, 166, 168.
Ordre de Léopold, the, 108, 125.
'Orlamonde', 140, 152, 162, 165.
Osiris cult, 134.

Palermo, 136.
Palestine, 137.
Palm Beach, 158, 162.
Paris, 13, 24, 35, 36, 37, 39, 40, 48, 51, 54, 58, 59, 61, 62, 65, 67, 68, 75, 79, 82, 88, 92, 97, 99, 100, 117, 127, 143.
Parnasse de la Jeune Belgique, Le, 18.
Pascal, 62, 139, 144, 150, 161.
Patriote, Le, 40.
Péguy, Charles, 71, 155, 171.
Péladan, 'Sâr', 48, 89.
Pelléas et Mélisande, 33, 34, **37–39**, 40, 41, 45, 51, 52, 54, 64, 65, 76, 77, 78, 85, 95, 98, 102, 104, 106, 108, 131, 153–4, 166.
P.E.N. Club, 162, 163.
Percheron, M., 29.
Philadelphia, 154.
Picard, Edmond, 11, 22, 30, 49, 134.
Piérard, Louis, 162.
Pirmez, Octave, 11.
Pisa, 136.
Plato, 21, 30, 148.
Plotinus, 21, 50, 140.
Pléiade, La, 15.
Poe, Edgar Allan, 5, 26, 38, 126, 134.

INDEX

Poincaré, Raymond, 54, 104, 114, 115, 125.
Poland, 119.
Poma, M., 6.
Poncheville, André de, 84.
Pond, Major, 127, 130, 131.
Portugal, 65, 143, 148, 150, 151, 152, 158.
Positivism, 20, 43, 71, 167.
Pre-Raphaelites, 12, 26, 28, 31, 38, 39, 49, 55, 170.
Princesse Isabelle, La, 143.
Princesse Maleine, La, 3, 21, 22, 26–27, 102.
Proust, Marcel, 136.
Puissance des morts, La, 121, 132.

Queen's Hall, London, 117.
Quenouille et la besace, La, 41.
Quillard, Pierre, 14, 29.
Quinze chansons, 32, 41, 50.

Rachilde, 61.
Redford, Mr., 75.
Régnier, Henri de, 37, 41, 78.
Reinhardt, 85.
Réjane, 78, 99, 102.
Renan, 62.
Renard, Jules, 61.
Retté, Adolphe, 29.
Retournemer, 55.
Réveil, Le, 35, 36.
Revue générale, La, 18, 20.
Rhode Island, 161.
Rimbaud, 84, 167.
Rockefeller Club, 153.
Rodenbach, Georges, 2, 4, 6, 9, 11, 12, 16, 17, 19, 22, 40, 48.
Rodin, Auguste, 61.
Rolland, Romain, 117.
Rollins Park College, Florida, 158.
Romains, Jules, 153.
Romanones Sr., 118.
Romanticism, 53, 64.
Rome, 116, 136, 143.
Ronsard, 138.
Rosicrucians, the, 48, 90.
Rosmersholm, 52.
Rosny, the elder, 104, 170.
Rossetti, Dante Gabriel, 32, 41.
Rothschild, Robert de, 37.
Rotterdam, 41, 51.
Rouen, 114.
Rouzaud, Mme, 135.
Royat, 122, 135.
Russell, Donna, 126, 131.
Russell, Henry, 78 n.; director of Boston Opera House, 104; produces *Pelléas et Mélisande*, 105, 121, 124; persuades Maeterlinck to visit U.S.A., 125; supervises visit, 126–33 *passim*.

Russell, Sheridan, 126, 127, 128, 129.
Ruysbroek, 16, 20, 63, 140, 169.

Sablier, Le, 144–50 *passim*.
Sagesse et destinée, 2, 57, 58, 59, 60, **62–63**, 68, 70, 91, 117, 123, 147, 166.
Saint Augustine, 145.
Saint-Brieuc, 143.
Sainte-Adresse, 114.
Sainte-Barbe, Collège de, 6 ff.
Sainte-Beuve, 136.
Saint-Georges de Bouhélier, 171.
St. Louis, Miss., 132.
Saint-Pol-Roux, 14.
Saint-Wandrille, Abbey of, 92, 95, 97, 98, 102, 104, 109, 110, 113, 138, 141.
Salazar, Dr., 143, 151.
San Francisco, 133.
Santa Barbara, 160.
Santa Monica, 132.
Santander, 134.
Sarcey, Francisque, 24, 39.
Schiller, 53, 155.
Schinznach, 5.
Schopenhauer, 47, 53, 62, 91, 149.
Schratt, Catherine, 155.
Schubert Theater, New York, 120.
Schuré, Édouard, 89.
Schurmann, 76, 81.
Sel de la vie, Le (sketch), 119.
Sentiers dans la montagne, Les, 121.
Sept Princesses, Les, 31–32, 33, 44.
Serres chaudes, Les, 4, 15, **19**, 20, 39, 126, 136, 143, 167, 171.
Serrure, Monique, 123.
Séverin, Fernand, 61.
Shakespeare, 23, 24, 25, 26, 52, 62, 98, 124, 145, 170.
Shaw, G. Bernard, 51, 52, 75, 155.
Sicily, 136.
Sobieski (liner), 162.
Socialism, 57, 70, 90, 110, 136.
Société nouvelle, La, 21.
Sœur Béatrice, 64, 73, 170.
Soir, Le, 111.
Sorcery, 43, 89, 168.
Spaak, Paul, 103, 162.
Spain, 65, 118, 119, 134, 152.
Spencer, Herbert, 70.
Spinnewyn, 72.
Spinoza, 145.
Spiritualism, 43, 89, 112, 130, 157.
Stanislawski, 101.
Stockhausen, George, 77.
Stoicism, 62, 149, 150, 168.
Strindberg, 49.
Surrealism, 171.
Sutro, Alfred, 51, 52, 55, 110, 117.
Swinburne, 75.
Swynaerde, near Ghent, 3, 7.

INDEX

Symbolism, 11, 14, 20, 22, 26, 30, 38, 40, 41, 52, 64, 126, 140, 145, 156, 165, 169, 170; *La Pléiade*, 15; Symbolist drama, 43-46, 166; Victorian opinion of, 51; later evolution of Symbolist writers, 56-57; rejection by Maeterlinck, 72; in *L'Oiseau bleu*, 120; Maeterlinck as creator of Symbolist drama, 171.
Symons, Arthur, 52, 75, 82, 172.
Syria, 137.

Tancarville, 121.
Tasso, 138.
Telepathy, 34, 112.
Tempest, The, 80.
Temple enseveli, Le, 69, 89.
Temps, Le, 75, 79.
Terneuzen, 4.
Tête d'or, 171.
Théâtre d'Art, 29, 32, 33, 37.
Théâtre de la Monnaie, 48, 49, 107.
Théâtre de la Porte St-Martin, 72.
Théâtre de la Renaissance-Cora, 143.
Théâtre de l'Œuvre, 37, 51, 71, 72.
Théâtre des Bouffes-Parisiens, 37.
Théâtre du Parc, 33, 39, 49.
Théâtre du Vaudeville, 27, 37.
Théâtre-Français, 71.
Théâtre Libre, 27.
Théâtre Moderne, 32.
Théâtre Mixte, 27.
Théâtre Réjane, 101.
Theosophy, 89, 134.
The Times, 52.
Thompson, Oscar, 153.
Toledo, 132.
Toulon, 87.
Trench, Herbert, 84, 99.
Trésor des humbles, Le, 28, 46, 53, 57, 63, 73, 120, 123, 126, 145, 146, 156, 167, 170.
Trois Justiciers, Les, 156.
Tunisia, 138.
Turkey, 137.

United States of America, 63, 65, 105, 117, 119, 121, 123, 124, 125, 132, 133, 152, 153, 154, 169.
Uzanne, Octave, 99.

Valéry, Paul, 11, 78.
Van den Bossche, Mathilde, *see* Maeterlinck, Mme Mathilde.
Van den Hove, Désiré, 10.
Vanderbilt, Mrs., 127.
Vandervelde, M., 110.
Van Eyck, Jan, 116.
Van Hamel, G., 51.
Van Lerberghe, Charles, 40, 86; at school, 7; friendship with Maeterlinck, 10, 35; interest in telepathy, 34; admiration for Maeterlinck, 61; organizes *Manifestation Zola*, 63; visits London, 64; opinion of *Monna Vanna*, 75; opinion of Georgette Leblanc, 78-79; death, 92; *Les Flaireurs*, 100.
Van Melle, Georges, 10.
Van Melle, Louis, 19, 21, 25.
Vannerus de Solart, Senator, 28.
Vedism, 146.
Veere, 50.
Venice, 163.
Verhaeren, Émile, 2, 12, 19, 22, 33, 40, 52, 53, 57, 63, 103, 104; and Collège Ste-Barbe, 6, 9; and *La Jeune Belgique*, 11; spiritual crisis, 20; leaves Belgium, 54; visits Maeterlinck at Nice, 117.
Verlaine, 13, 17, 29, 36, 142.
Verneuil, 114.
Verstraeten, Auguste, 13.
Verviers, 36.
Vie de l'espace, La, 139-40.
Vie des abeilles, La, 4, 69-71, 89, 108, 110, 138, 166.
Vie des fourmis, La, 138.
Vie des termites, La, 138-9.
Vielé-Griffin, Francis, 53, 126, 144.
Villa des Abeilles, 103, 114, 116, 118, 121, 140.
Villa des Quatre Chemins, 87.
Villefranche, 140.
Villiers de l'Isle Adam, 19, 22, 25, 26, 28, 52, 89, 150, 169; meeting with Maeterlinck, 14; turns Maeterlinck from Realism, 16; visits Ghent, 17; influence on Maeterlinck, 43; Maeterlinck's tribute to, 143-4.
Voix de France, La, 160.
Volta Congress, 143.

Waller, Max, 11, 12.
Wallonie, La, 11, 171.
Wauters, Joseph, 110.
Whistler, 37.
Whitman, Walt, 48, 126, 134, 154.
Wilde, Oscar, 51, 62, 172.
Willems, 1.
Willy, 78.
Wilson, President, 131.
Witley, Surrey, 117.
Wolff, Albert, 109, 127.
Wondelgem, near Ghent, 83, 102.
World War, First, 113 et seq., 124.
World War, Second, 150 et seq.

Xau, Fernand, 87.

Yeats, W. B., 52, 75, 86, 143, 172.
Yellow Book, The, 51.

Zola, 56, 63, 90.
Zoroaster, 134.
Zweig, Stefan, 154.